Miss Addie's Gift

Portrait of an American Folk Artist

Kate Merrill

Miss Addie's Gift; Portrait of an American Folk Artist

COPYRIGHT @ 2018 by Kathleen E. Merrill

Cover art: Kate Merrill

MJS

Merlin-Janus Studio, Inc.
Mooresville, NC

Publishing History
First Edition 2018
ISBN-13 978-0692390139

Published in the United States of America

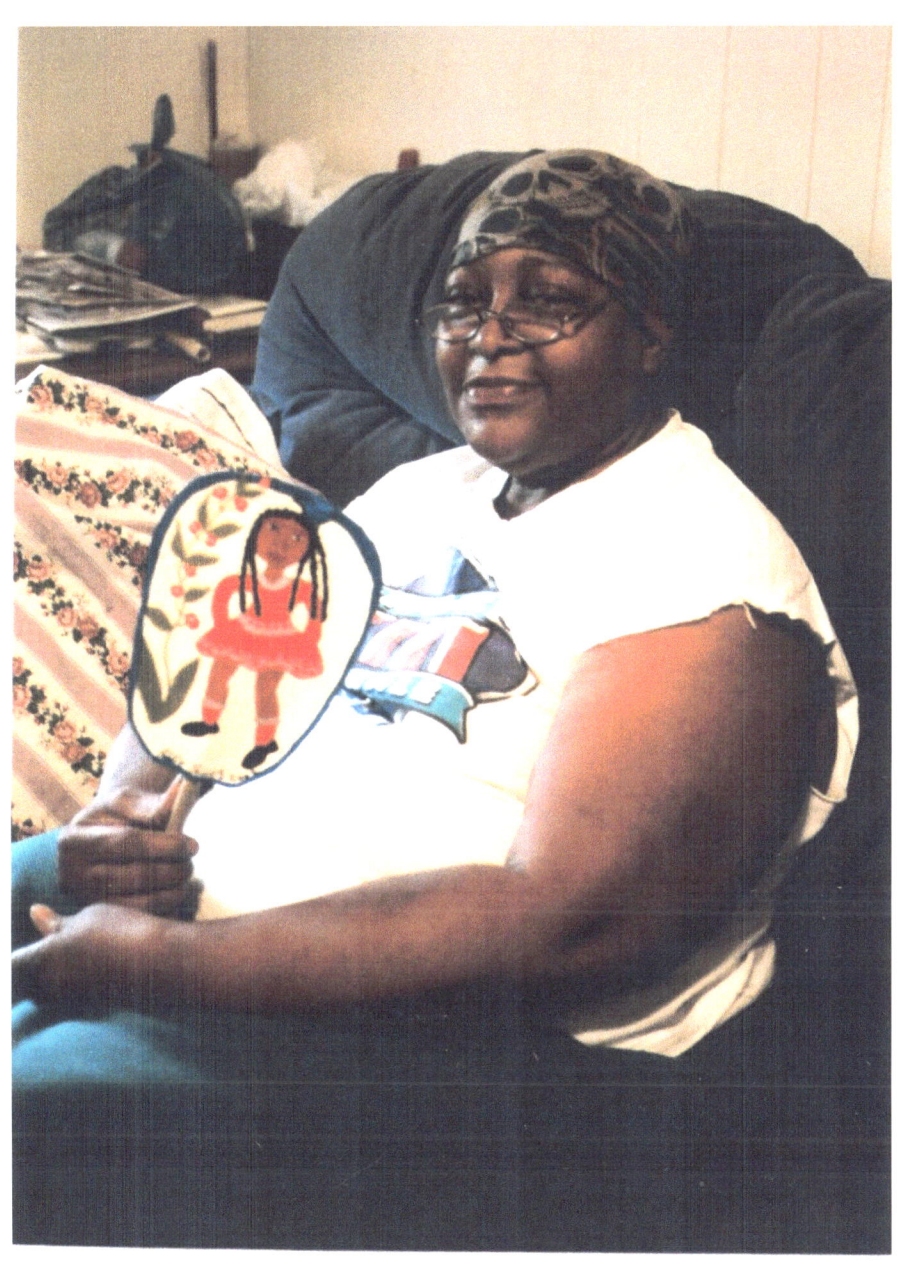

Addie James at Home

CONTENTS

FOREWORD

I met Addie James late Sunday afternoon, July 22, 2001. As usual, my partner, Susan Jennings, and I were off to a late start. We were on an adventure, disguised as a mission, to a sleepy little dot in the North Carolina foothills called Ferguson.

We had set aside all thoughts of the gallery, which would resume business as usual Monday morning, and we were ready to relax and explore. Susan was hoping to locate her grandfather's old home in North Wilkesboro, while I was focused on finding Whippoorwill Village, which included the one-room school house and the nearby gravesite of legendary Civil War era murderer, Tom Dooley.

But as shadows grew longer, we realized Pop Pop's house would not be found without more specific instructions from Susan's family, and that the Village would close before I captured one remnant of the Dooley legend. We almost missed the gravel road leading to Whippoorwill Village, and as we drove in, all the other visitors were leaving for the day.

Magical light bathed the meadows, and majestic foothills slept on the horizon. I scuttled about collecting information about Tom Dooley, while Susan drifted, as though drawn by a magnet, to a cardboard box filled with paintings. They were created on cardboard, old book covers…anything the artist could find.

Susan corralled me and dragged me into a log cabin, where the rough-hewn walls were alive with paintings by an artist from nearby Statesville. Miss Addie herself was seated near an electric fan, directing its breeze with one of her own, hand-painted fans.

Love at first sight. The art and the artist enchanted us. Each work was an authentic joy: colorful children at play, intimate domestic scenes, imaginary African landscapes, and extravagant fashion studies. While Addie, clad in an earth-tone caftan, presided over them all like a proud Buddha. She met our wild enthusiasm with a warm, half-smile and watched our antics through dark, amused eyes.

When we described our gallery and expressed an interest in showing her work, she said hanging her art in a *real gallery* was her lifelong dream. As we talked, we confirmed what we already expected: Addie was a self-taught artist with a treasure trove of accumulated work…hundreds of paintings…stored in her home. She also wrote poetry, designed fashions, and had exhibited in small local shows for many years. And while Addie was genuinely humbled by our interest, she already had a healthy appreciation of her own efforts. She saw herself, quite correctly, as a serious, dedicated painter. Her lack of formal training did not diminish her sense of self-worth, and this balance of unselfconscious humility and ego are key to any artist's success.

Addie did not drive. She depended on family and friends to take her where she needed to go. Nonetheless, we agreed that sometime someone would help her pack up a carload of art and bring her to our Davidson gallery. This settled, we all wandered out of the cabin, where the shadows were longer and heat shimmered in the grass. As I watched Addie buy a half-bushel of corn to take home for Sunday dinner, I knew I would write *Miss Addie's Gift.*

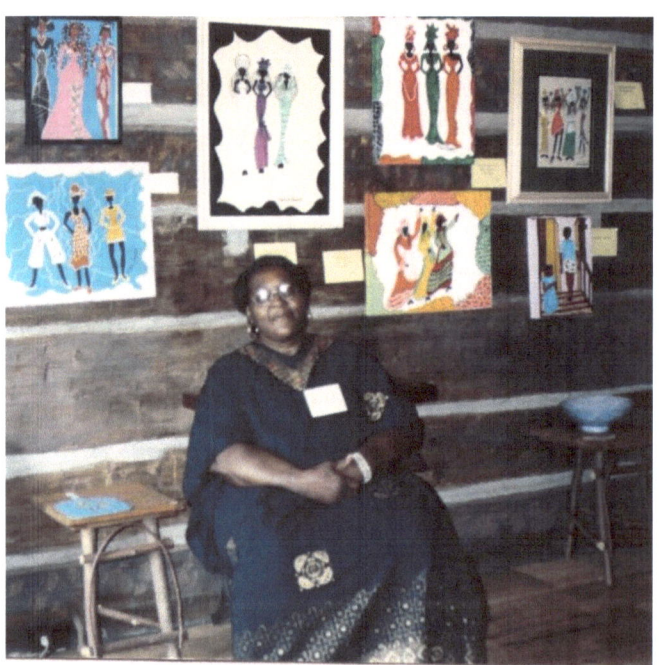

I'VE BEEN THROUGH THE STRUGGLE
The life and times of Addie James

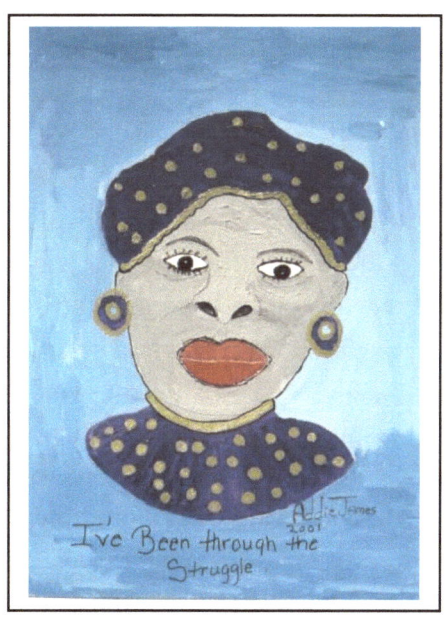

I've Been Through the Struggle
18 ½ x23 ¾   acrylic on mat board

By April 10, 2002, almost nine months after first meeting Addie James, I drove down a country road looking for Miss Addie's little brick ranch house. The azaleas and dogwood were in full bloom, and already new leaves hung heavy in the trees. The temperature hovered in the high eighties, proving summer had come too soon.

By then Addie and I were getting to know one another. Her daughter, Madaron, had driven her down from Statesville to our Davidson gallery several months after we met. We had purchased 285 of Addie's paintings, we had presented a One-Woman show for her in February, and we had sold a record number of pieces. Already Addie had won a loyal following and we had agreed to do this book together.

Still, I had never visited Addie's home. I got lost only once on the way, and I came prepared with my tape recorder, note pad, camera, and the gallery checkbook. I knew from past experience that Addie's new work would be irresistible, and that I would purchase yet another carload of treasure. I was right.

Morning sun baked the wooden deck when Addie greeted me. She wore a white tee shirt advertising the Charlotte Hornets basketball team. The shirt was smudged with paint and adorned with a single safety pin. A dark green skirt and a patterned headscarf completed the outfit. Although I was nervous about this first interview, Miss Addie put me at ease as she led me into a small living room just off the deck.

Everything was exactly as I had imagined. The tiny space included a well-worn sofa, cluttered coffee table, TV, and several chairs. I understood Addie shared this little house with her daughter, son-in-law, and three grandchildren, and I marveled at how they all could coexist in such cramped quarters.

Addie explained that the couch was her only studio. While the family swarmed around, she alone owned rights to the end of the sofa. She would clear a small area on the coffee table, set up her paints, and create all her art from this narrow vantage point.

As we settled side by side on that sofa, the wall behind us was crookedly hung with family photos and a framed display of old Confederate dollar bills, yet all I could see was the opposite wall. There, randomly propped on hooks, were Addie's recent paintings…dozens of them vibrating, calling out to me. More art littered the floor. Work was stacked on every available surface amid a tangle of bamboo poles she was decorating. I saw hand-painted fans and two whimsical birdhouse, (which I vowed to keep for my own collection), and, oh, that door!

Each wooden panel of the door leading to the deck was painted with a distinctly different Addie James scene. A less timid collector would rip the door from its hinges, leaving the family exposed to the elements, and then install the door as a work of art in his own home (or donate it to a museum).

As it was, I calmly agreed we should open the door so that any breath of air lingering outside might flow into our hot space and allow us to begin the interview. Naturally, my tape recorder would not record, my camera was jammed, and clearly all the gods of modern technology had conspired to defeat our noble purpose. Only Madaron, Addie's daughter, arrived to save us. She came home to bring her mom a McDonalds sausage n' egg biscuit (Addie had not yet eaten that day) and she graciously set up her twin boys' karaoke machine, complete with a microphone, so that we could begin what was to be the first of several wonderful sessions.

And Miss Addie
started telling me
her life…

ADDIE LEE FRANCES MADDOX was born August 11, 1943, in Anderson, South Carolina. Her great grandmother was a slave. Her mother was Inez Maddox, and her father, Willie Snow Maddox, was a brick mason by trade.

My daddy was born during Christmas. There was a big snow that year, and that's why they put "Snow" in his name.

While they lived in South Carolina, Inez and Willie gave birth to four daughters: Gladys, Betty, Addie, and Janie. They also had two sons: Aaron and Clifton. The family then moved to Statesville, North Carolina, where a third son, Willie, was born. One of seven children, Addie lived in Statesville all her life.

When the family first came to North Carolina, Willie could not find work as a brick mason, so he took a job for the town of Statesville:

Daddy worked for the city driving a trash truck. Oh, we couldn't wait 'til he got home. He brought boxes of candy, fudge candy, home...and dolls, and different things people would give him. And that was like Christmas every day. And we couldn't wait to see what he had, 'cause another person's junk is another person's treasure. I found a lot of treasure in there...a lot of treasure.

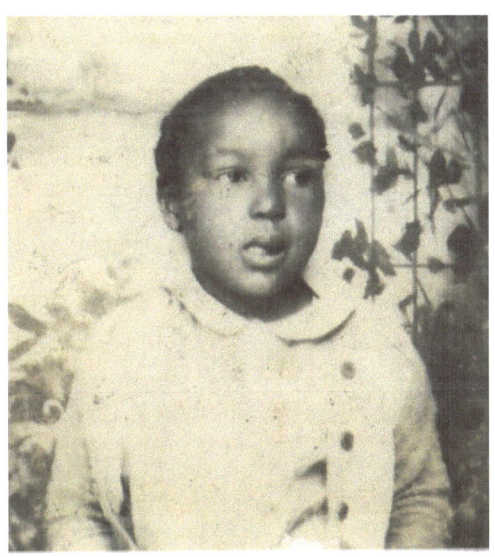

only existing photo of Addie James as a child

Addie's earliest memories evoked a big, barn-like structure where the Maddox family lived near the railroad tracks:

First house I lived in was Templeton Hill. The railroad track was behind the house and down the hill. And when we heard the train coming we went running. We thought the world was coming to an end, you know?

Although that house was gone, and Addie was not precisely sure where it once stood, a vision representing the house often appeared in her paintings. No doubt the image was somewhat idealized as a white box-like structure with happy children playing in the yard, and yet that interpretation recurred again and again:

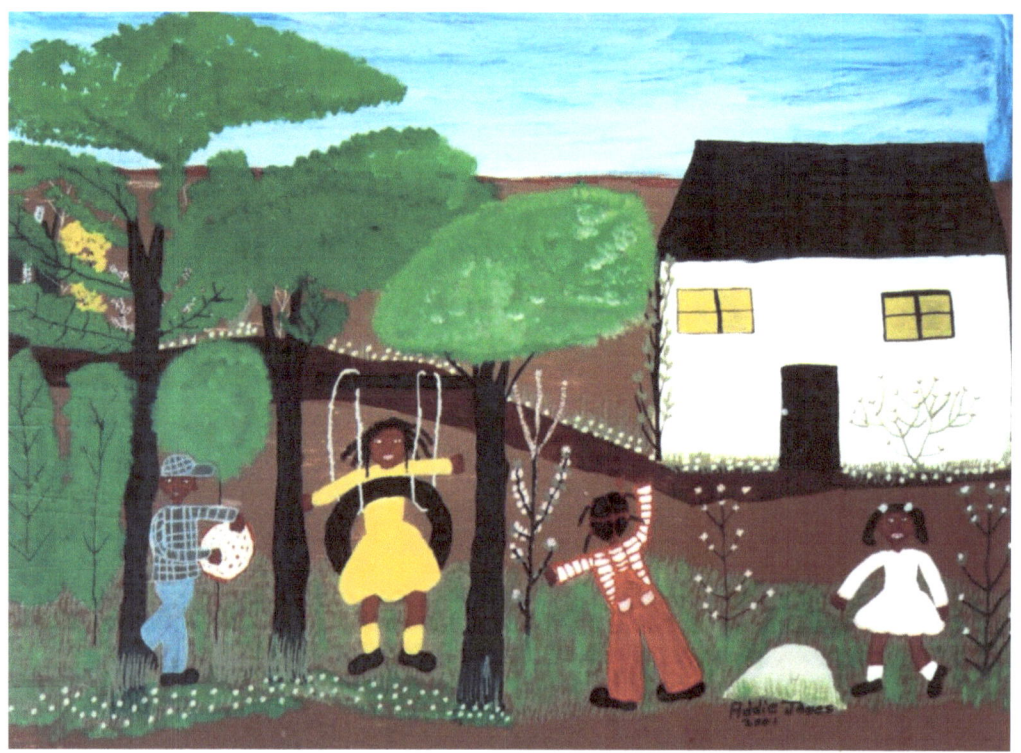

Playing at the Swing 20 ½ x29 acrylic on mat board

"Little Addie" was another recurring image in the artist's work. A young girl, always seen from the back, always dressed in overalls with pockets, with her hair parted into four quadrants and braids, appeared in many paintings. This figure represented the youthful artist looking into the scenes of her life.

Children loved to find Little Addie in the paintings. Indeed the exercise worked well for adults too. Unlike children, adults often forgot to look closely, and finding Little Addie helped to combat this tendency.

Although the house near the railroad tracks was primitive, lacking all modern conveniences, the family was happy and life was full. The siblings played together and walked along the tracks to Morningside School, an elementary school for black children.

Addie was a spirited student, full of herself and driven by an impulse to create. She was a natural leader who spoke her mind, held her own, and often moved against the grain:

You know, I'm a Leo and I was always a leader. Like, I was at school one day, at the front of the school where there was a big tree, and it was May Day. And a bunch of kids always snuck off, the bad ones, and they'd be smoking. I went up to them and they say "Do you want to smoke?" And I say "No, and you shouldn't be smoking neither. You can call me chicken, duck, hawk...whatever you want to call me, but I won't smoke because I got a mind of my own and I don't want to!" Those were my words.

Throughout her life, Addie confronted adversity, poverty, racism, and personal loss with the same positive approach she developed as a child. She brought this same confidence to her art.

Kids Talking 11x14acrylic on canvas

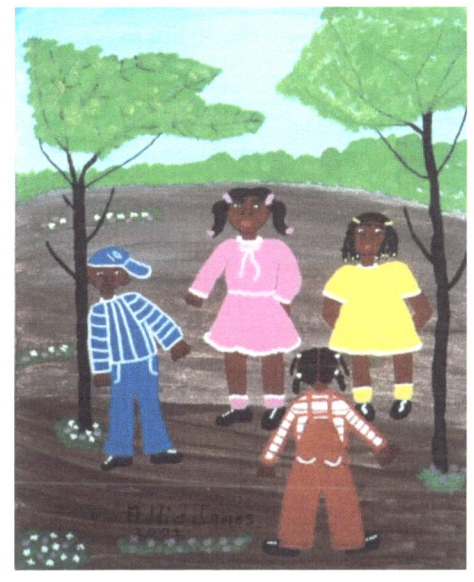

This ability to look beyond negativity and injustice served Miss Addie well. Arguably, her hometown Statesville was neither the best nor the worst place to survive as a black woman. While the town had taken giant leaps beyond inequality, there was still the Ku Klux Clan active in Addie's youth as well as a *back door policy* in force, especially at eating establishments.

I was in about seventh grade when I started painting. I started drawing paper dolls for children and they would pay me for them. So I made a little money. They paid me fifty cents, or something. I made the clothes to go with them, too.

Addie continued to paint, write poetry, and compose songs. Her early life was a continuous chain of happy memories, strung together like a necklace of pearls. The children enjoyed school in the fallow months and worked in the summers:

Well, back then they would let you out of school early to pick cotton, and we'd be on the back of a truck and when we'd go by the school we'd always lay down so the kids wouldn't see. It was embarrassing, you know, to have the kids see us in the back of a truck.
But I was never in the cotton patch. I was in Hollywood, and I was out there dreaming. That was what got me through the day farming...was dreaming, was seeing myself in the limelight.

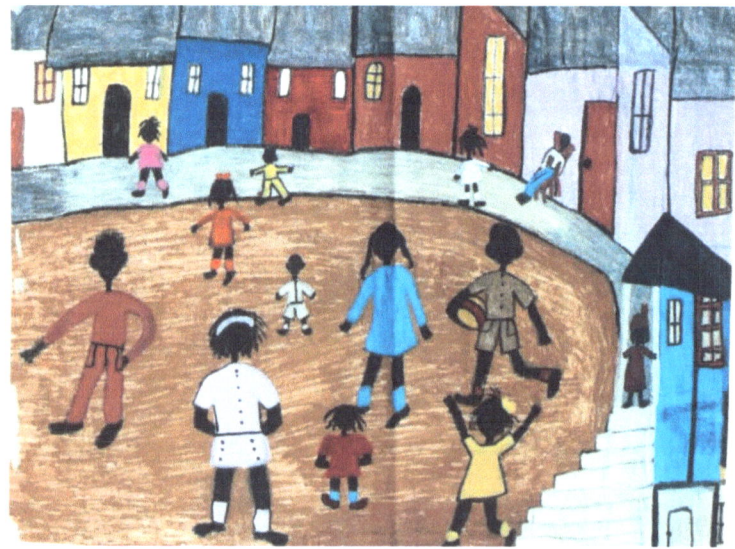

City Playground 15 x 19 acrylic on cloth

14

Also in summer, the Maddox family made a pilgrimage to the old home place in South Carolina:

> *It was an old farm place, an old house, you know? We did crops for this man. I forget his name, but we did sharecropping. Mama used to be out in the field picking cotton when we were little. Her and Daddy'd be working in the fields and they'd put us in a pasteboard box, and, you know, they'd come back and check on us every now and then. They had to work for a living.*
>
> *And the place didn't look too beautiful to me, you know? I wasn't too inspired. I loved the trees and the surroundings, but the house held a lot of bad memories, to hear Mama tell it. They had such a hard time.*

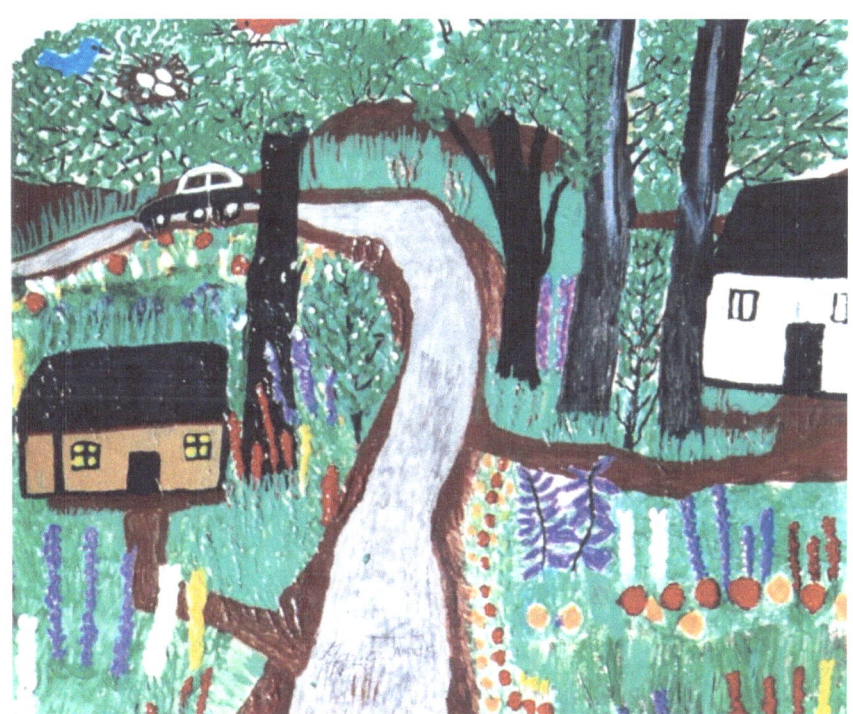

Addie James *Family Woods*
12 ½ x 14 ½ acrylic on paper

Eventually the family moved from the house near the railroad tracks to a new place on Belmont Street. During this period, Willie Maddox found work laying bricks, Inez had a job in a clothing factory, and everyone in the family farmed the land:

Well, it was a big apartment. There was a family downstairs, the one that owned it, and we was upstairs. We had enough room, and that was a big apartment...big front porch.

And that was when we done a lot of farming. We would work a farm right there on Route 64. And I remember that farm had the best walnut trees on it. The best walnuts you ever tasted. And I would always get me a bunch of walnuts and crack 'em and that was some good eating. And we would make walnut cakes and walnut cookies and they were just the bomb!

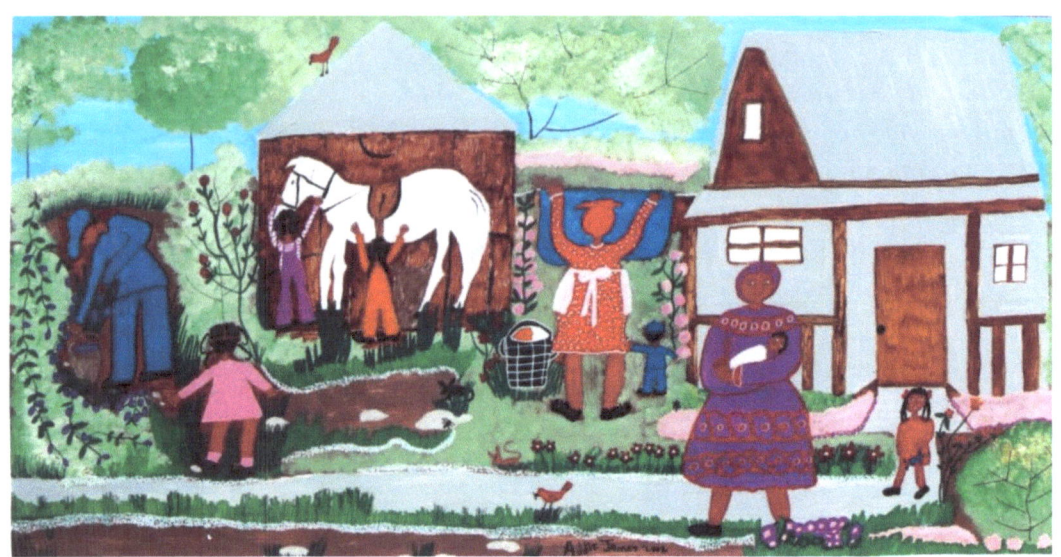

Family farm Work 24 x 48 acrylic on mat board

After the Morningside School, Addie went on to Unity School, which took her through twelfth grade. By then her father, Willie, had died. He left the family with a good social security check, but everyone understood they still needed to work:

Daddy died when I was about eleven, and the social security check helped Mama with the bills. She'd give us the money, and we'd catch the bus and go uptown and buy what we wanted.

When Daddy died, Mama was working in a miller place, where you twist the mill out? Everybody worked in the family. Oh, yeah, we raised chickens and lived off the land.

Miss Addie seldom revealed sorrow or regret, but as she described her time at Unity School, her voice dropped to a whisper and she averted her eyes:

I went to the twelfth grade, but I didn't graduate... I was pregnant with my first child. That's what happened.

Clearly Addie's life changed forever during her senior year. Her first child, Angela Faye, was born prematurely in 1961. Arriving after a seven- month pregnancy, the child weighed two pounds and three ounces. Now married, the young mother was forced to drop out of school. After that, Addie was blessed with new babies almost every year: Jerry was born in 1962; Ricky was born in 1963, and Christopher was born in 1965.

While her marriage ended unhappily, with Addie divorcing her husband after the birth of their last son, children had always been the joy of Miss Addie's life. Motherhood was depicted time and again in her art…lovingly, tenderly, with the maternal bond strong and in tact.

Madaron, Addie's last child, was born in 1968 after she met Robert James, with whom she captured a second chance at love.

Baby and Me
10 ¼ x14
Acrylic on mat board

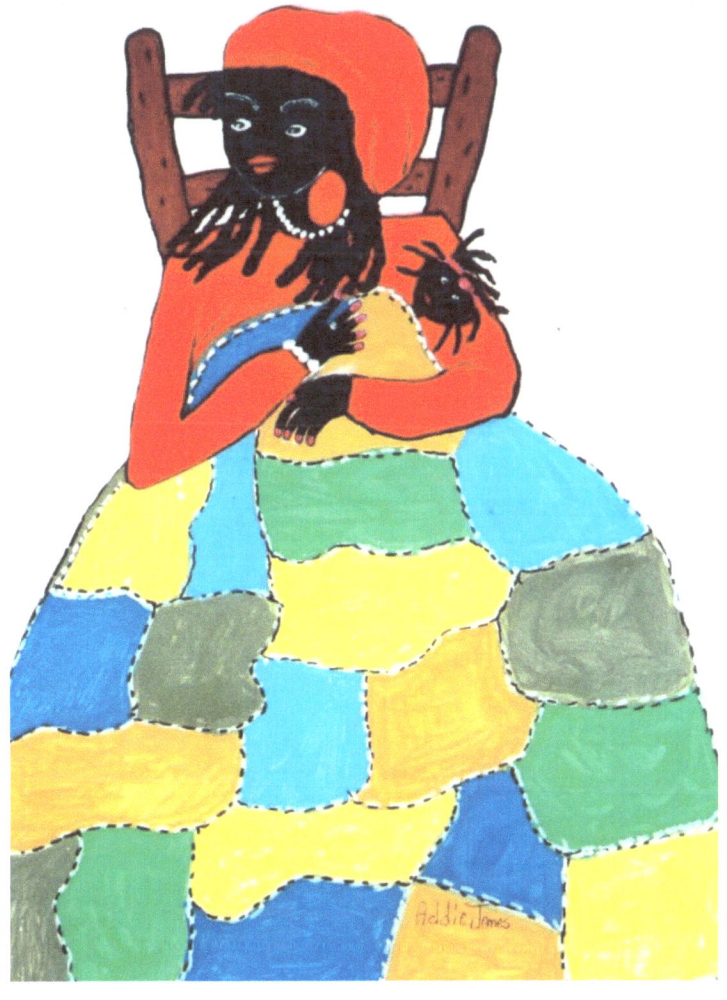

I married Robert James in 1969. He was from Georgia, and he brought my brother, Clifton, home one night. And he was so tall and handsome. And when he come into the house, I looked at him, and he looked at me, and we just knew.

He went one way, and I went another, and I said, "He's got to like me, I got to have him!" And he was thinking the same thing. And we started talking and I said, "I know you probably don't want me because I got all these kids…"

And he said, "No, I think you're a nice person and I would like to come see you again…"

From then on he wined me, and he dined me. Every day when I come home from work, he would take me out to eat, and we were just SO HAPPY!

He made me feel so good, and he kissed me every day before he left. He would buy me dinner because we worked different shifts. And he'd take me to the movies, and we'd have a GOOD time.

Robert was from Georgia. He took me down to Georgia to meet his parents and everything. It was a BIG old deal, and everybody liked me.

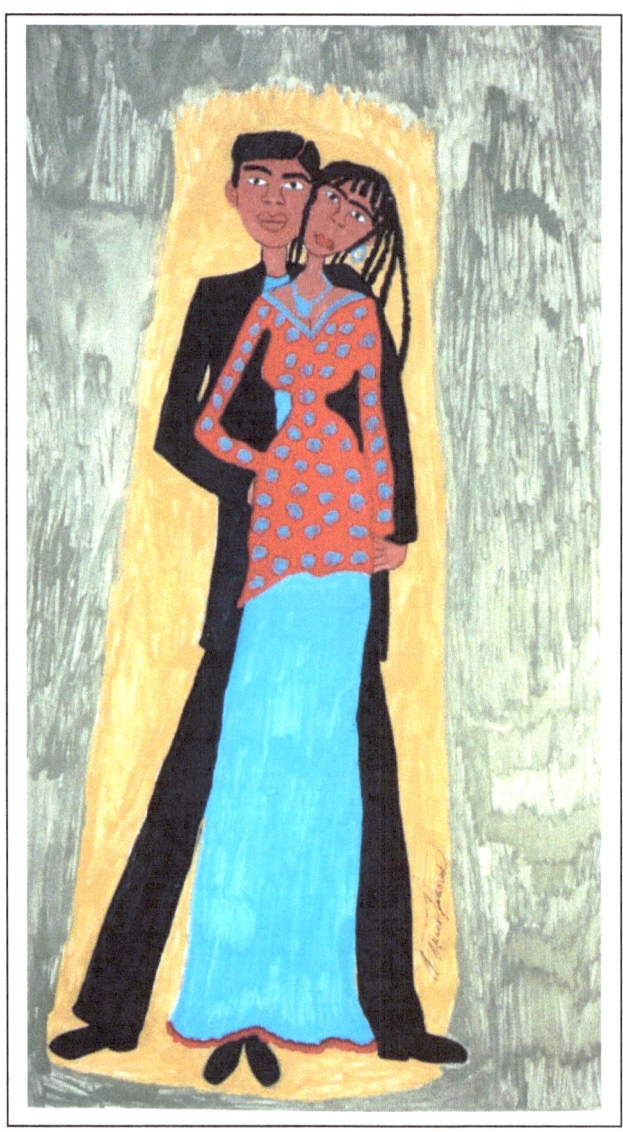

Honeymoon 9 ¼ x 16 ¾ Acrylic on mat board

We lived together at first and saved money, and then we went and got married, and we bought this house in 1971. And that's my love life.

I don't got no love life now, there's just me and Jubie. (the nickname for Willie, Addie's youngest brother)

But Miss Addie also had six grandchildren, and they were her delight. Although her three sons had no children, her eldest daughter, Angela Faye, gave birth to Ashley, Dacota, and Michael. Addie's youngest daughter, Madaron, and her three children: Kesha and the twin boys, Christian and Christopher, all lived with their grandma.

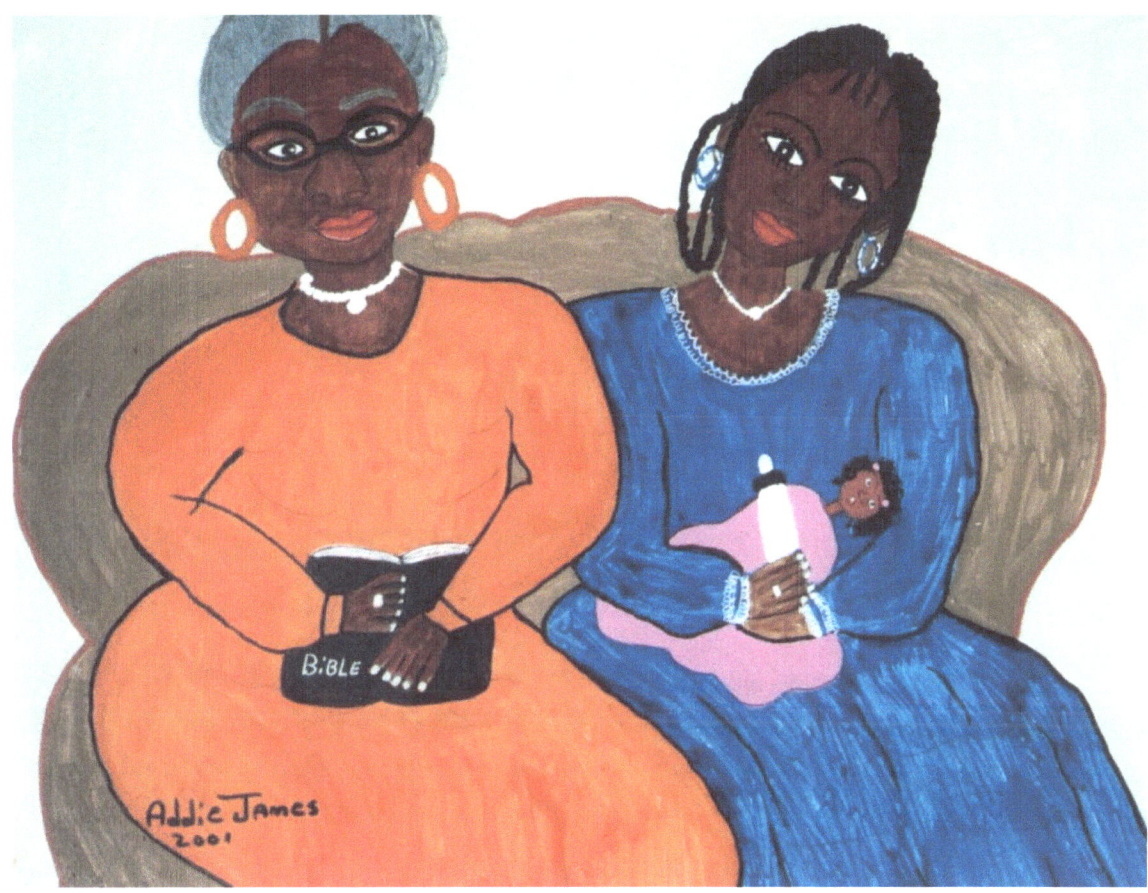

Addie James Mother and Daughter10 ½ x 13 ½ acrylic on mat board

Yet, along with the blessings of family and children come the inevitable sorrows. Miss Addie's husband died on October 5, 1993, and her first-born son, Jerry, to whom this book is dedicated, was *a tall, handsome man* who died of AIDS exactly one year later. Addie's son, Ricky, who was also an artist, *got mixed up in the drug world. He's the only one of my children a lot like myself.*

So Addie had lost family to death, to imprisonment, and even to murder by gunshot of a nephew too young to die. Yet, she remained strong and positive. She was sustained by her faith and by her gift. If any good came from her tragedies, an intensified focus on her painting was that good.

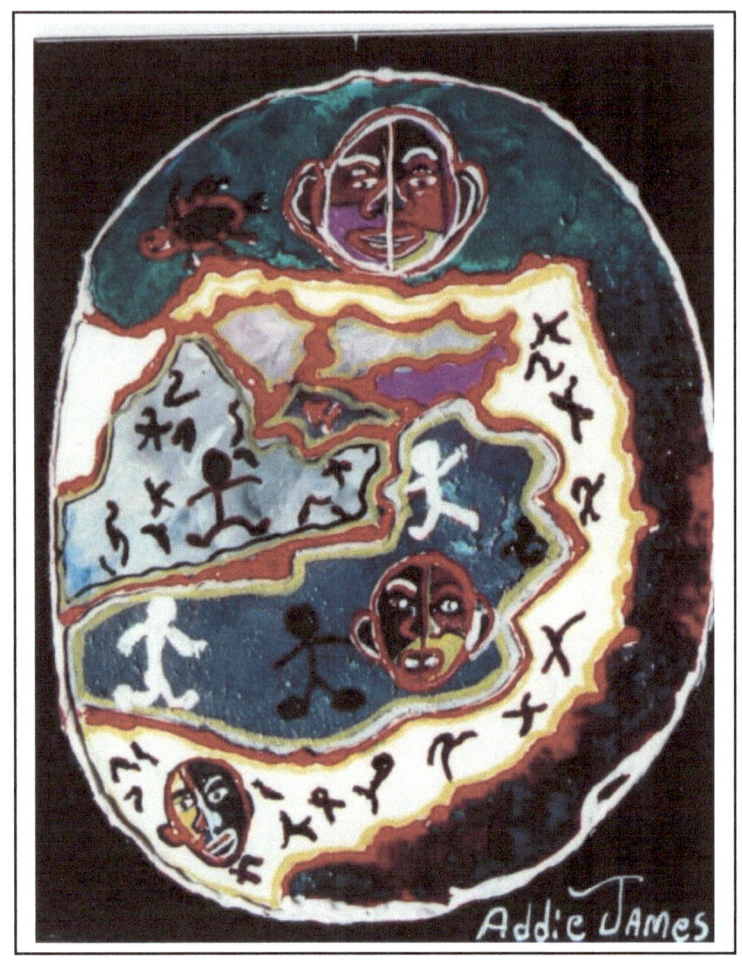

Mix Up 7 ½ x 9 ½ mixed media on mat board

In her time, Addie labored in the fields, worked in a clothing factory, and dedicated herself to motherhood. Through all those years, art was her mainstay, her one constant in a mixed up world. When she titled a painting *I've Been Through the Struggle*, we must believe her.

The family got together for cookouts and things like that. The picture FAMILY GATHERING puts me in mind of my sisters and cousins, you know? The girl in red is my niece. She's got long hair and she's so pretty! The handsome man beside her is my brother, Jubie (Willie). That's my brother Boot (Aaron) in the overalls and hat, and that's my mama, because Mama used to smoke a long time ago. And the man in the glasses is my uncle, the one who used to pinch me all the time…

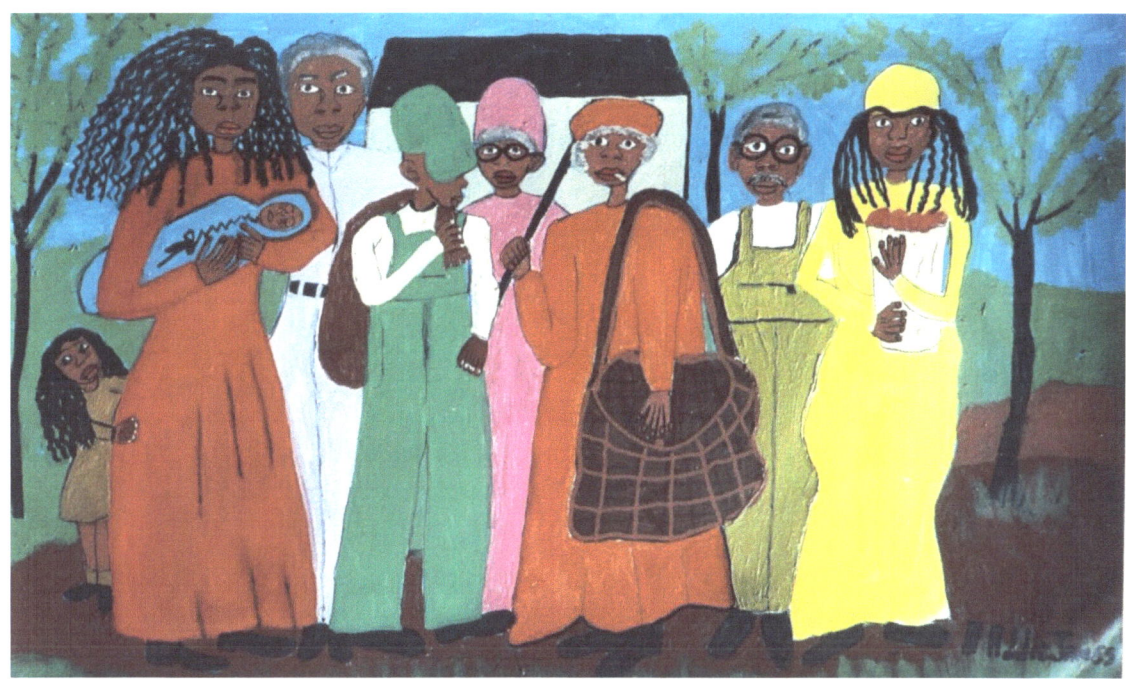

CHILDREN OF THE FIELDS

By Addie James

Brought forth before
The morning sun,
Laborers of earlier times, working crops that
Were never done.
Poor and forever hungry, flour sack clothes,
Raggedy and torn.
Having very little self-worth,
From the day they were born,
Generation conceiving many
Toward the working fields, always trying
To get ahead. Imagine the voice of my mother
As she bids her goodbye
Through the shadows of the morning that touch
The sky.
Many decades have come and gone, only the memories
Of children
Shine like the sun,
Make a silent sound.
Through the eye of this generation
I can still see
The children running around.

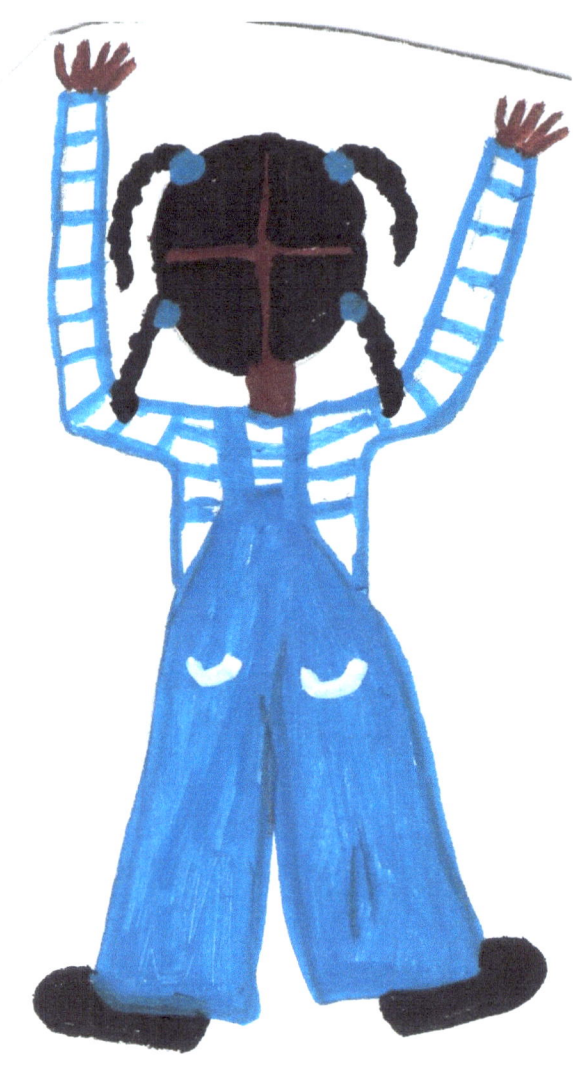

When *Little Addie* appears in a painting, she represents a memory from the artist's life.

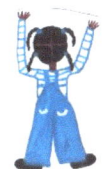

YOU GOT IT GOIN' ON…
But what is it?

Most potential art collectors have one burning question: *What do you call this kind of art?* They want to know the style, and they need a label in order to place the artist's work into a neat little category. Critics and academicians also suffer from this impulse; we are all human. Our minds wander in a confusion of media bombardment. Our modern lives are complex and cacophonous, and we hunger for order and clarity. The visual arts, subtle and subjective as they are, beg to be boxed, and throughout art history, we have obliged them.

Lumping is a good word, and ever since it became important to make sense of human scribbling, lumping art into categories became an art form its own right.

In modern art history, starting in the Nineteenth Century, someone decided the best way to do this was to add the suffix *ism* to groups of art which were alike in style or intent: Classicism, Romanticism, Impressionism, Fauvism, Cubism, Expressionism…you get the picture.

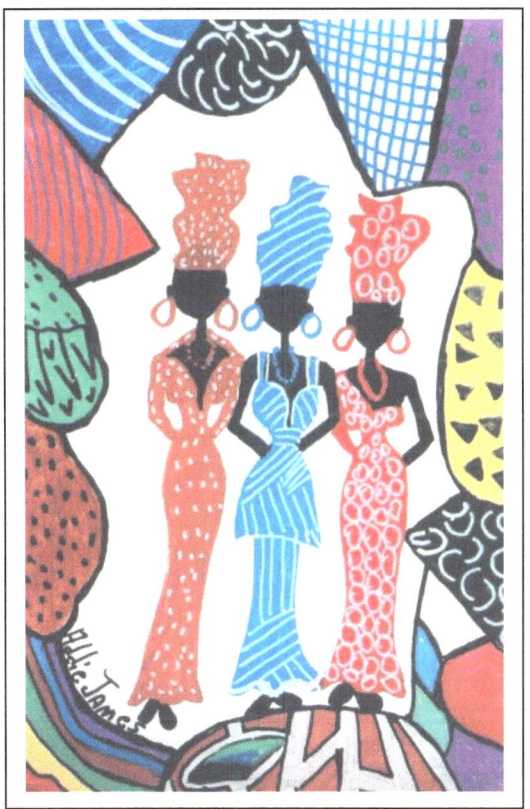

You Got It Goin' on…
8 x 10 ½ acrylic on canvas

23

It was determined that almost any painter could be lumped into one category or another, even if one had to bend, fold, and mutilate to put him there. But what if he just won't fit? Voila! We have a new category, very chic these days: *Outsider Art*, handy for misfits, especially when that painter has received no formal training.

So, what is Addie James' art? Can it be categorized? Many have tried. Visitors to her shows tend to call it *Primitive*, *Naive*, or *Folk Art*. All agree it is *African American Art*. Currently it is stylish to use the term *vernacular*, which is defined as the ordinary, everyday language of a people, native or indigenous to a specific region.

In his 1959 textbook classic, Mainstreams of Modern Art, John Canaday describes the American Primitives, *whose art has been lifted in recent years from a level of interesting novelty to the respectable one of an important national expression.* He describes the self-taught amateur painters who painted friends and family and familiar places: *Such painters may be merely inept, or they may have a degree of awkward charm dependent on the painter's innate sensitivity to decorative color and pattern.*[1]

Canaday cites works by Edward Hicks (1780-1849), whose best-known work was *The Peaceable Kingdom*, and the French painter, Henri Rousseau (1840-1910), *who first set about reproducing the real world as photographically as he knew how, and then discovered that he had created a world of enchantment instead.*[2] He next describes how the art dealers of his time are scrambling to discover other exceptional Primitives, but that usually these *others at best turn out to be charming but inconsequential, bizarre but only bizarre, or sincere yet somehow at once ponderous and shallow.*[3]

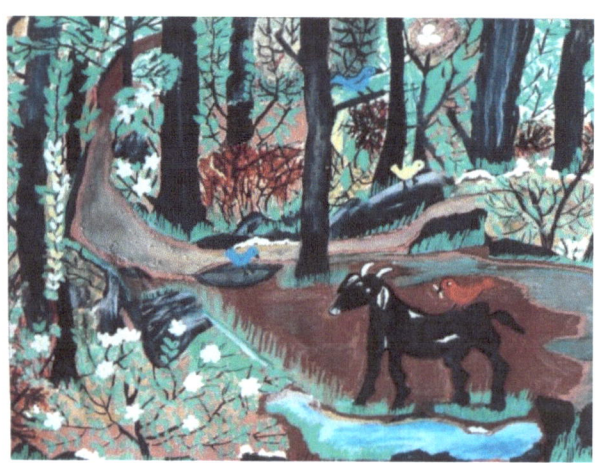

Addie's woodland paintings
could be compared to
Edward Hicks' *The Peaceable Kingdom*.

Addie James *The Woods, 15 ½ x 18 ½ acrylic on paper*

[1] *Mainstreams of Modern Art*, John Canaday @1959 Holt, Rinehart and Winston, p.258
[2] *Mainstreams of Modern Art*, p258
[3] *Mainstreams of Modern Art*, p.392

Henri Rousseau's *Young Girl* could be compared to Addie's *Sasha.*

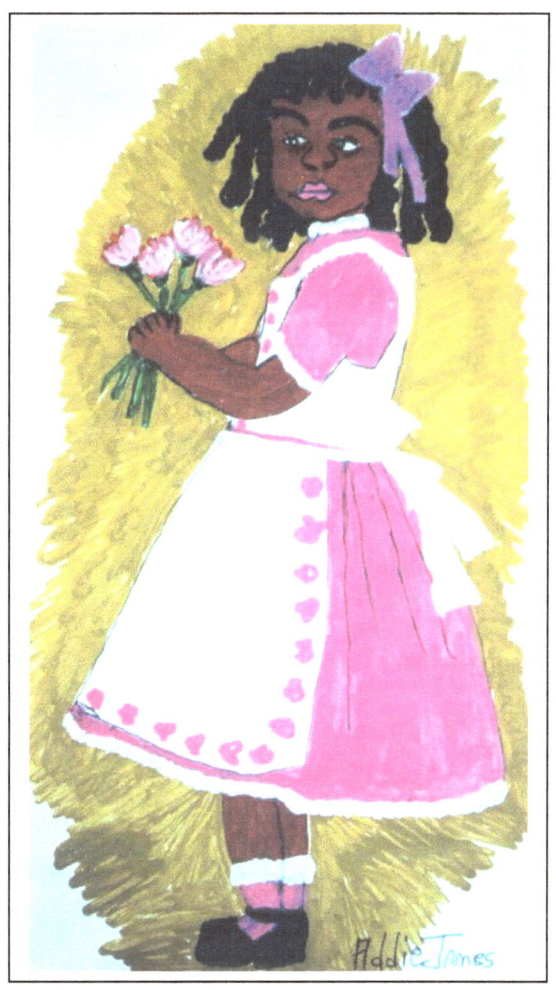

Addie James: Sasha
6 ¼ x 11 acrylic on paper

Interestingly, Canaday allows one notable exception: Horace Pippin (1888-1946), *whose intimately observed genre scenes and his engaging historical pictures, are close to the tradition of American folk art.*[4]

Which brings us back to square one, to where my personal interest in Addie James had its roots. Horace Pippin, one of the first prominent, self-taught African-American artists, rose from obscurity to national fame in the 1940's, and made his home on Gay Street in West Chester, Pennsylvania. His house was three blocks down the street from my first gallery, The Merrill Collection. For ten years I walked in his footsteps and lived among the landmarks featured in his paintings: his humble brick row house, the county courthouse, and the local art center at the end of our street, where Pippin first exhibited his work.

---

[4] *Mainstreams of Modern Art*, p.392

Pippin's ghost led my partner, Susan Jennings, and me to begin a gallery tradition in 1986, of presenting annual Black History Month shows. And as we forged new relationships with marvelous African-American artists in the Philadelphia area, some self-taught, the issue of what constitutes *primitive*, as opposed to *naïve* or *folk art,* became an ongoing question.

Addie's *First Christmas Alone* could be compared to Horace Pippin's *Christmas Morning Breakfast.*

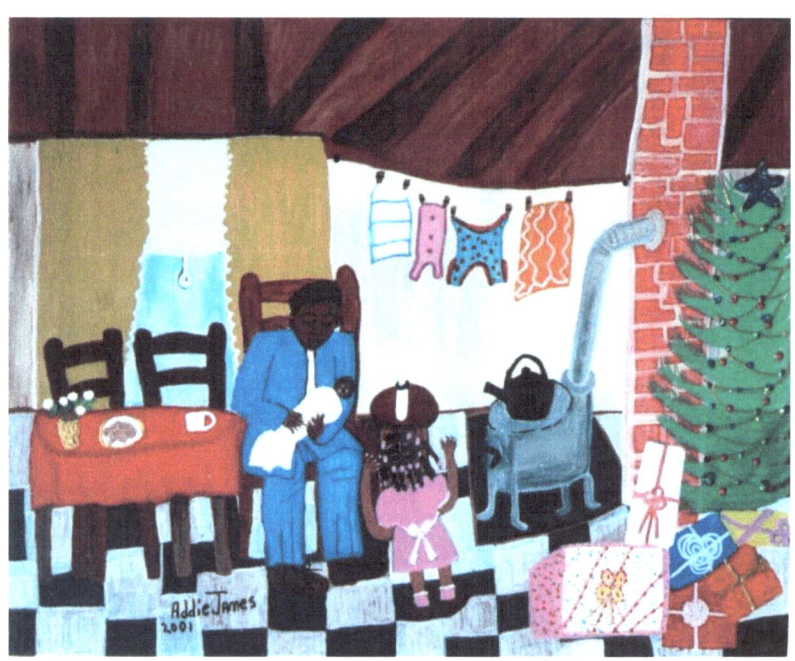

First Christmas Alone
16 x 20 acrylic on canvas

Horace Pippin, along with his reviewers, critics, and devotees, had struggled with the same question four decades ago. The fact that Pippin was often called a Primitive reflected the definition at that time: no formal training, but creative by instinct. *The benign art world usage of such adjectives as naïve, primitive, and instinctive notwithstanding, there is no question that the terms had racial overtones when employed by some commentators to describe Pippin.*[5]

One hopes that today, with the dawning of the Twenty-First Century, with political correctness etched in the American psyche, racial overtones are no longer a factor in art criticism.

_____

5 *I Tell My Heart, The Art of Horace Pippin* @1993 Pennsylvania Academy of Fine Arts, p11

Yet where do we place Addie James? One collector said Addie was like Grandma Moses (1860-1961), the humble farm woman from Eagle Bridge, New York, who wowed Manhattan with her first solo show at the age of eighty-nine.

Fact is, Miss Addie's work bears little resemblance to the bucolic landscapes of Anna Mary Robertson Moses, who still ranks as perhaps the best known of all American folk artists. True, both are self-taught women artists who found recognition late in life. Addie finally enjoyed her first solo show in 2002, at the young age of fifty-eight, and while comparisons are inevitable, they are not necessarily valid.

It is interesting to note that Addie James was geographic kin to several North Carolina artists who have soared to international fame. The haunting, allegorical paintings and murals of Ben Long, also from Statesville, command not only a high price, but also intense critical acclaim. More to the point, African-American painter Romare Bearden (1912-1988), from nearby Charlotte, enriched the world with his stunning collage technique. He was an outspoken advocate for black artists and now ranks among the most important artists of the Twentieth Century.

Addie's *New Home* is much like Romare Bearden's serigraph: *Home to Ithica.*

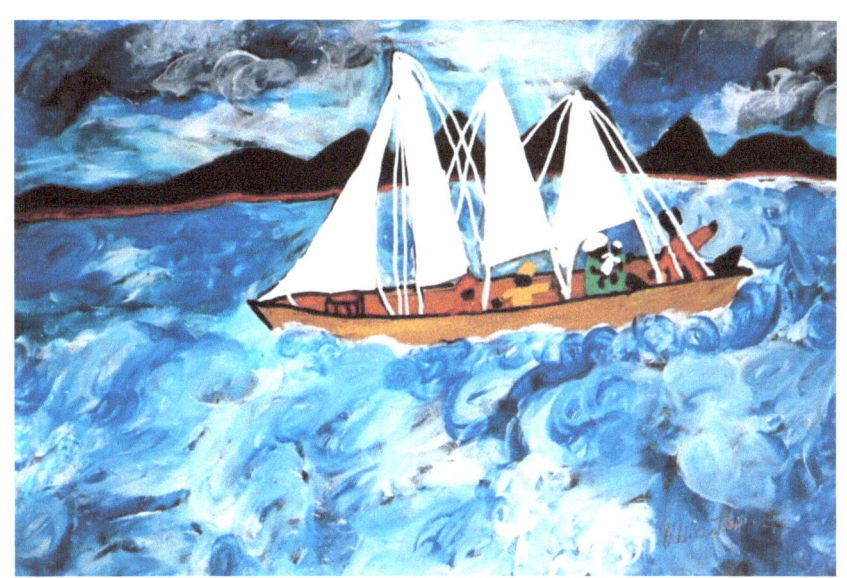

Addie James   New Home
12 x 18 acrylic on panel

Yet Addie's famous neighbors were highly trained, with additional schooling in Europe and advantaged exposure to the culture, trends, and machinations of the contemporary art world. So while it is tempting to draw comparisons here, again it is not valid. Indeed Miss Addie, having little exposure to the worlds of Long or Bearden, drew no influence from them.

In order to move closer to Addie James, we must view her art in the context of African-American artists who are self-taught and who, like Addie, have lived their entire lives in the South.

Once we have narrowed our vision this far, we can bisect that group once again into two generations: those who have lived through segregation and the Civil Rights Movement (like Addie's parents, uncles, and aunts), and those like Addie, who were young adults in the politically active 1960's and 70's, when great gains in equality were achieved and many promises were made. (It is for Addie's children and grandchildren to decide the value of those achievements and determine which promises have been kept.)

Art historian Edmund Barry Gaither likens art by this group of self-taught black Southern artists to *blues, work songs, and gospel---musical traditions with roots in the experience of black poor and working class people---vernacular art prizes first-person narrative, compelling personal visions, and spiritual interventions.*[6]

Now we are getting very close. Of artists from the earlier generations, Clementine Hunter, born around 1880 on Little Eva Plantation in Louisiana (alleged to have been the model used by Harriet Beecher Stowe for the plantation in Uncle Tom's Cabin) was a kindred spirit to Addie James. Unlike Addie, Clementine was illiterate, one-step removed from slavery, and had to wait until late in life, until her work in the cotton fields and as a cook was done, before she took up a paintbrush in the late 1940's.

Like Addie, *Clementine was always a nimble-fingered and outstandingly capable woman. She liked everything she did to be done right and to look nice, and she always knew what "looking nice" was all about.*[7]

Also like Addie, *Clementine Hunter painted on anything she could find---cardboard, old pieces of used wrapping paper, empty bottles, shoeboxes. She painted the pictures she could see without even opening her eyes: a girl bringing slops to the hogs, women scrubbing the wash in big tubs under the trees, the church, the plantation house, gourd picking, weddings, funerals, a wild Saturday night at a roadside honky-tonk. She painted the Nativity, black angels dressed in white and red gowns floating through the air. She painted her feelings about people and nature*[8].

---

[6] *Testimony: Vernacular Art of the African-American South*, "Witnessing: Layered Meanings in Vernacular Art", Edmund Barry Gaither, et al @2001 Harry N. Abrams, Inc., p 67
[7] *Contemporary American Folk Artists*, Elinor Lander Horwitz, J. Roderick Moore, Consultant @1975 J.B. Lippincott Company, p.44
[8] *Contemporary American Folk Artists*, p.47

Many of Addie's paintings can be compared to the art of Clementine Hunter. Addie's *Party Time with Kids* is similar to Hunter's *Negro Wedding.*

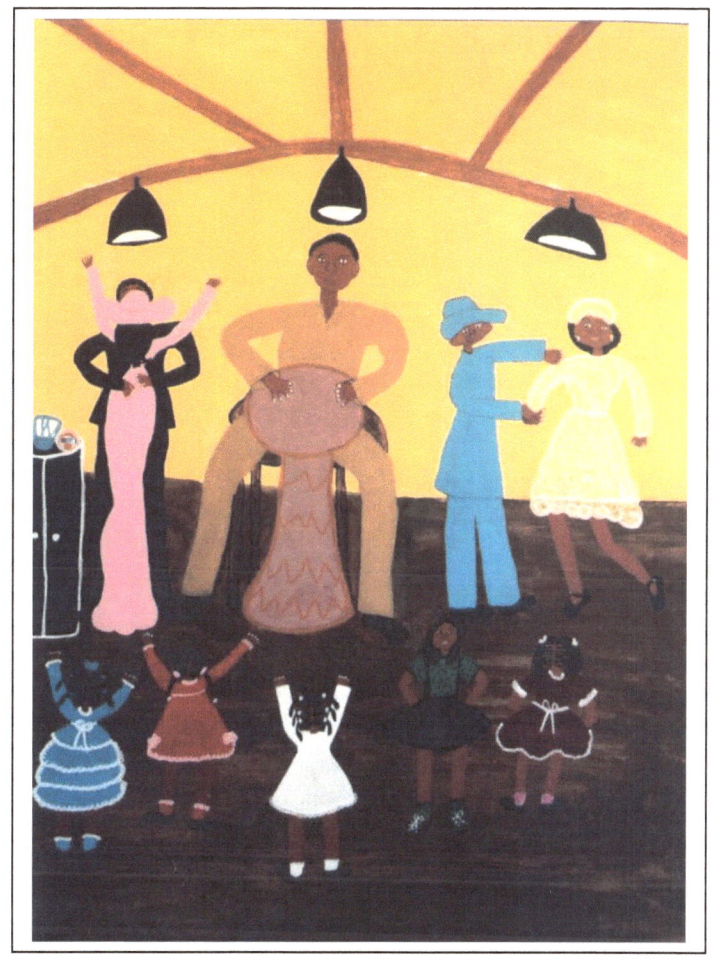

Party Time with Kids
30 x 40 acrylic on mat board

Moving closer to home, *paintings by the self-taught black artist Minnie Evans (1892-1987), apparently spoke volumes about the effects of racism and segregation on black aspirations and dreams in Jim-Crow era North Carolina. The white angelic choir in Minnie Evan's "A Dream," (1959) was entirely conceivable in a society where, for blacks as well as whites, a spiritual and divine realm---and all that was considered "good" and "beautiful" in the culture---had to be white.*[9]

It is interesting that Clementine Hunter on her Louisiana plantation boldly painted black angels in 1940, while Addie James, forty years later, has clearly gotten past the notion that only white is beautiful.

---

[9] *Black Art and Culture in the 20th Century*, Richard J. Powell @1997 Thames and Hudson, LTD, p.99

Minnie Evans's floating prophets in *Dream: Prophets in the Air* could be compared to Addie's

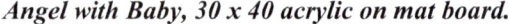

Angel with Baby, 30 x 40 acrylic on mat board.

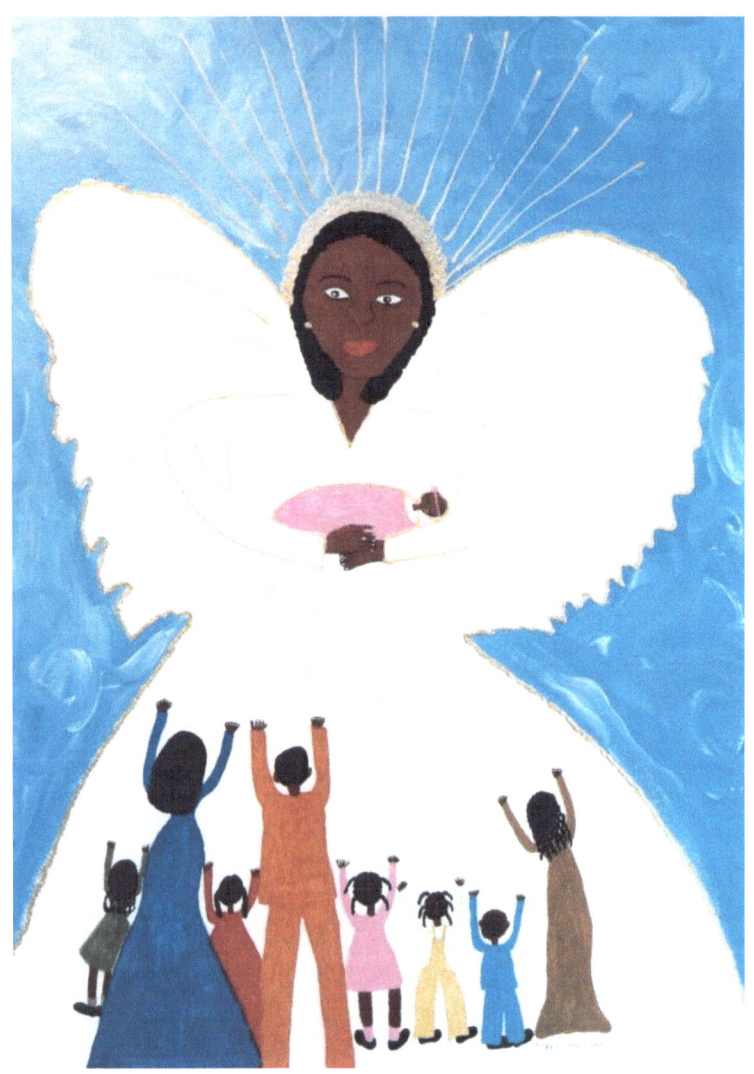

Of Addie's generation, Leroy Alman (1938-1997) from Tallapoosa, Georgia, was an ordained minister and nondenominational evangelist who was best known for his painted, carve wood relief work, yet his religious subjects compare to Addie's.

The fact is, every region has its own favorite folk artists, many of whom bear some resemblance to one another. Because they are self-taught, they may have similar approaches to perspective, often depicting the most important figure in a scene as larger-than-life, regardless of his proper proportion.

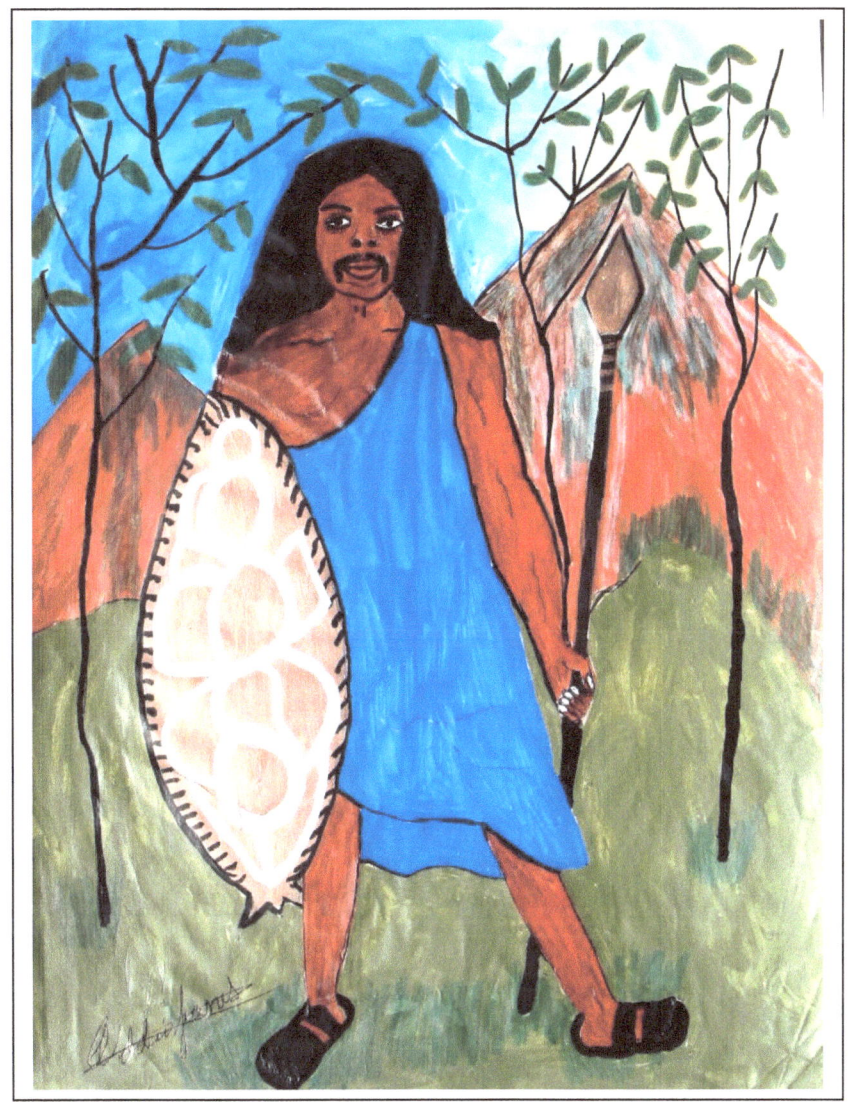

David, 10 ½ x14acrylic on paper

Self-taught African-American artists usually focus on everyday scenes from their own lives, with an emphasis on figures and relationships. One notable exception to this is a universal interest in creating scenes of Africa. Few of these painters have actually seen Africa, yet the media offers rich images to a culture searching for its roots. A perfect example of this is Addie's *David* as an African warrior.

As we continue to generalize, self-taught painters often take a similar approach to nature, with leaves on trees either carefully delineated, like Horace Pippin's, or puffy as clouds with stick-like branches, like Addie James'. As with figures, animals and birds are presented with unnatural prominence according to their relative importance in the scene.

Most haunting of all the similarities are the religious overtones that resonate throughout African-American art. The Christian tradition surfaces in virtually every folk artist's repertoire, lending depth and spirituality to otherwise simple human scenes.

Where strong similarities exist, powerful differences also occur. The first obvious and distinctive feature in Miss Addie's art, one that separates her from all the others, is her intense use of color. Addie's color is vibrant and pure; her yellows, reds, pinks, oranges, and sky blues are knock-your-socks-off bright. While many folk artists use somber, mixed earth tones, Addie does not…ever. When Addie does mix, the resulting coral or purple is Day-Glo hot.

The pink, yellow, and emerald green buildings in **Project Kids** vibrate off the canvas, as do the pigments in **Colors**:

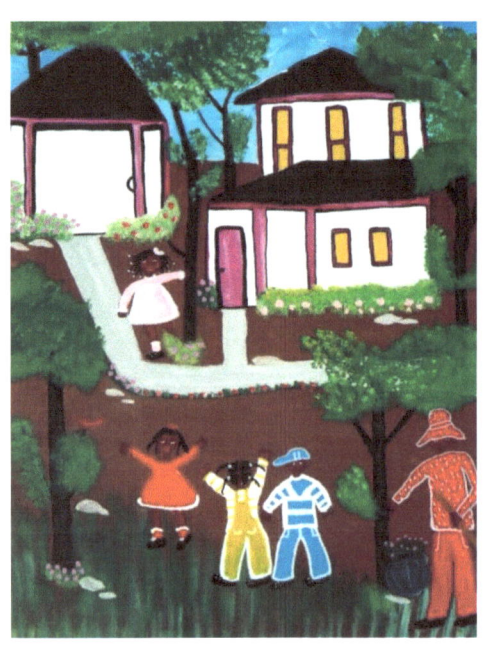

Colors
20 x 24 acrylic on canvas

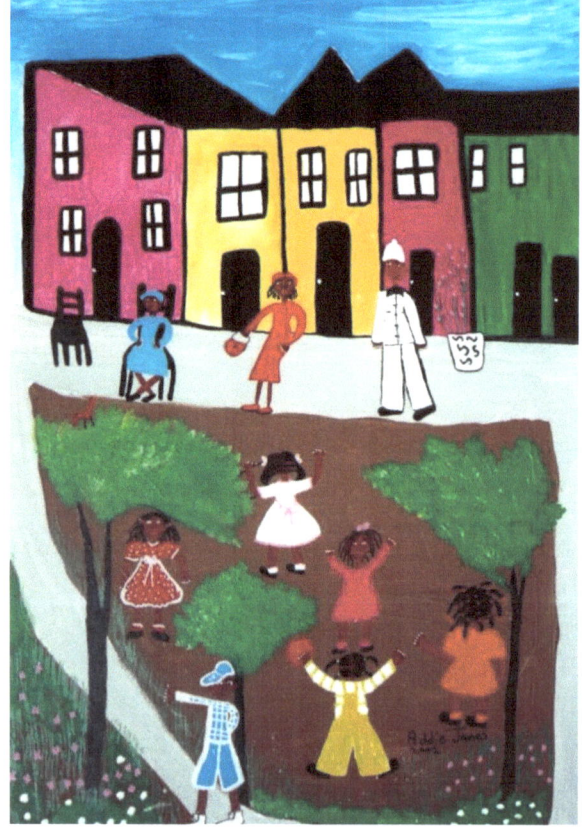

Project Kids
24 x 36 acrylic on canvas

The second distinctive feature of an Addie James piece is often texture. The artist may use sparkling glitter…silver, gold, or ruby to decorate a fancy dress, necklace, or fingernails. She switches from matte finish to glossy black enamel to paint hair. And for her painting ***The Cotton Patch***, Miss Addie laboriously removed the cotton from Q-Tips and pasted them to her panel:

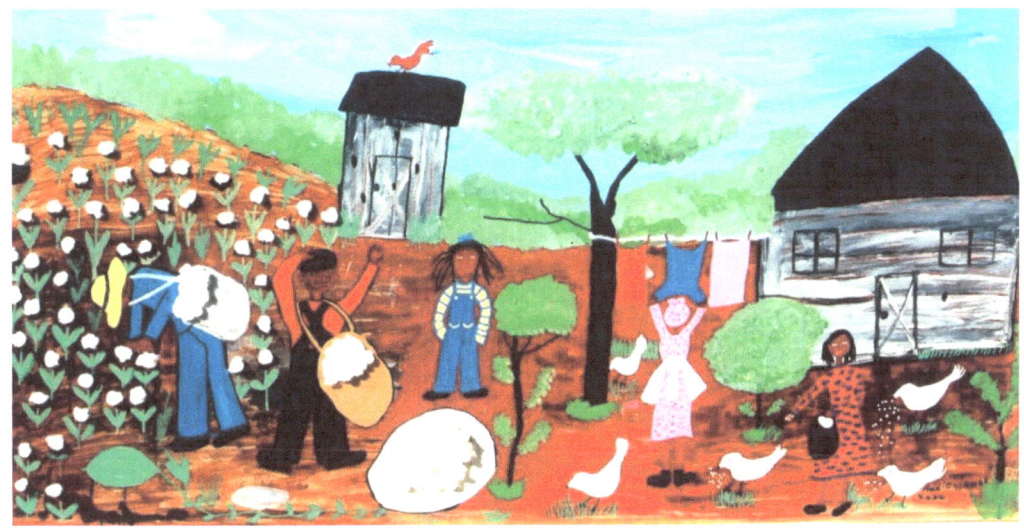

Addie James: ***The Cotton Patch***, 19 ¾ x 39 ¾ acrylic and cotton on Masonite

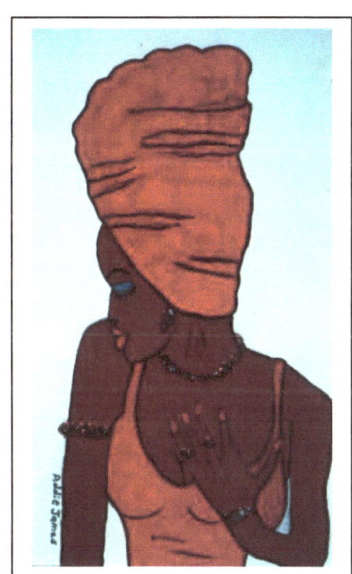

Beauty, 8 ¼ x 14
acrylic & glitter on paper

The final distinctive difference in Miss Addie's work was *tone* or *theme*. While many of her counterparts explored the dark side of living in black America, especially the discordant ugliness of racism, Addie's thrust was always positive, hopeful, and infused with joy. One collector noted this saying: "But I've always heard if art makes you *smile…* it isn't *serious* art."

Serious art? The pages of art history books are filled with humorous, whimsical, and other critically acclaimed works

that not only evoke a smile, but sometimes inspire outright laughter.

33

In the final analysis, no matter what you call it, Addie James' style appeals to almost everyone. It crosses cultural, socio-economic, and racial borders. Collectors who usually prefer conservative, traditional art surprise themselves by selecting one or more of Miss Addie's works. Ruth Pittard, who had never before purchased a painting, bought numerous pieces during *MEET MISS ADDIE*, the artist's first one-woman show that opened February 2nd, 2002. Later Ruth presented a letter to Addie, which eloquently expressed her feelings:

Miss Addie,

Thank you so much for sharing your paintings with us. They are a path to God for me, a way that God speaks to me through you and your marvelous painting people. In this very hard and cynical time, when innocence seems lost, goodness appears to me in your paintings. They speak of seeing the best in people, of reflecting love by living in our everyday life, surrounded by children, being with those we cherish, working with the earth. Now, as your paintings live in my house, in every room, I am reminded every day of the connections with which I am blessed---friends, family, nature, young people, old people---all of Creation around me representing how blessed it is to be alive and loving.

Monica, an 8 x 11 acrylic on paper,

originally hung in Ruth Pittard's Office of Community Services at Davidson College. And over the years, Ruth has collaborated with Addie to create several illustrated children's books.

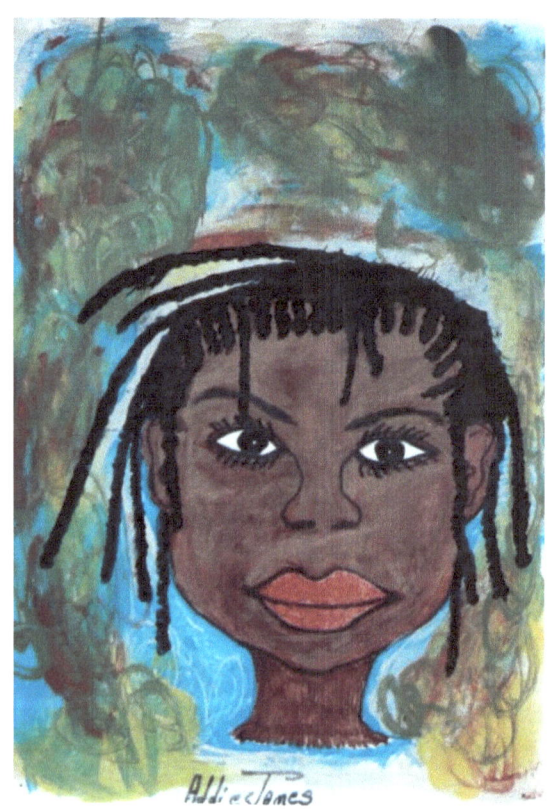

Alvera Brown, a postal worker in Charlotte, happened to spot Addie's show invitation as she sorted mail. She jotted down the information and made the trip. Not only did she meet Miss Addie, but she also acquired **God is Good** for her budding collection.

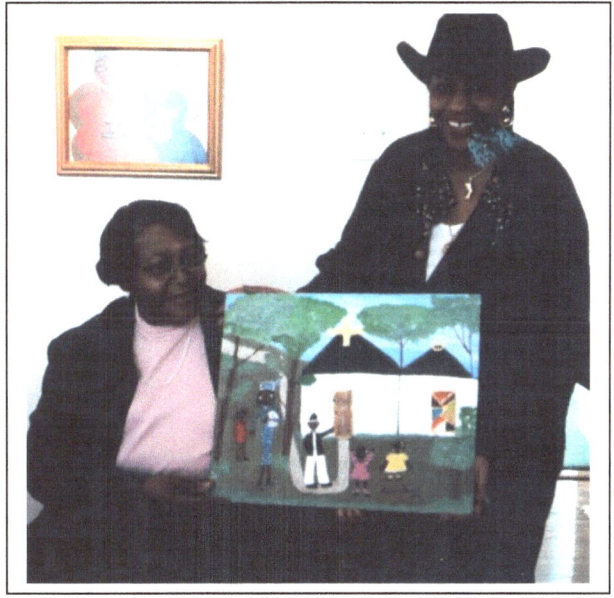

Somehow special things happened when people connected with Miss Addie and her art…

Fred and Kathy Marks lived in Addie's hometown, Statesville, where Fred was Addie's physician. Yet he had never seen Addie's work, nor had Addie revealed that she was an artist. Enchanted by her paintings, Fred purchased a large collection for his office, while Kathy chose several for their home.

After that, Miss Addie saw
Just Like Sisters,
16 ¾ x 16 ¾ acrylic on mat board,
when she visited Dr. Marks' office.

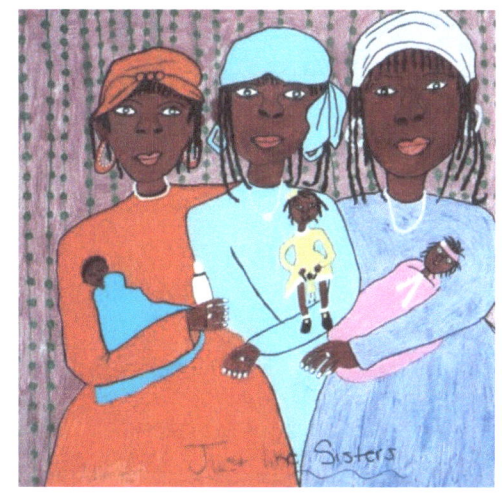

So, Miss Addie, You got it goin' on, but what is it? Regarding her style, The Charlotte Observer's Mary C. Curtis reviewed Miss Addie's show and got it right:

Art experts define and dissect what's called outsider or primitive art, art by untrained artists. Definitions are too narrow for Addie James' gift.[10]

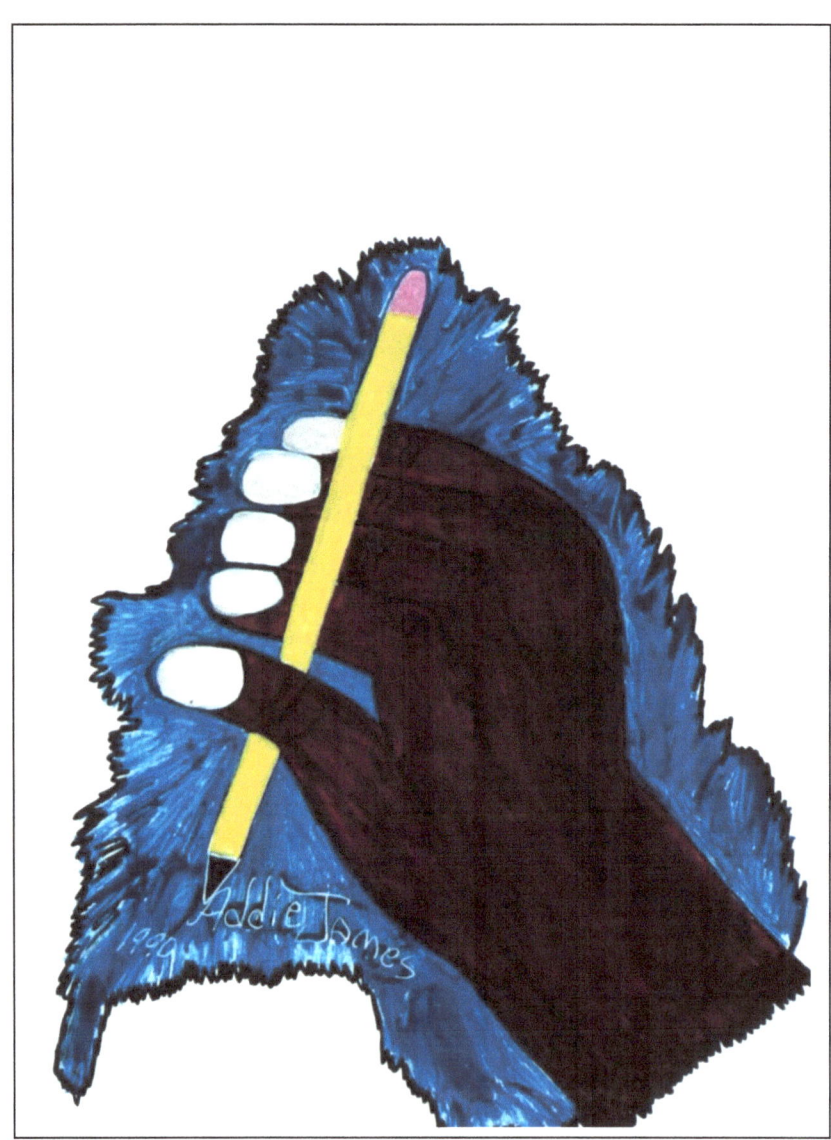

Artist's Hand
9 x 14 acrylic on mat board

---

[10] "From Miss Addie, the art of the smile" Mary C. Curtis, Charlotte Observer, February 10, 2002

LOOK AT ME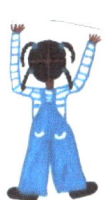

When earliest man took up a chalky stone, a burnt stick, or a primitive carving tool, his first impulse was to create a likeness of himself. Along with the urge to make his person *fine* by decorating and clothing his body, he needed to depict himself in relation to the world around him. This obsession has persisted from prehistoric times to modern day.

The desire to replicate one's own image is a human need that goes deeper than vanity, deeper than the wish to leave a pictorial history of a people, and deeper than the therapeutic value of drawing a place for oneself in a chaotic world. Ultimately, to record one's image on a cave wall, a canvas, or videotape is to cheat death. It is a bone-deep bid for eternity that likely will not go away anytime soon.

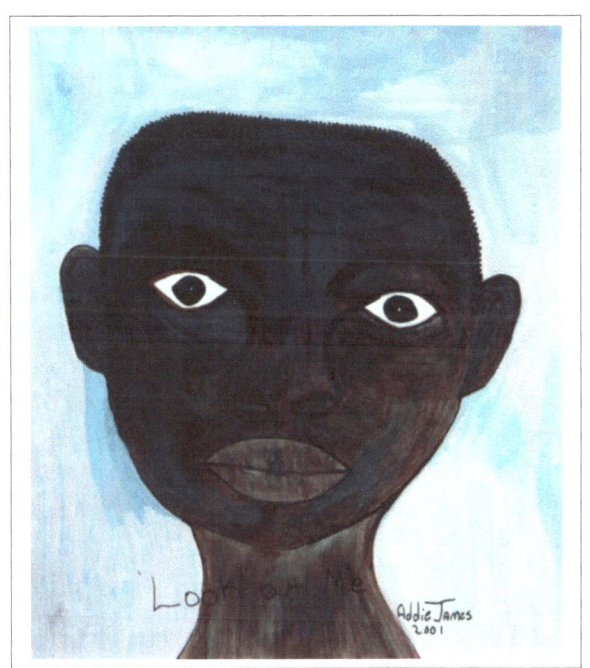

Look at Me 18 x 21 acrylic on mat board

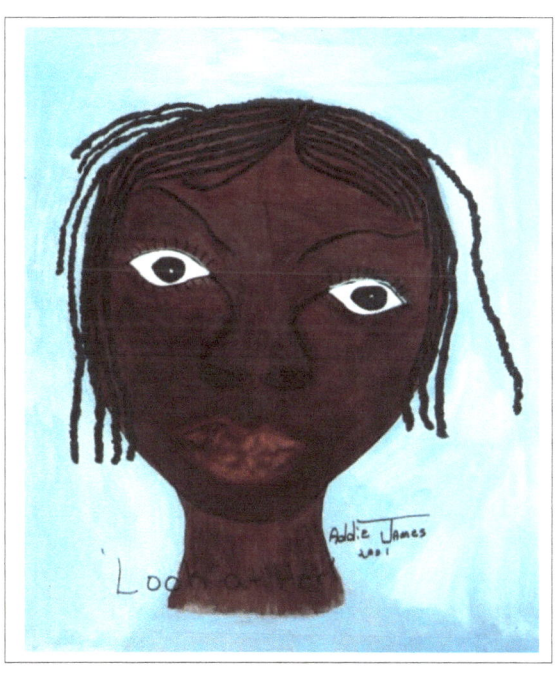

Look at Her 18 x 21 acrylic on mat board

Art history reflects this impulse century by century, and as we enter a new millennium, the technical means of creating our own image have advanced well beyond primitive man's imagination. The motivation, however, has not changed. At one time or another almost every artist attempts portraiture, and Addie James is no exception.

Miss Addie's paintings *Look At Me* and *Look At Her* evoke innocence and a sweet naiveté that sometimes defines her work. The young boy insists: *look at me*! He will not be ignored or overlooked. At the same time, they are *his* words that spill over onto the young girl's portrait: *look at her*! Seemingly she does not speak for herself.

Historically, beautiful young black women have been the *objects* of admiration, but in this case, the boy's words inspire us to look beyond the girl's physical beauty to her strength. This insistence reflects more directly on the boy's integrity than the girl's silence, for as we explore Addie's art and her personality, we understand that the girls and women she depicts are mute only when they *choose* to be.

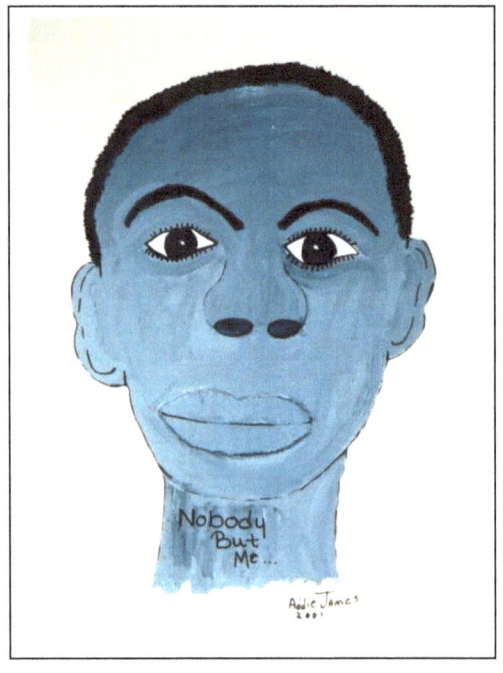 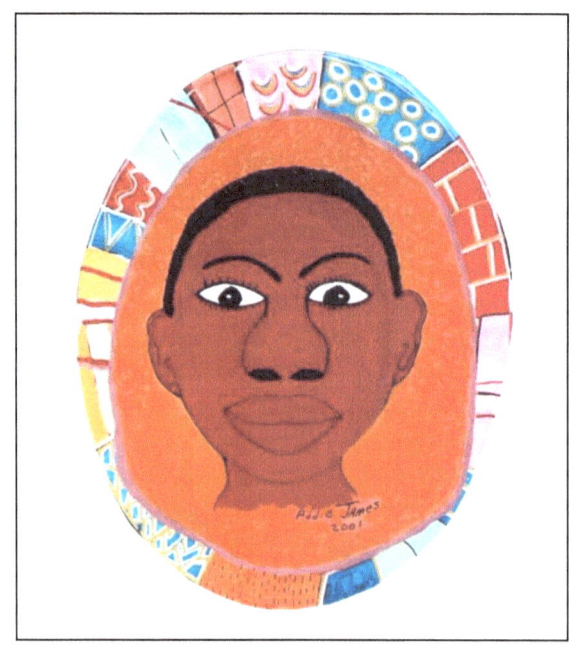

Nobody But Me
17 ½ x 23 acrylic on mat board

Brown Boy
16 x 20 acrylic on oval canvas

Nobody But Me and *Brown Boy*, like many of Addie's portraits, have less to do with specific personalities than with the expression of an idea.

Nobody But Me is a strong phrase implying black pride and solidarity, and yet there is nothing militant about the subject. As always, Miss Addie made her point gently, without a trace of rancor.

Brown Boy celebrates the color of African-American skin, which the artist enjoyed painting in all its rich hues from pale gray through chocolate brown to charcoal black. It seemed when Addie painted very pale skin…light gray…as in *I've Been Through the Struggle, Nobody But Me,* and *Young Man,* the color also implies sadness.

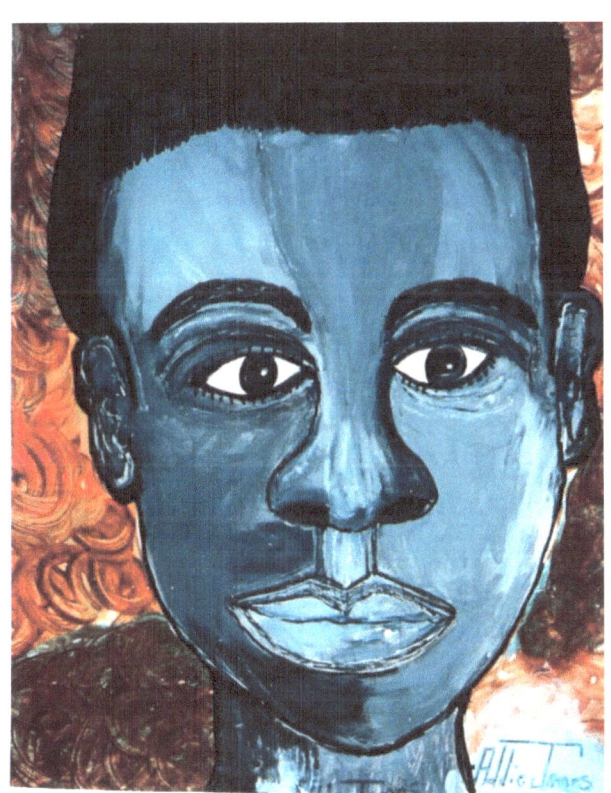

When I start a portrait, I be thinking of people I've seen on TV, or maybe at church. And sometimes I just draw from my own mind to create a person.

I think about my grandchildren and other little children I see. Some children I see are so sad, and when I make it in the world, by the help of the good Lord, I'll go back and help those children, because they really need help.

Young Man 10 x 21 ½ acrylic on paper

The vast majority of Miss Addie's paintings feature girls and women, but in her portraits, male images dominate. *Young Man* is a more specific portrait, a combination of her favorite brother, Jubie (Willie Maddox) and Jerry, the beloved son she lost.

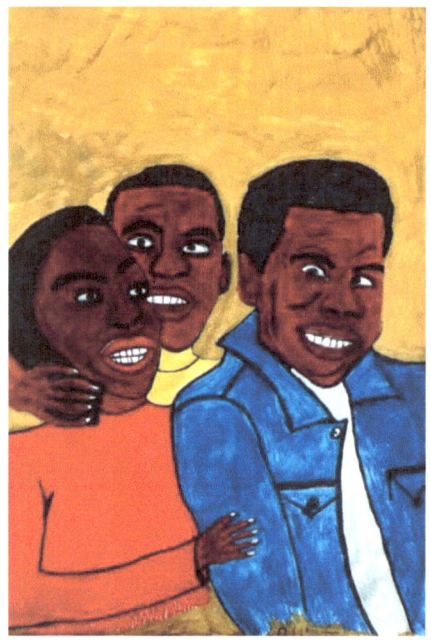

Old Times presents three distinct people, uncles and aunts, as they reminisce about the good old days.

Old Times
10 ½ x 14 acrylic on paper

**When Miss Addie *did* create a woman's portrait,
it was often about high style and glamour.**

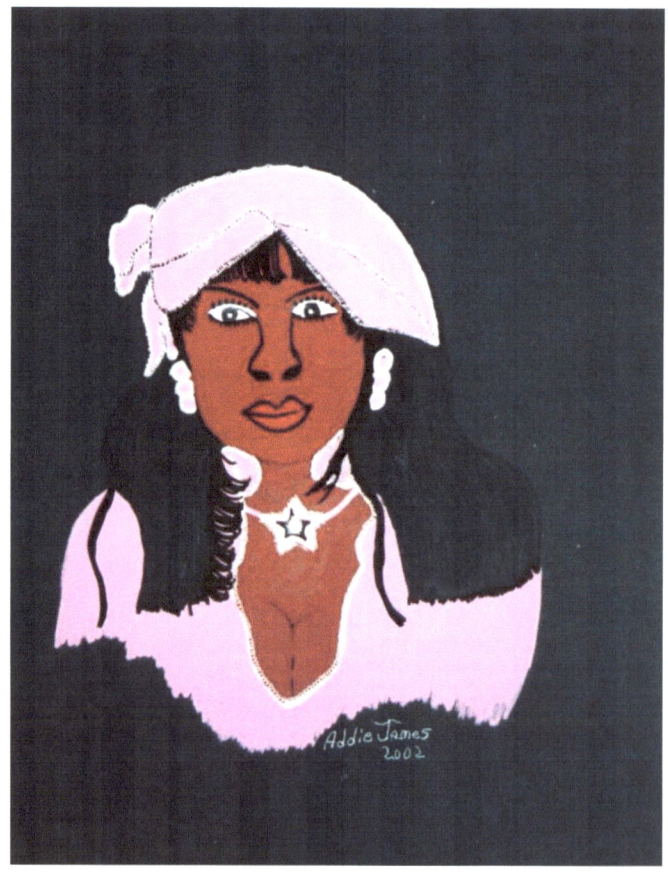

Lady in Pink
15 x 17 ½ acrylic on mat board

VISION OF BEAUTY
  *by **Addie James***

If you are searching for me, let me help you,

Because I am more than you can see.

Look first through the outer being.

For I am hidden far beyond your seeking.

I am calm, peaceful, beautiful, and pleasant.

I wait to be recognized.

But most times I am not rewarded a prize.

Most people spend a lot of time

Adorning their outer parts

Forgetting that I am closer to their hearts.

You may say I'm a mental image.

Or you may call me a dream.

Whichever the case may be, give up.

My identity is *Vision of Beauty*.

And, oh, by the way, you are part of me.

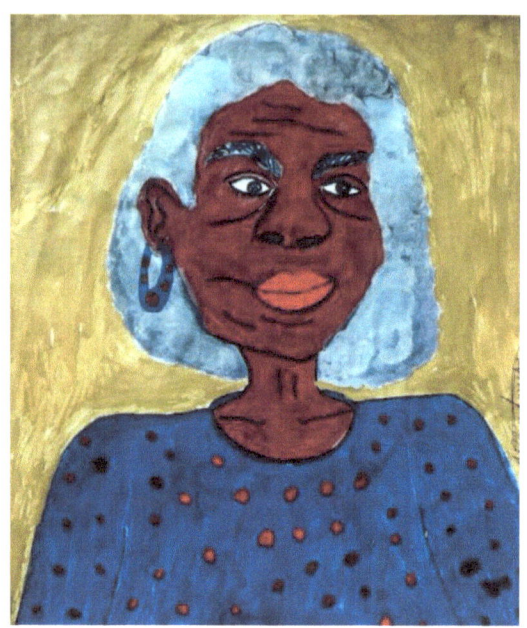

Aunt Addie
10 ½ x 12 ½ acrylic on paper

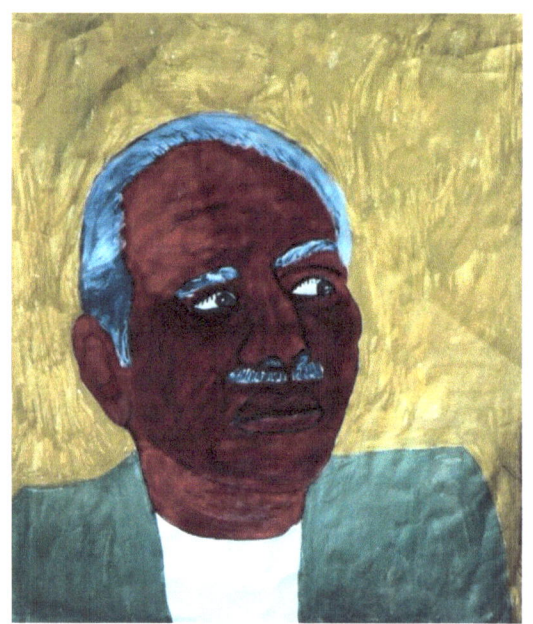

Uncle Benny
10 ½ x 12 ½ acrylic on paper

That's my Aunt Addie and Uncle Benny. Because I was named after my Aunt Addie,
I sort of placed them both in my mind, you know?

LIFE IN THE COUNTRY

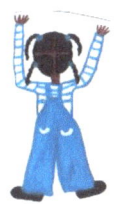

When I met Addie at her house on May 8th for another interview, it was hot enough to brew sun tea on the deck and fry an egg on the tin wash bucket. The scent of honeysuckle hung sweet in the still air, and as I surveyed the neighborhood where Addie lived, I tried to imagine the fields and forests which surrounded the little house when Addie and her new husband, Robert James, bought the place in 1971.

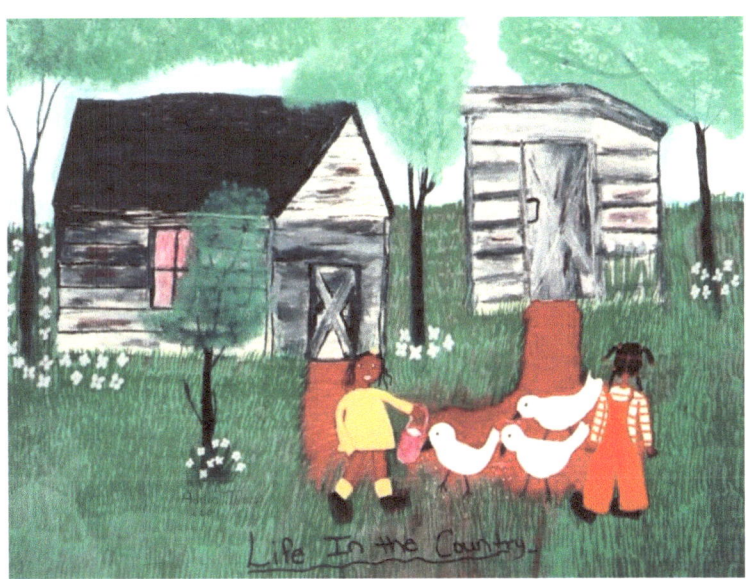

Life in the Country
17 ½ x 23 acrylic on mat board

By then I had discovered that like so much in North Carolina, many of the places Addie described from her childhood had been torn down or altered beyond all recognition. My research had confirmed what Addie had already told me: her old houses were gone, her grade school was now a funeral home, and even a street name had disappeared. The colorful fabric of her past had been woven into a fine quilt that lived only in her memory.

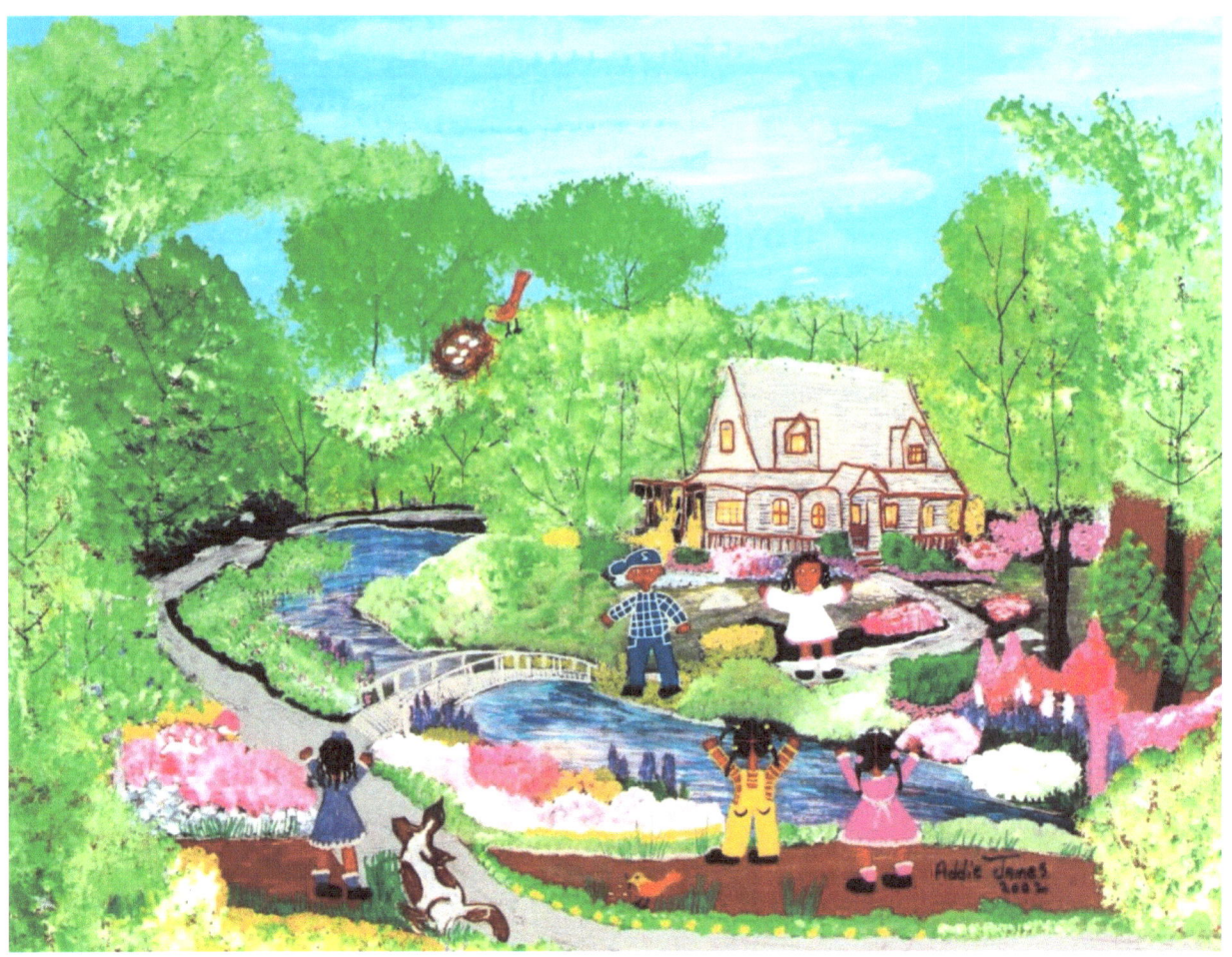

Springtime
22 x 28 acrylic on gray poster board

And do you know in those days you could find a pink dogwood in the woods? You can't go to the woods and find a pink dogwood tree now. They're all white. But they used to be pink, with the prettiest flowers. I was thinking about that when I painted **Springtime.**

Yet these long-gone images from Miss Addie's memory became

alive in the here and now when she captured them on paper or canvas.

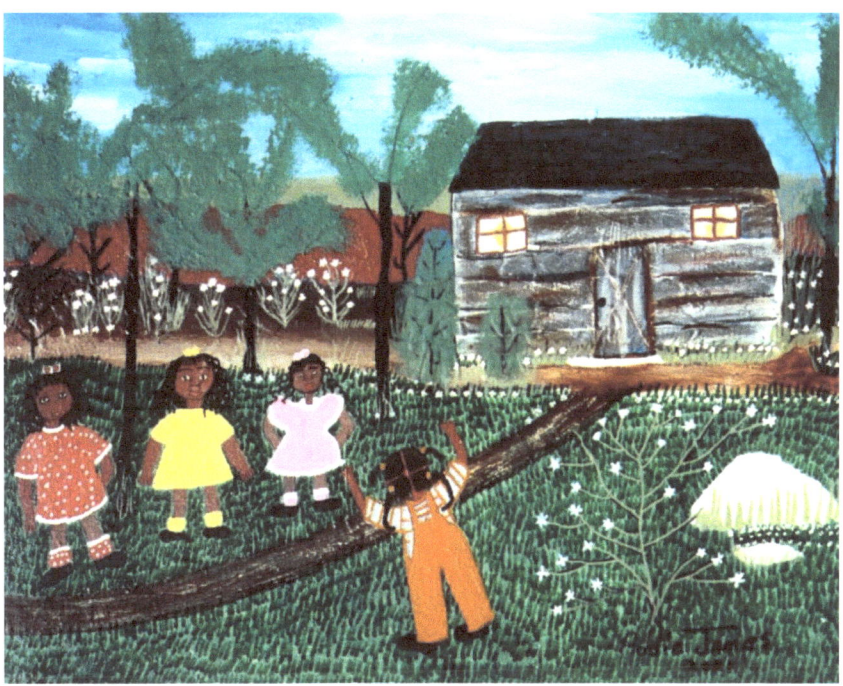

Having A Good Time
16 x 20 acrylic on canvas

They got some log cabins in Harmony, and I put these chickens and kids around them, and that's what come into my mind when I drew Having A Good Time.

Clearly the paintings depicting Miss Addie's life in the country are among her most powerful works simply because they are narrative and heart-felt. Each of these scenes is fully realized, with a complete foreground, middle ground, and background. Each one tells a story from her life, from the birds in the trees to the mice in the grass, so that even without Addie's commentary, we would learn to know her.

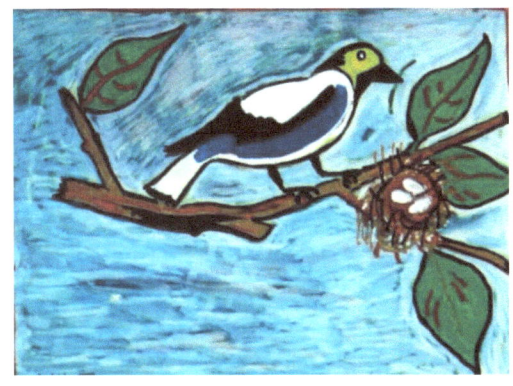

Bird Nesting 8 x 10 acrylic on paper

Boy, I was something! I wasn't like the other kids. I didn't get into trouble because I was always busy reading... always trying to invent something, you know?
I didn't like crowds of people.
I'd like to talk to the trees better than I would people.

45

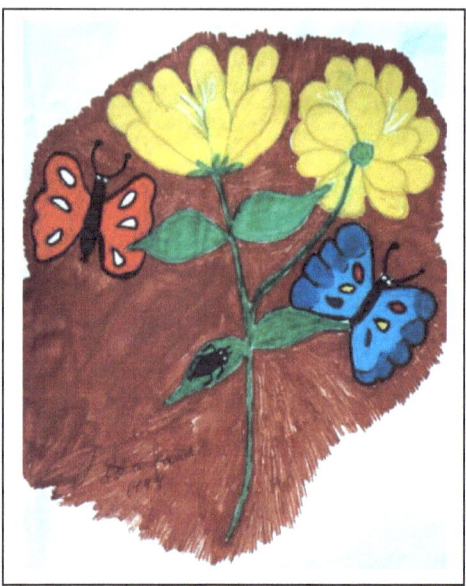

Bug and Butterflies
9 x 11 ½ acrylic on paper

They called young Addie "Demp" because she had dimples: *But I guess I grew fat and they grew out.* Her best sidekick was her sister, Janie, called "Dot." Next to Addie, Janie was the youngest Maddox girl, and together Demp and Dot had marvelous adventures:

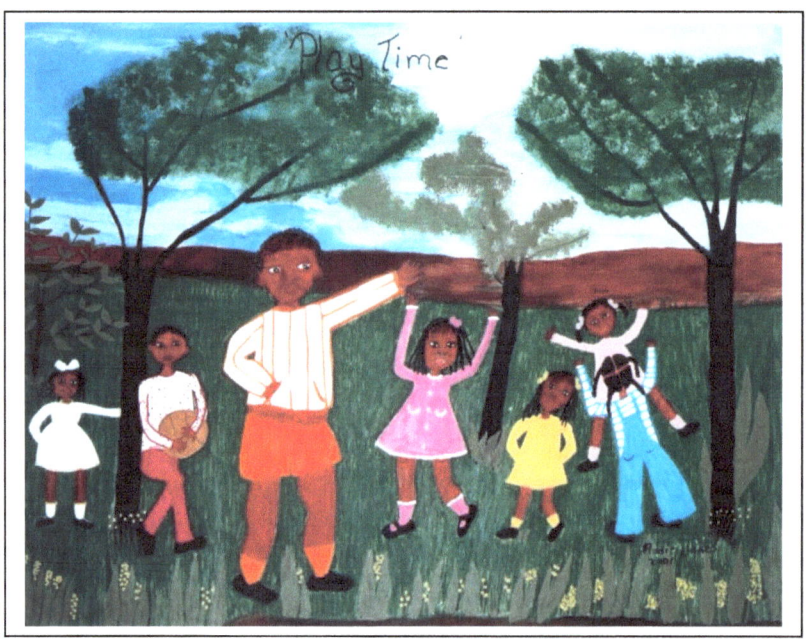

Play Time
21 ¾ x 27 ¾ acrylic on mat board

What we did for fun was me and my sister would sit and draw, and make things, and look at Daddy whittle out dolls. He would sit down and whittle out a jumpin' jack doll...every part of it moved. And he would make slingshots and bow and arrows.

And we would play in the branch and get clay. We would never buy clay; we would always get it out of the branch. We would dry it in the sun. We made little buildings, and we made farms. My sister had a farm, and I had a farm...little house, just everything. It was so much fun! We had the whole family to go into it.

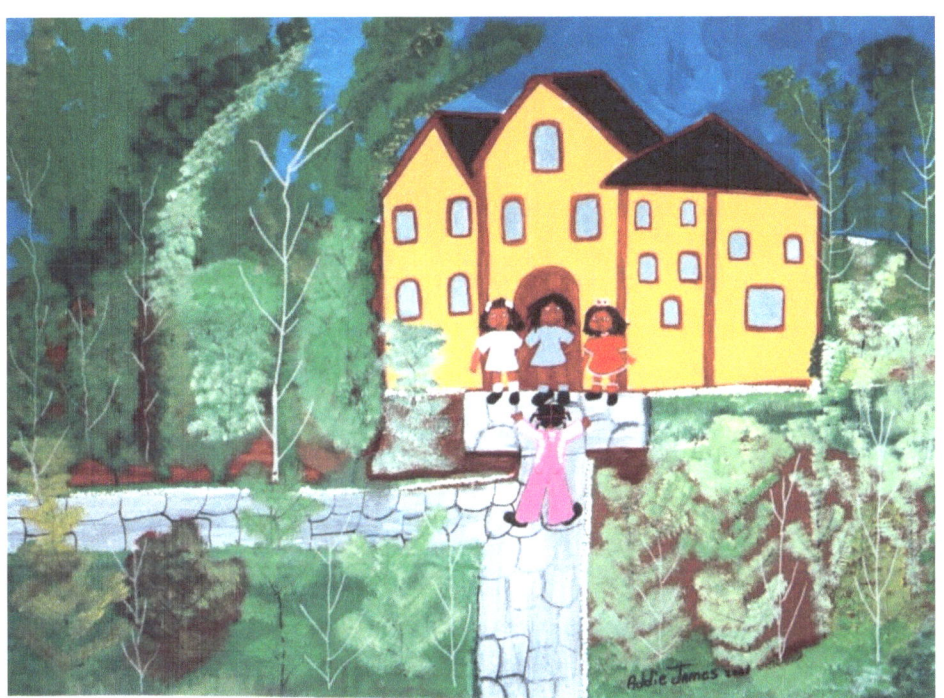

Girls at the Big Yellow House
20 x 28 acrylic on gray cardboard

But in *all* adventures Addie was the ringleader. In *Girls at the Big Yellow House* the little Addie figure in pink stands on the sidewalk telling her sisters Gladys, Betty, and Janie *what is what.*

In this painting the yellow building represents a school, but in many other works it puts Addie *in mind of the house where we lived in Belmont. There was a lot of woods and stuff around it.*

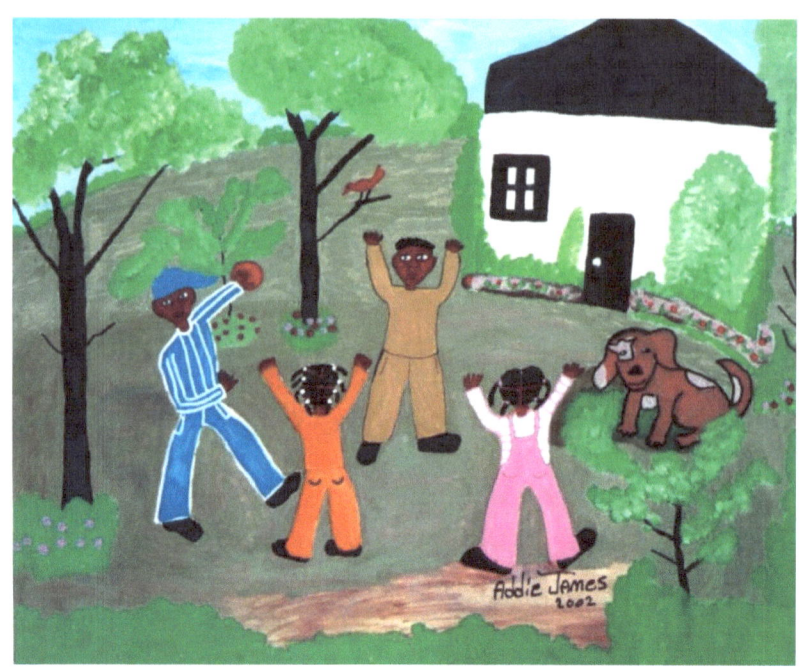

Kids Playing With Dog
16 ½ x 20 ½ acrylic on mat board

In other paintings Addie featured a small *white* house: *My sister, Gladys, lived in a little white house like that. Only she's added on to it now. It don't look like this now…*

On the subject of pets:

 We had a little brown dog once with a little black nose, but I didn't like pets. I liked drawing, designing clothes, inventing something…trying to make the world a better place, but, no, I'M NOT AN ANIMAL PERSON. I'M REALLY NOT.

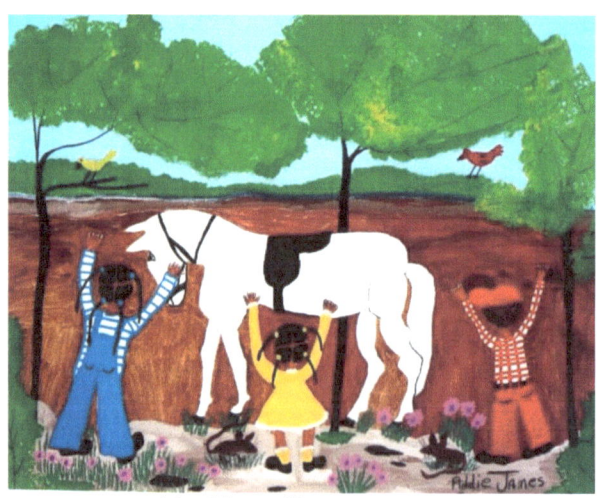

16 x 20 acrylic on canvas

Maybe Miss Addie was not an animal person, but she loved to draw herself and her pals in the company of animals. The idea of enjoying four-legged friends was more appealing than the reality:

Now I went to ride on a horse one time, and I got thrown on my leg when I jumped. I was scared of the horse, and I jumped clean over his head and never got back on. I didn't like the feel of the horse to my skin.

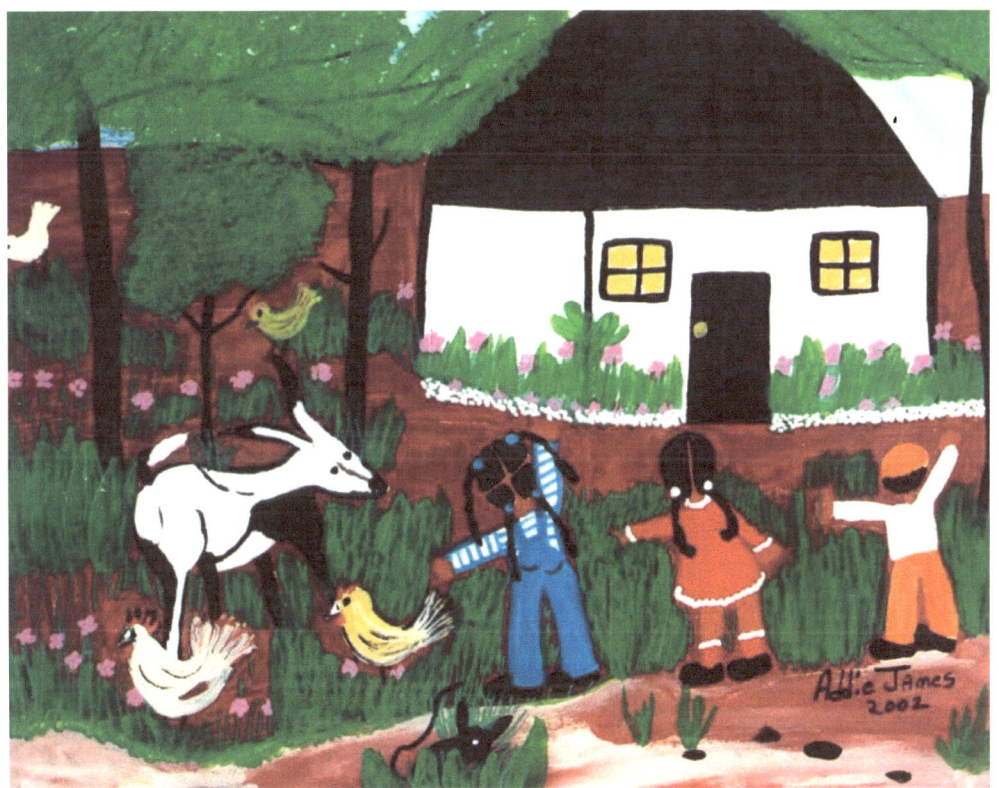

The Billy Goat, 11 x 14 acrylic on canvas

They got goats where I live now...right back there. And they got chickens, and I go back there and talk to them sometimes.

You need not visit Paris to imagine the Eiffel Tower. Addie painted children on camping trips and playing at the lake. These activities were not part of her childhood experience...not as one would assume from her paintings. Nonetheless, they came to life in her work.

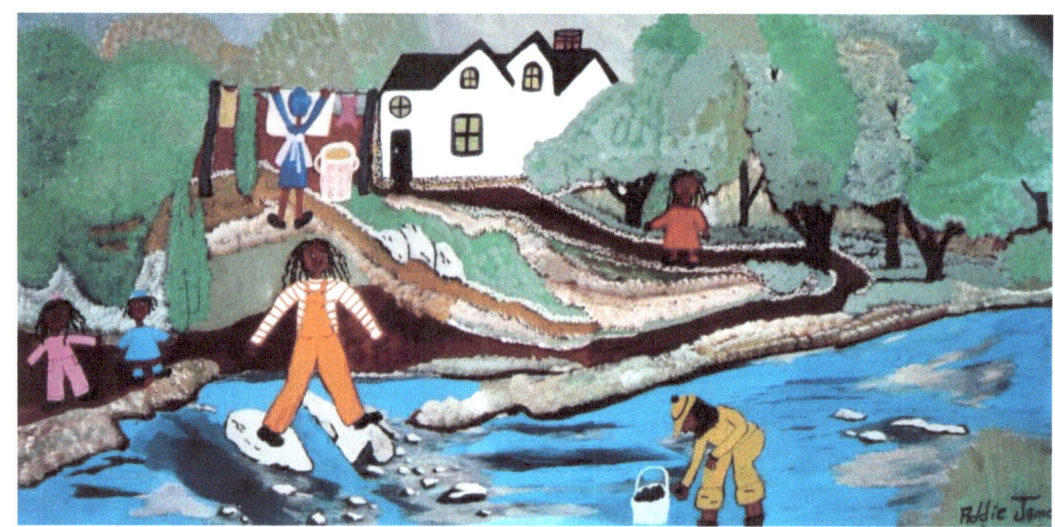

A Day at the Lake
19 x 38 acrylic painted over a reproduction on canvas

I'd gather up all the kids in the neighborhood ˈand take marshmallows and watermelons and hot dogs…and a flashlight for protection, and we'd go way deep in the woods. Those were very good adventures.

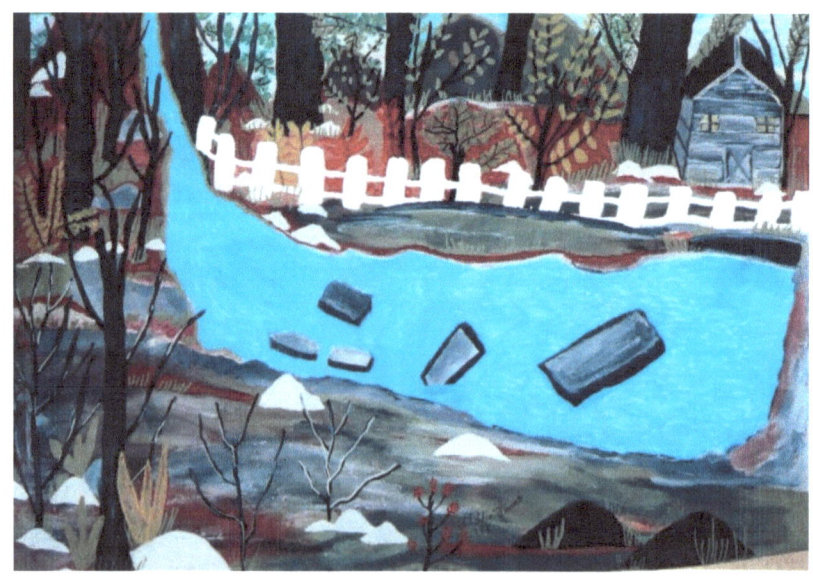

River Front
15 x 22 acrylic on paper

Occasionally Miss Addie created landscapes without people. Scenes like *River Front* may spring from her memories of the home place in South Carolina, or she may have visited the nearby Catawba or Yadkin Rivers. All the same, she did not trust water: *I will never get in a boat!* She did, however, love the mountains:

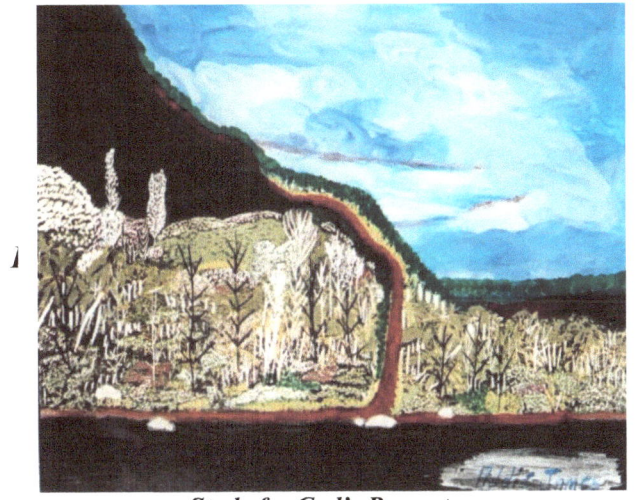

and I love the mountains. I love the outdoors and the trees, and I see a spot and I'll name it on my own.

Study for God's Present
10 x 12 acrylic on paper

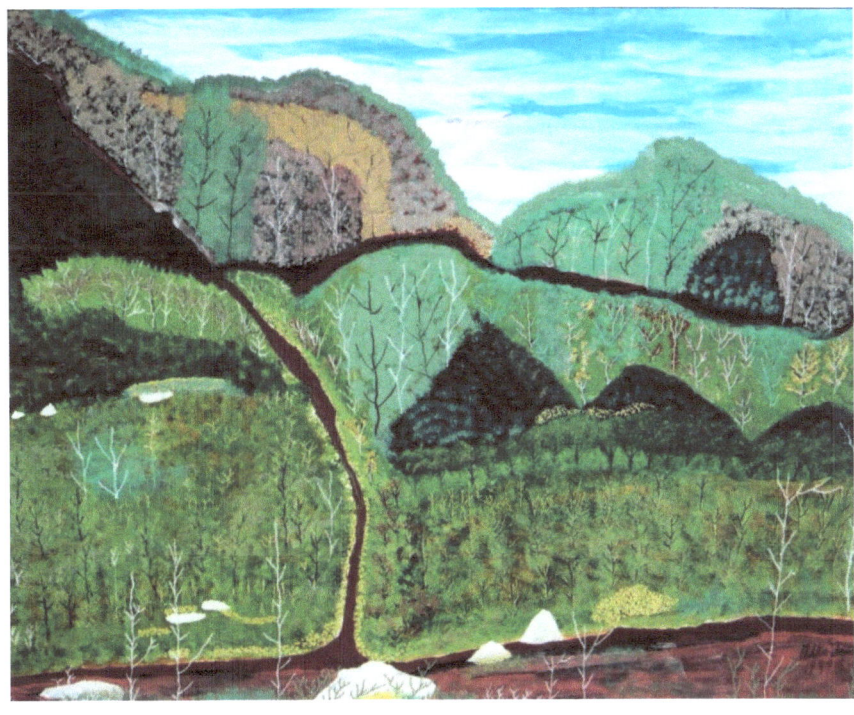

God's Present
23 x 29 ½ acrylic on
gray poster board

As a group, Miss Addie's *life in the country* paintings are close kin to what most critics call "folk art."

They enchant the most cynical beholder with the sheer joy of her expression.

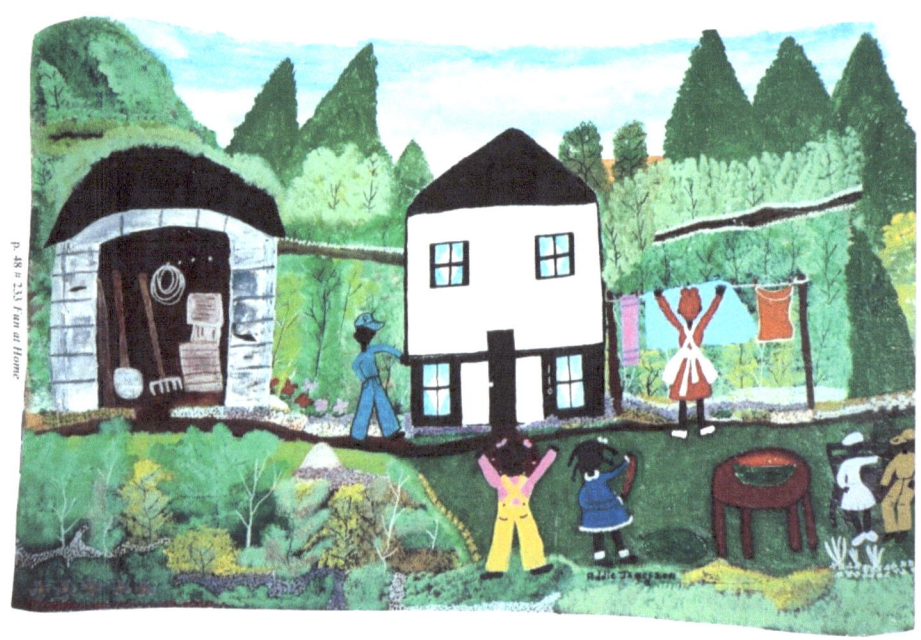

Fun at Home
22 ½ x 35 acrylic on gray cardboard

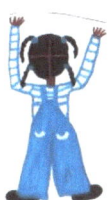

LIFE AT HOME

Like Addie's country paintings, her *life at home* **series** depicts fully realized scenes from her childhood. Only now we must leave her beloved outdoors and come inside to the warmth of her family circle:

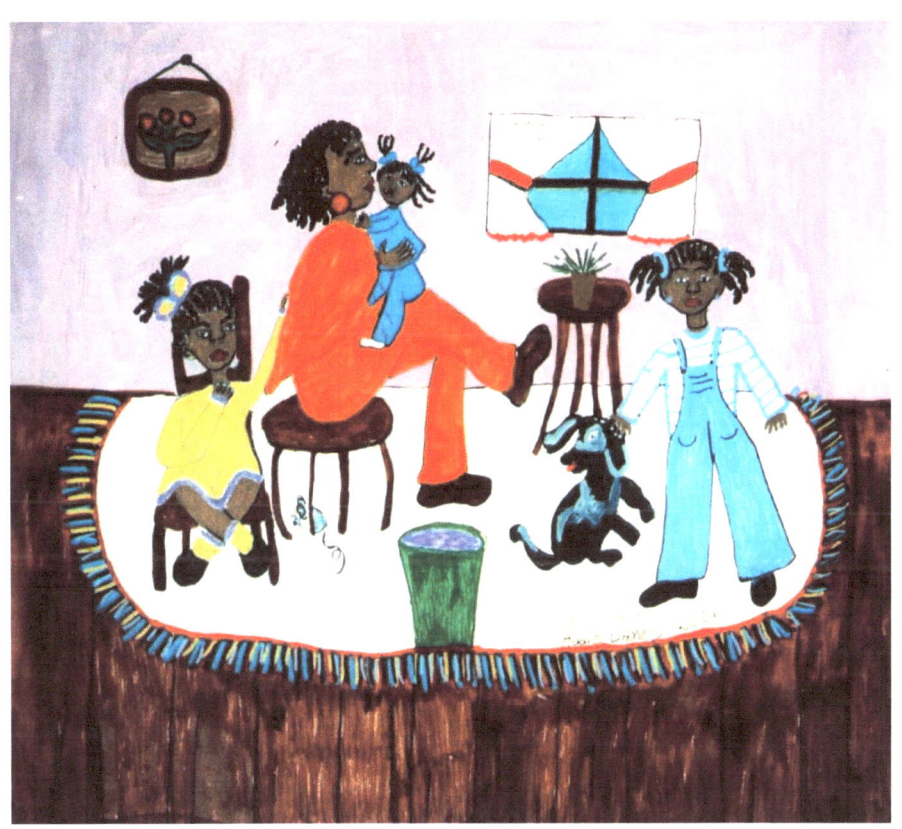

At Home
13 ¾ x 16 ¾ acrylic on mat board

The dog sees the rat under the chair, and the little girl in the yellow dress sees it, so she's trying to tell her mama. But Mama's too busy with the baby.

53

No doubt Addie's mama was always busy, especially when the kids were home from school!

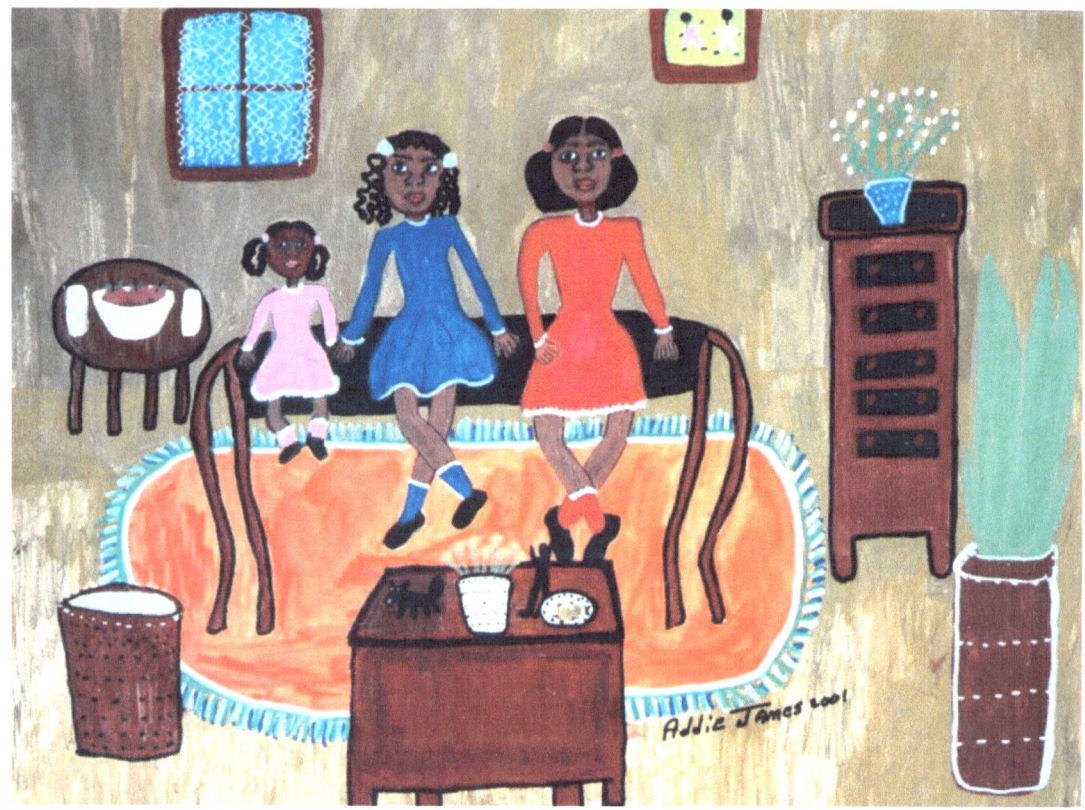

TV Time
12 x 16 acrylic on mat board

Me and my sisters used to sit and watch TV. That was Dot, and that was myself, and that was the little girl used to come over to our house all the time.

Well, we had an old black and white TV. Of course, before we got a TV we went to each other's houses, a bunch of people to look at TV. And when we got our first TV, that was the most exciting thing in the world!

I used to love to watch little Michael Jackson, I Love Lucy, *and* Soul Train. Soul Train *was the main thing, and it was GREAT!*

The elements in *TV Time* recur in many of Miss Addie's interiors. The plants, the dresser, the lace at the windows, the ebony sculptures on the TV…these items appear time and again. Best of all, we get reproductions of the artist's own paintings on the wall. It is a bonus to acquire additional paintings within a painting…two or more Addie James originals for the price of one!

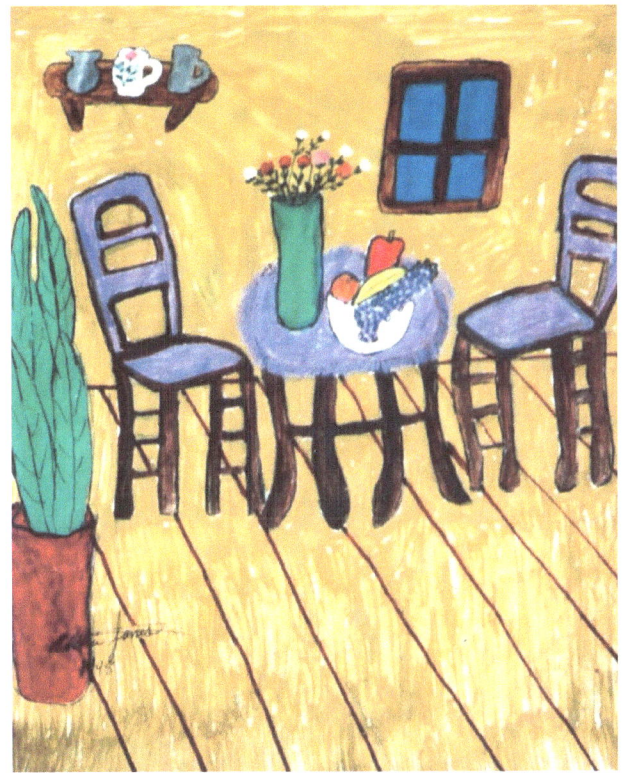

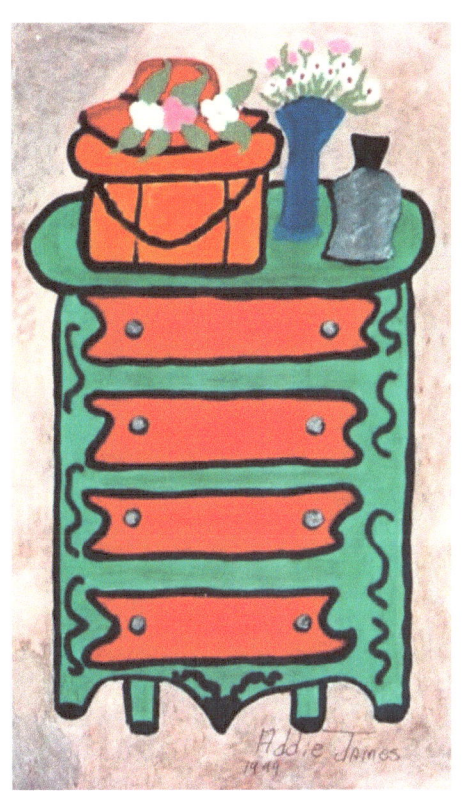

My Room
8 x 10 acrylic on paper

Red Drawers
8 ¼ x 11 acrylic on paper

These things I draw out of my mind, but I used to have a cactus like that. And I used to have a hatbox and a hat like that, and I drew a dresser to put them on. And my son, the one that died, had a bottle of cologne. It was Avon cologne. And I put that all together.

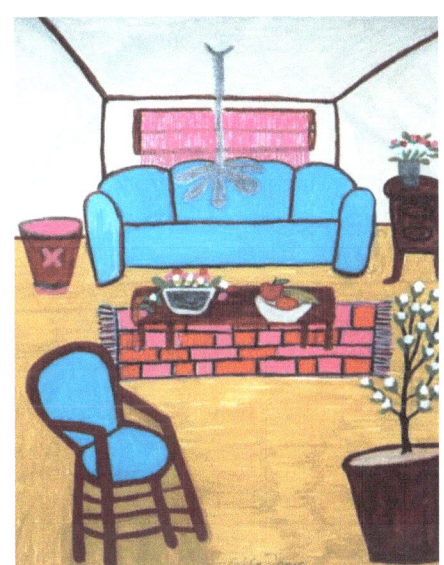

That's my old couch now.
And I had a table like that one.
And I had that big plant right there.

Blue Couch 12 x 16 acrylic on paper

Addie's blue couch was her studio. All her creations were born as she sat in its cushiony depths, painting almost every day, often into the night. Her family testified that they had to wrestle the paintbrush from her hand in order to get her to eat or go to bed.

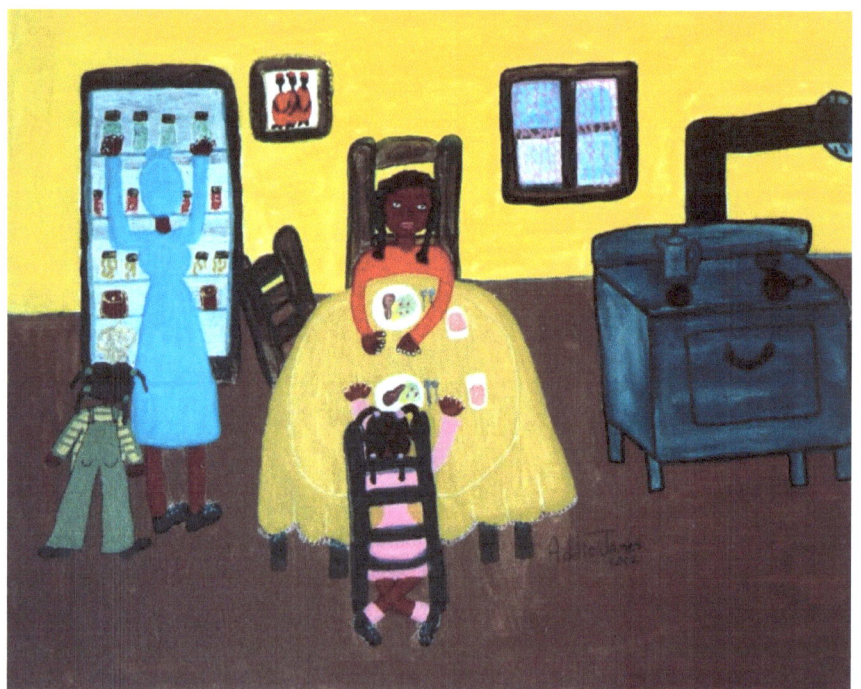

16 x 20 acrylic on canvas

At Addie's house, as in most homes, family life revolved around the dinner table. Cooking and eating were the clocks that set the pace and rhythm of the daily routine:

We had a wood cook stove, and Mama had to can all the time, and it was a great time. We didn't have electric lights back then. There were no fans…and that was a GREAT time back then.

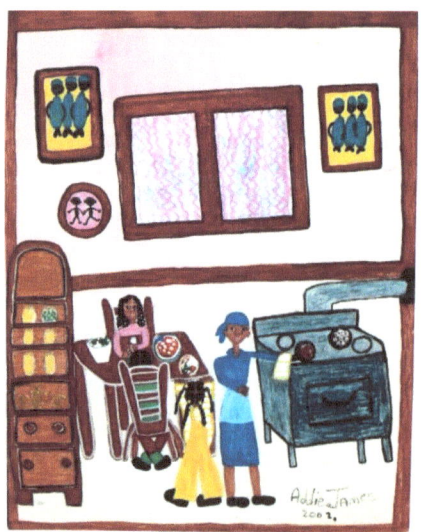

We had already established that Addie's mama was busy, but so were the kids. Even on a rainy day, after school let out, there was never an idle moment.

Cookin' Dinner **16 x 20 acrylic/canvas**

56

When we come home we had our lessons and we had to get our work done. We had to draw water. There was only one well in the community on Templeton Hill, and we had to walk down the street and carry buckets of water, enough water as we were going to use. And then we'd get our wood in and cut the wood. I had to iron and wash the jars so Mama could can in them...and I'd peel apples.

And THEN we'd get our baby dolls and make clothes and play...things like that.

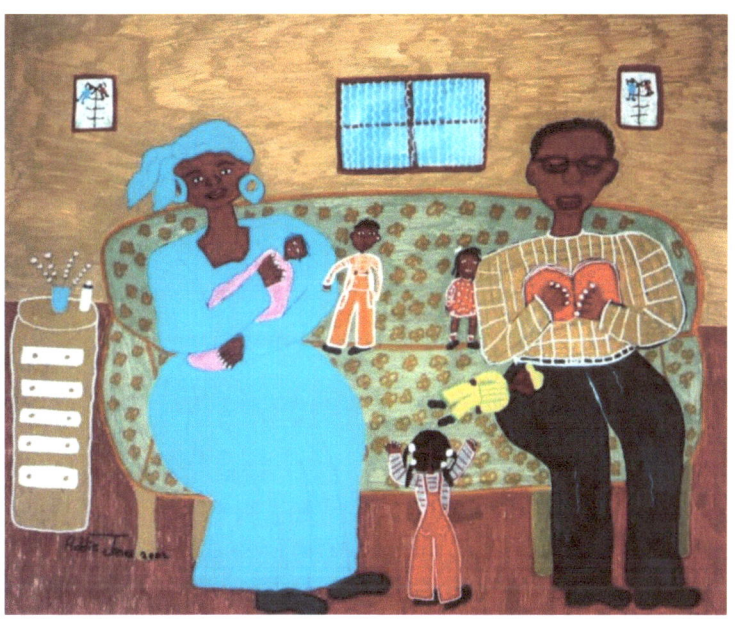

Father Reading Bible to Children
19 ¾ x 24 acrylic on mat board

Addie said *I don't remember nobody ever reading to me,* and yet in the idealized world of her imagination, children were supposed to be read to before they were tucked into bed. The Father in this painting is reading the Bible instead of the *true love* stories Addie actually preferred, so this world is good indeed.

I shared a room with my sister, Janie. Oh, Lord, we had a big iron post bed. She slept on one side of it, and I slept on the other.

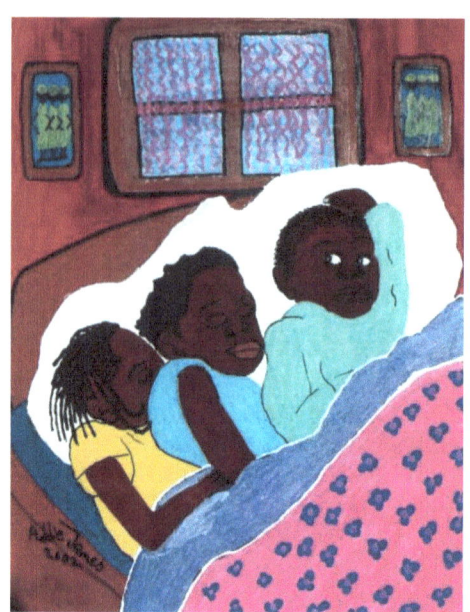

Bedtime **11 x 14 acrylic on mat board**

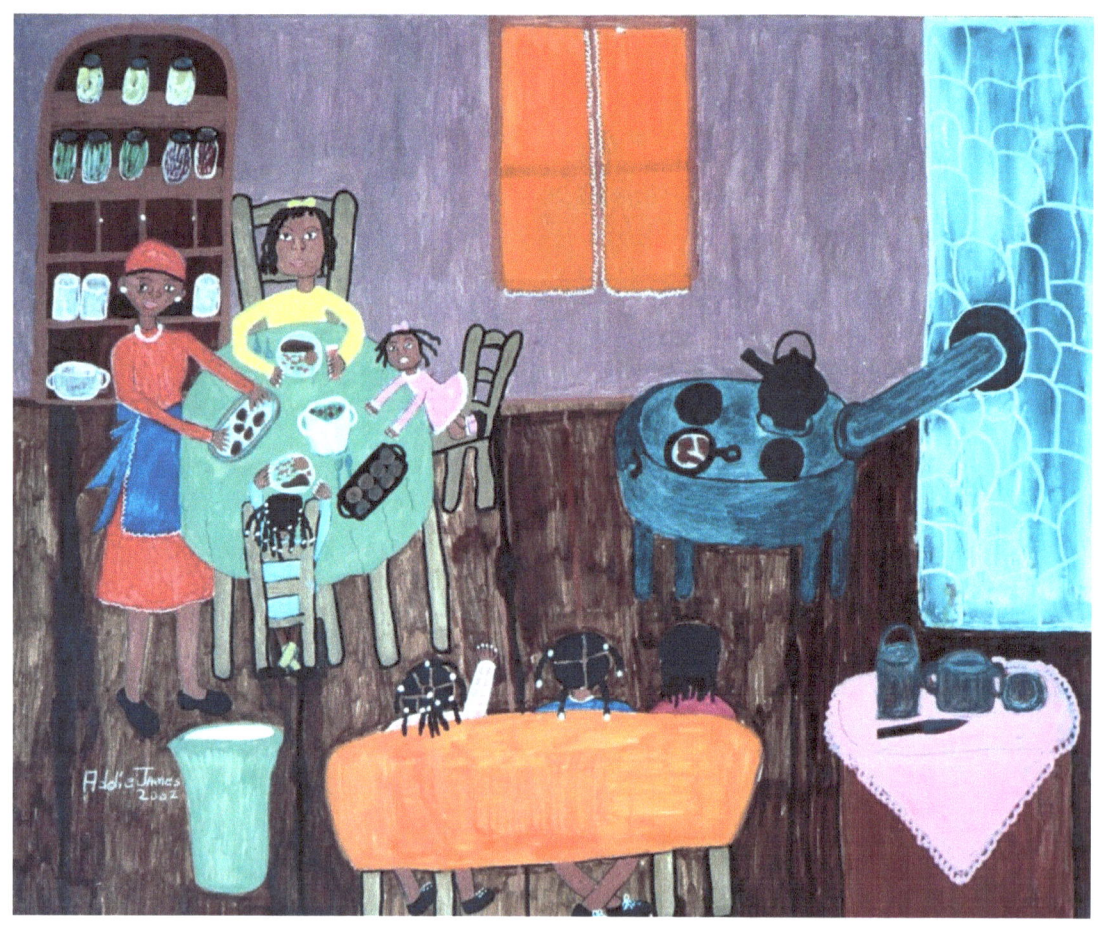

Back in the Day, **16 x 20 acrylic on mat board**

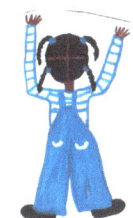

CHILDREN DON'T GO ON TREES

If only one word could be chosen to describe the content of Miss Addie's art, that word would be *children*. While the artist boasted a wide range of styles, children play throughout her entire repertoire. From the fully realized folk scenes to the design statements, children are the emotional key that unlocks Miss Addie's world and draws us inside. The children are an irresistible force.

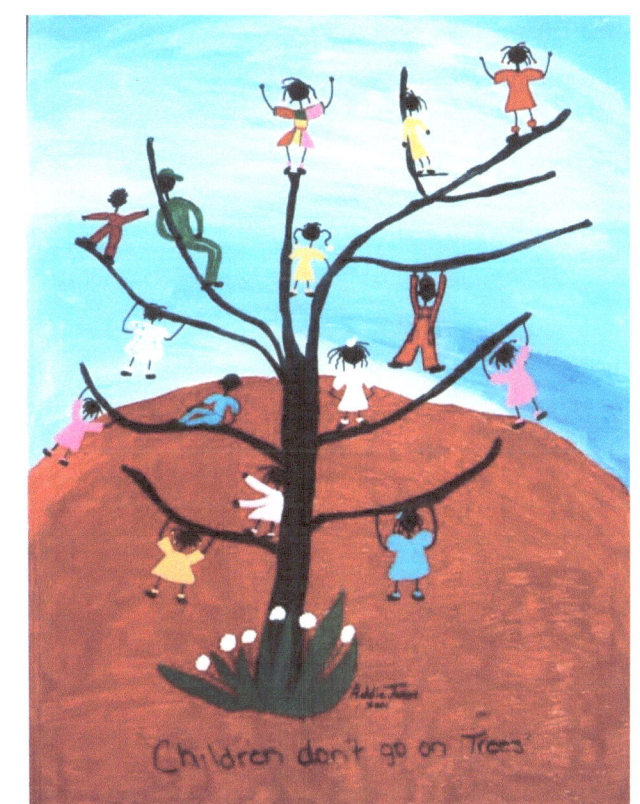

Children Don't Go On Trees
is an exquisite example of Addie's
boundless imagination
and her tongue-n-cheek humor.
Is the title a command warning
the little ones not to climb
lest they fall?
Or is it word play
implying that children
are rare and precious?
Indeed, they do not *grow* on trees.
Ask Addie,
and she will reply
with a sly, enigmatic smile.

Children Don't Go On Trees

18 ½ x 23 ¾ acrylic on mat board

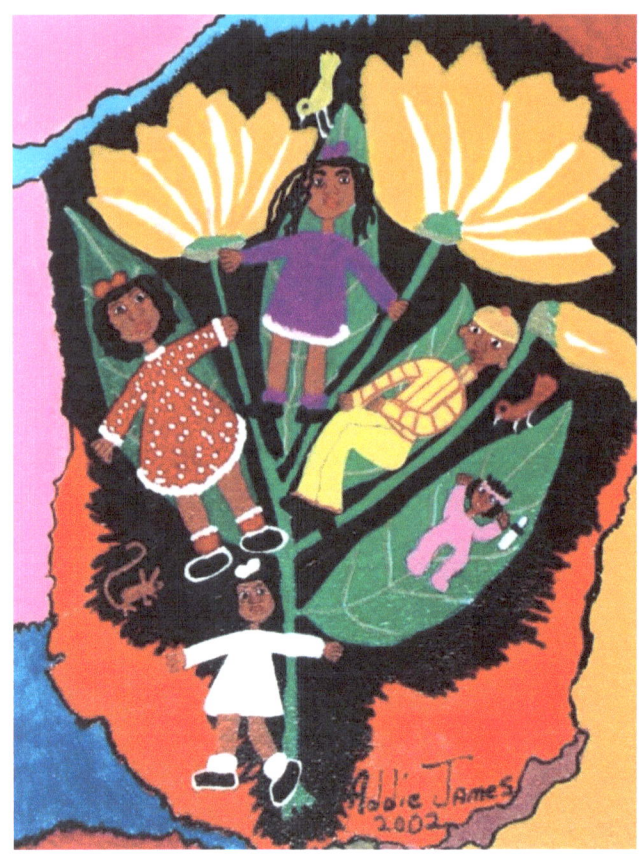

Expanding on this theme,
Flower Children…Again
Gives form and faces
to the stick- like figures
from the tree,
and they become *specific* children.
Is this another play on words?
Are these kids simply blossoms,
a part of nature…?

Flower Children…Again
10 ½ x 13 ½ acrylic on mat board

Or are they actually *flower children* from the turbulent sixties? It is true that Addie James came of age during the decade of drugs, sex, and rock n' roll, and yet it is impossible, knowing her, to place her in that culture.

Children growing on trees…? I don't know. Ideas just pop up in my head and I go for it. I used to love climbing trees, though, and swinging on those monkey vines. But I was no tomboy. I LOVED to dress up!

On one hand the artist drew the *Little Addie* figure in overalls, looking every inch the tomboy. On the other hand, she created dozens of little *pretty prissy girls* (Addie's description) wearing an amazing array of dress- up dresses.

I love drawing little girls.
I love drawing their clothes…
little socks and bows.
And then I get to thinking
I got to draw some little BOYS
whenever it hits me.

But I love drawing little girls
better than I do little boys.

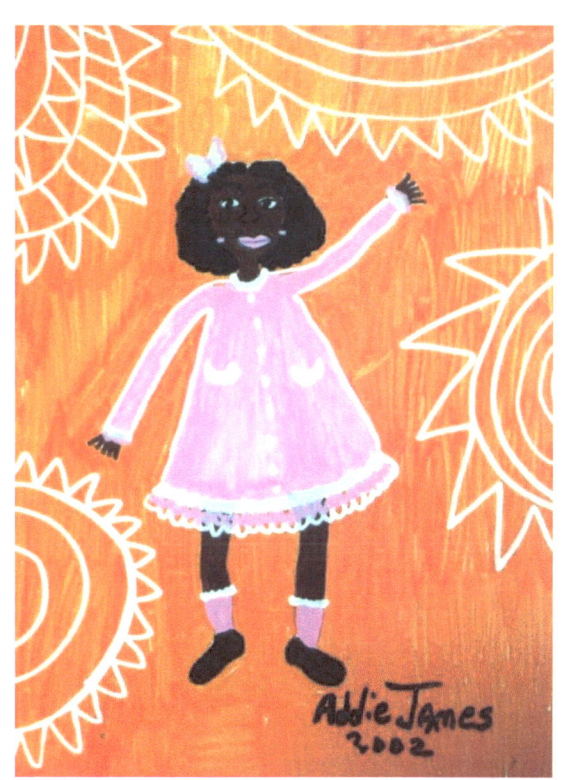

Goin' Dancin'
8 x 10 acrylic on mat board

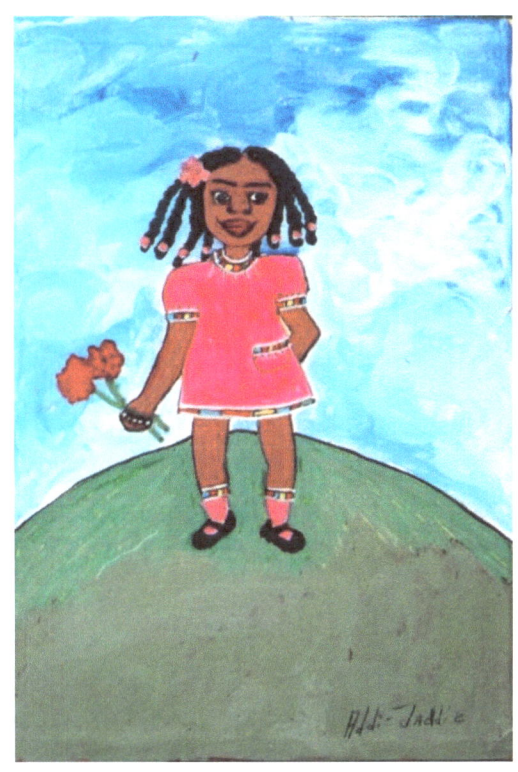

Pink Dress, 8 x 11 acrylic on book cover

   Pink Dress is especially interesting not only because it depicts a little girl on top of the world, but also because it was painted on the marbled green cover of a book that had fallen apart.

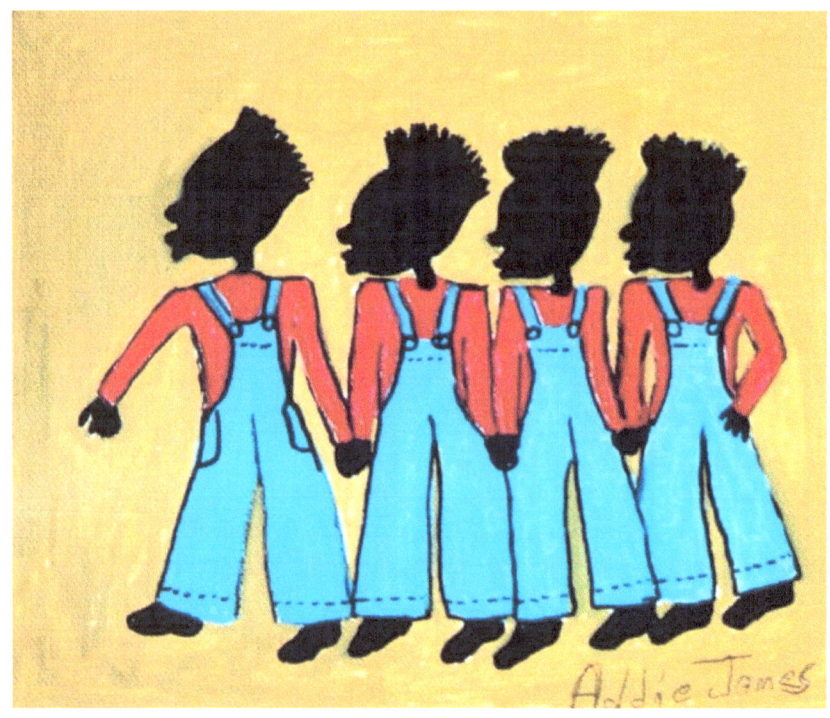

Follow the Leader
7 ¼ x 9 acrylic on paper

Often when it *hit* Addie to paint boys, they were presented in a highly stylized, repetitive group as in *Follow the Leader.* The black-silhouetted heads, the square red shoulders and the echo of blue dungarees reveal a sophisticated technique evoking both movement and rhythm.

By contrast, *Young Tiger Woods* is a very specific young man lifted directly from the media and transformed by Addie's imagination. While the high-stakes world of professional golf was far beyond the artist's realm of experience, Addie understood nature, human and otherwise.

Perhaps that explains why Tiger is holding a robin's egg rather than a golf ball.

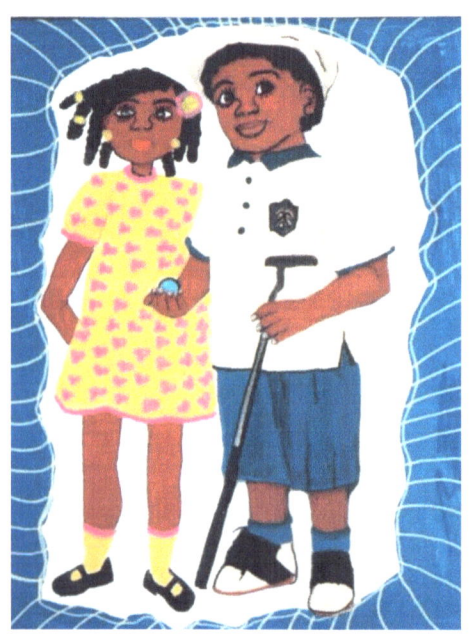

Young Tiger Woods, 8 x 10 acrylic on paper

62

As with all children, school was a dominant factor in young Addie's life. She and her siblings attended Morningside School. Just as all the children in her art were black, so too were all her classmates. This clip from her hometown paper explains:

Desegregation
Nineteen hundred and fifty four was a significant date in American history as in that year the Supreme Court declared schools segregated on the basis of race to be unconstitutional. In a follow-up case, the court ruled that desegregation should proceed with "all deliberate speed." That phrase was an apt description for the pace of desegregation in Statesville city schools as it was 1963 before the first few students, nine in number, attended a formerly all-white school. In 1964, a suit in federal court began to speed up the process of integration so that by 1970 integration was considered complete.[11]

Because Addie left the school system in 1961, before integration began, she grew to adulthood in a relatively segregated society.

If people wonder why Miss Addie's art featured African American subjects almost exclusively, they need to remember that art reflects life. Addie's exclusion of other races was not so much a conscious decision as a natural inclination to paint what she knew best.

And going to school was always a great adventure:

We walked to school on the railroad track every morning, and I will never forget...Old men used to gamble on the tracks, and there lay three hundred dollar bills on the track. Three hundred dollars...hundred dollar bills!

And I FOUND them, and I didn't tell my brothers and sisters. I put that money in my pocket, put a little tissue on top of it. And I gave my sisters some change when we got to the store, and I said "Y'all can buy y'all some candy." And, oh, they were so happy! They said, "Where did you get that money?" And I said, "Some change was on the railroad track, and I found it."

I am GOOD at finding things.

---

[11] Statesville Landmark and Record "Statesville City School System is Now Almost 100" Bill Moose, Sunday, March 3, 1991.

And I will never forget, when we got home that afternoon, there were Mama and Daddy. I gave them the money, and they were so excited. They locked themselves in the kitchen, and they didn't come out for a long time. I guess they were counting them three hundred dollar bills.

And they went to town. We had an old Studebaker car. And when they come back Mama had bought a little silk dress with a cape on it, patent leather shoes, socks, and hair ribbons.

I will never forget that Easter, 'cause I know I was the BOMB! We three girls, we were so pretty! Mine was blue, one was pink, and the other was purple. And patent leather shoes I had been dreaming about! And I told Mama, "Mama, the Lord has made way for us." I told her, "I have been dreaming about this Easter a long time."

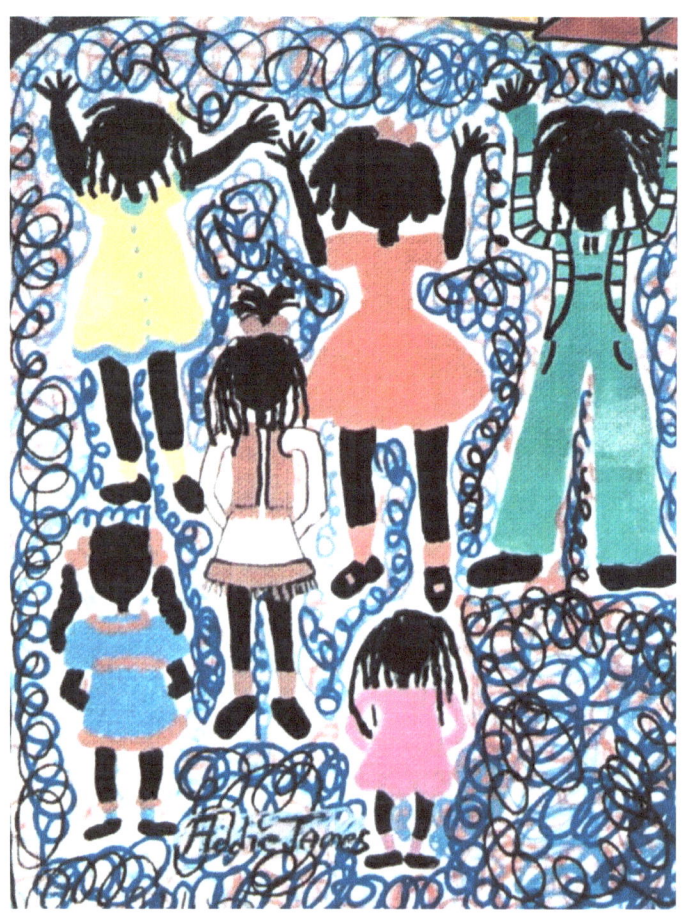

Girls in a Puzzle
8 x 10 ½ acrylic on paper

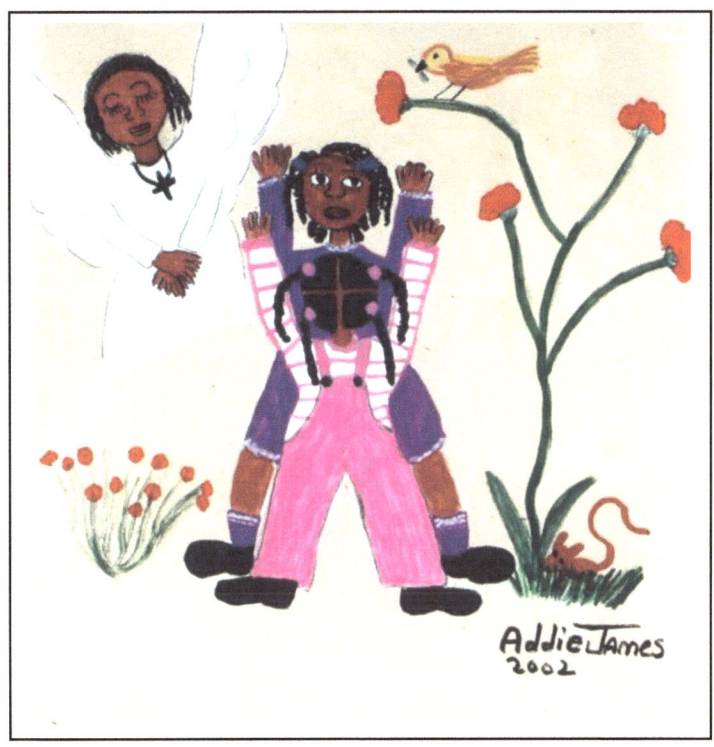

An Angel Over Us
8 ½ x 8 ¾ acrylic on mat board

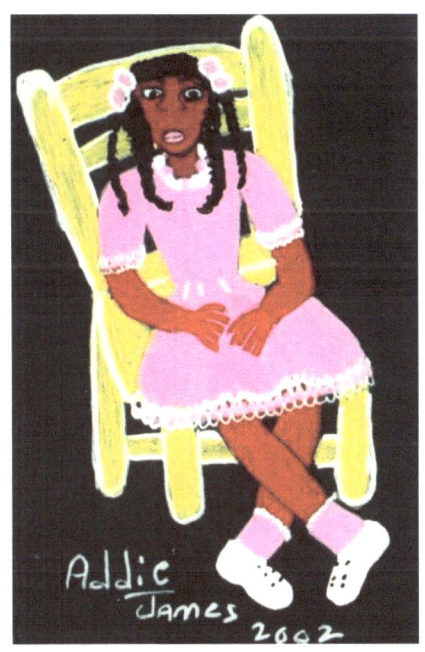

Thinking, 5 x7acrylic on black mat board

Many of Addie's childhood adventures were enacted on the lively stage of her imagination. In quiet times she read books, wrote poetry, and dreamed about becoming a famous actress:

At the Morningside School I was in Cinderella, Rumpelstiltskin, and Hansel and Gretel. I was in all those shows and I used to love to act. Acting was my dream.
But the only movies we got to go see were like Samson and Delilah… the Bible pictures. We didn't go to the movies that much.

Box Kids
5 x 7 acrylic on black mat board

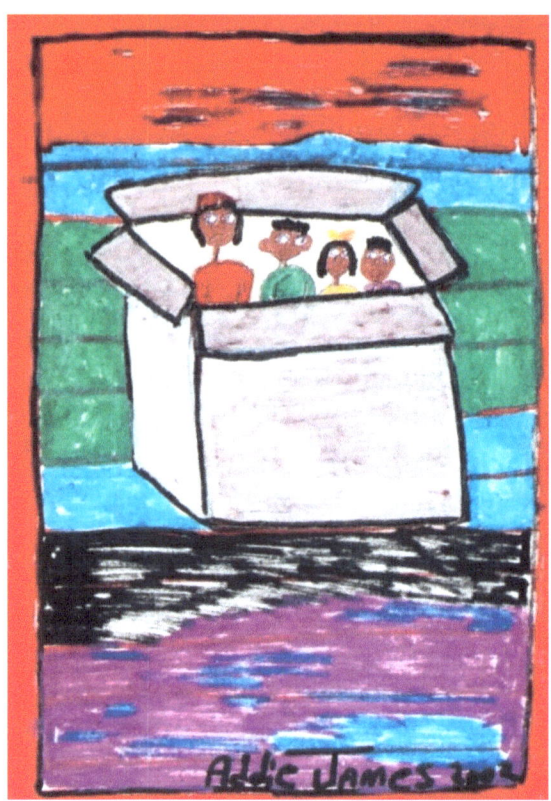

And like all children, Addie knew the joys of playing house:

We used to make tents and put everything in them. Children today don't know how fortunate it is to have a big pasteboard box.
If we got a hold of a big pasteboard box, it was the most glorious thing you ever seen!

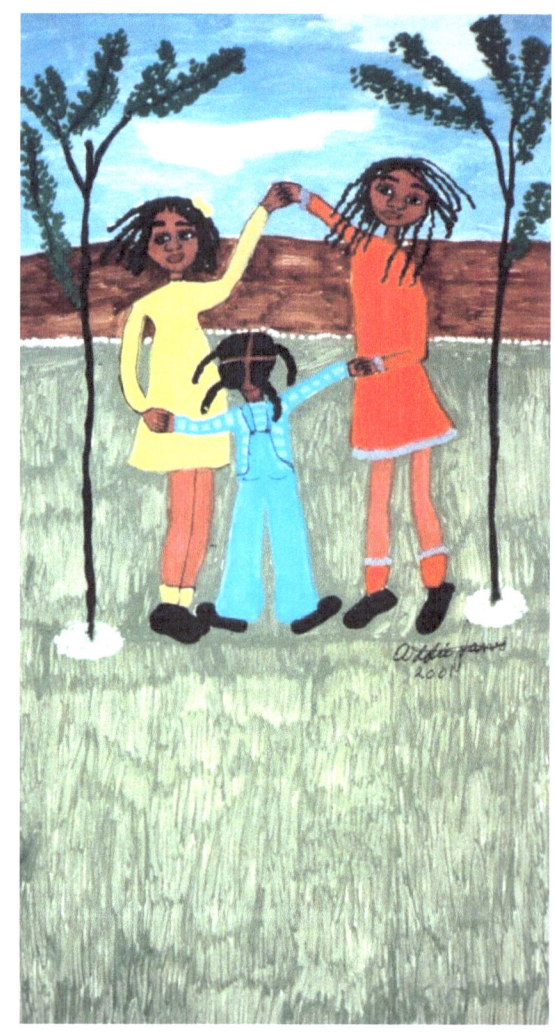

THE MAGIC OF 3

If we were forced to highlight one aspect of Addie's *composition*, we might note that the artist most often arranges her figures in groups of three:

I don't know why, really.
Well, it's in the Bible and three means a lot to me.
Three comes natural.

Another thing that came *natural* to Miss Addie was a deep conviction of her own self- worth. Never tell her how to paint. And never tell her not to eat the cookies and candies she adores. Even when she was a child, no one crossed Little Addie:

One thing about it when I was growing up...NOBODY ever beat me up. Still, old as I am today, nobody ever beat me up. I wouldn't let them.

And even in school when I got something right and my hand was up, I would REMIND that teacher that my hand was up, so don't give ME a bad grade. That's the way I was.

They didn't mess with me because I didn't allow them to. I was always horrified to see other people messing over people and bullying people. I wouldn't let them bully me.

I guess I could say I bullied THEM.

YOU CAN LEARN
*by **Addie James***

Gotta book…can't read
Got money…can't count
What's going on? Is there something you want
To tell me about?
You know kids today…I pray and pray
Both night and day
Praying to God He will change their ways.
You KNOW God will change your ways.
Let God turn it around!
Got a book….can't read. Got money…can't count.
COME ON NOW,
Don't that make you want to shout?

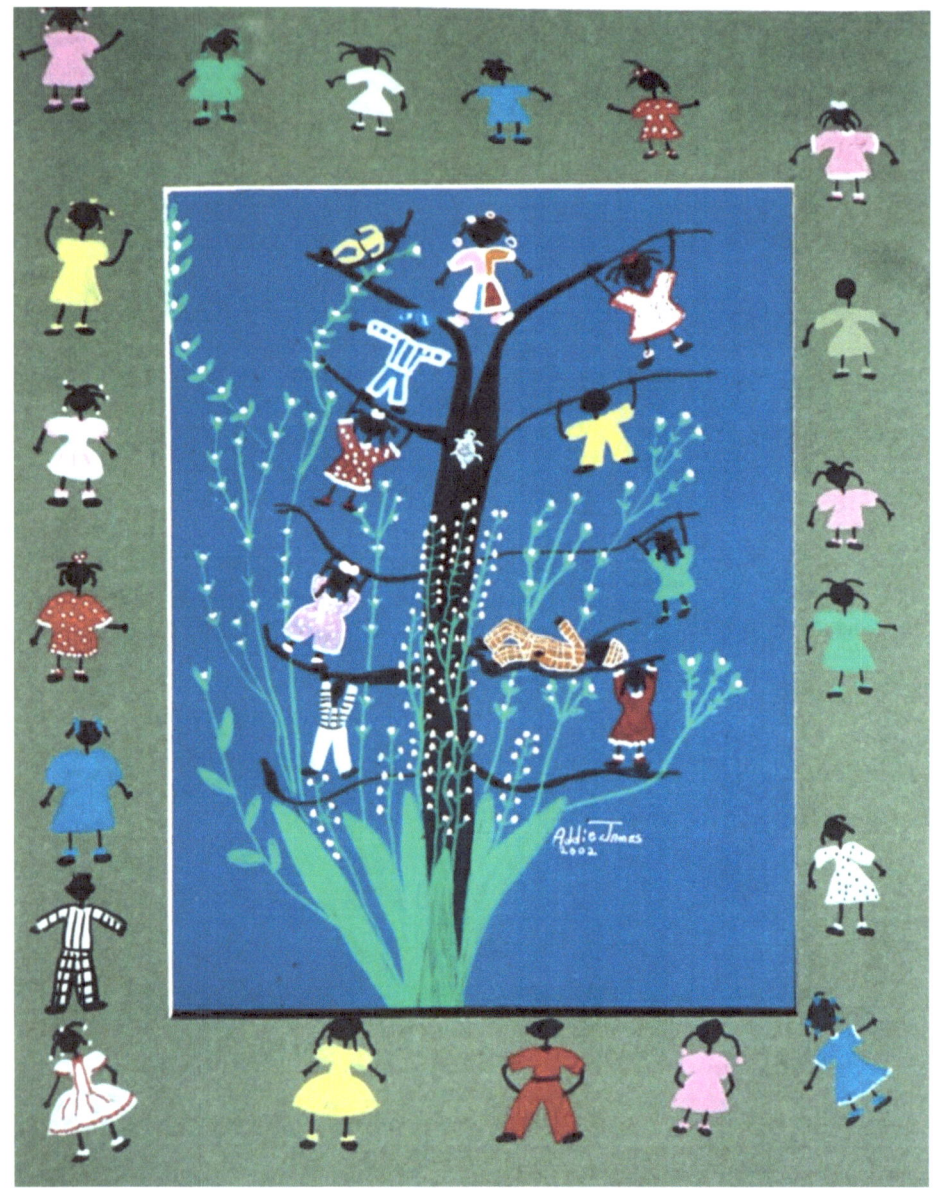

Tree Children

16 x 20 acrylic on mat board

Sometimes Miss Addie decorated

a mat, lending impact and emphasis

to the featured subject.

THE FOUR "F's"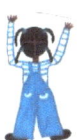

We breathe in, we breathe out. We eat, sleep, laugh, cry, love and hate…the human condition vibrates with predictable rhythms common to us all, but for Addie James that rhythm included making art. Night and day, painting was as vital to Addie as the oxygen filling her lungs, and the byproduct was an enormous volume of paintings, which reflected the artist's daily moods and her ever-changing interests.

When challenged to catalog this hugely diverse output of shifting subjects and styles, it helps to sort the work into categories. So far we have looked at Addie's portraits, her full-blown scenes of life in the country and at home, and her stylized *tree children.* The next groups can be examined as **THE FOUR "F's":** *fashion, friends, family, and faith.*

FASHION

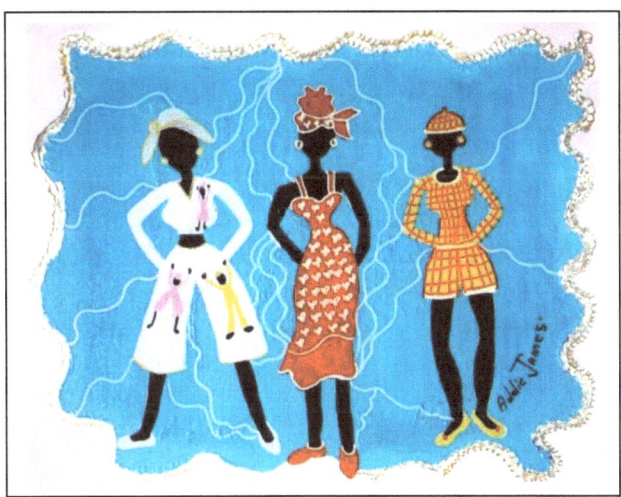

We Got Class, 16 x 20 acrylic on canvas

Of all Miss Addie's subjects, *fashion* was her *passion.* These painting expressed her lifelong interest in clothing, sewing, and high style. The fashion pieces showcased the artist's gift for composition and pattern, and they revealed sophistication totally unexpected in a self-taught artist.

When Miss Addie focused on fashion, she brought all her trademark powers to bear.
The power of three
is evident in many of these works as her models with *attitude* threaten to strut right off the canvas.

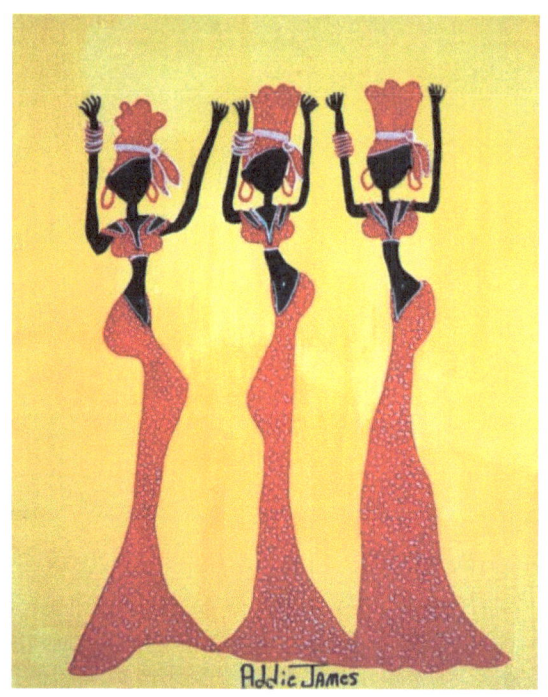

Polka Dots Hallelujah
16 x 20 acrylic on canvas

Whether she featured a funky pair of decorated culottes, pseudo-African peasant garb, or slinky urban wear, Miss Addie's creations were *haute couture* statements which were uniquely her own.

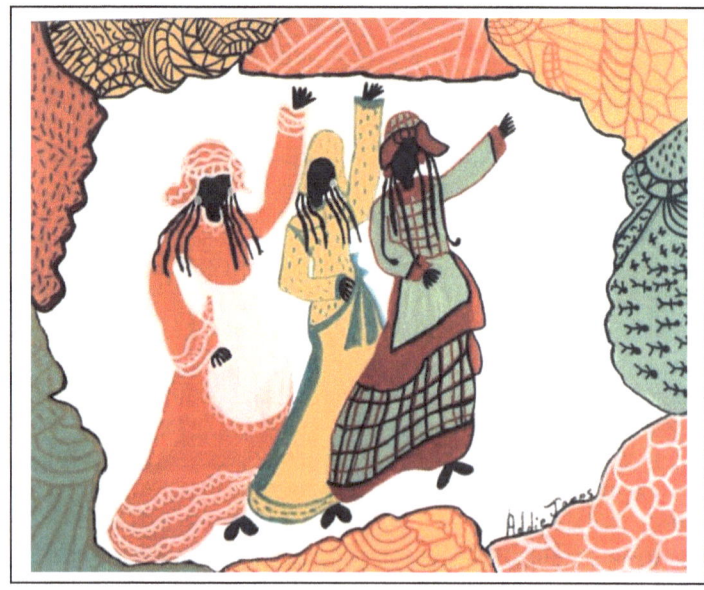

Shouting Sisters   **16 x 20 acrylic on canvas**

The elegant technique of using **black silhouette figures** to shift the spotlight to Addie's fashions speaks volumes about the artist's keen sense of design.

Whether Addie was born with this talent, or whether she acquired it over years of practice is a mystery. Certainly no one taught her the fundamentals of color, composition, and line, but the most scholarly, highly-trained painters will agree that Miss Addie's results *are to die for*.

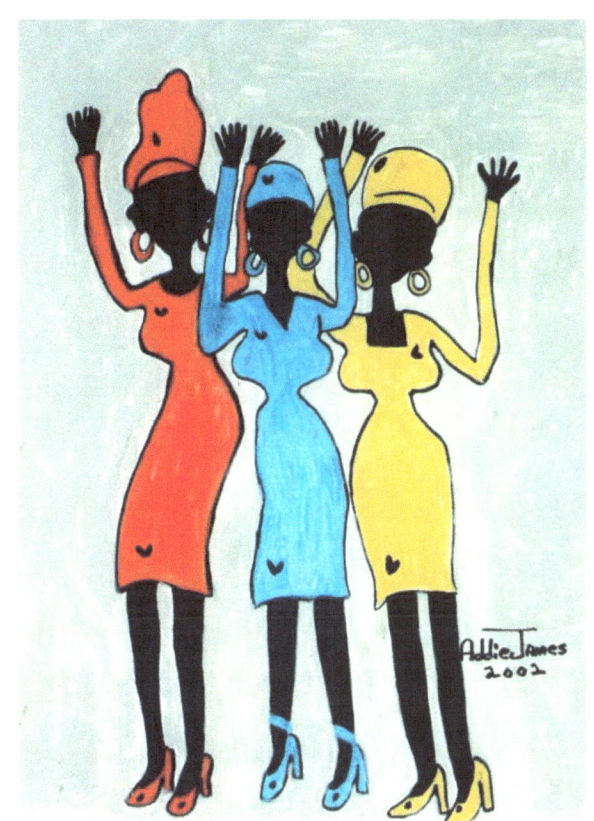

Fashion Hallelujah Girls
10 x 13 acrylic on mat board

It is in Addie's fashion studies that the distinctive **hallelujah girls** first breathed life. With arms joyously lifted to Heaven, the hallelujah gesture became a signature in many of Addie's paintings.

Three Hallelujah Girls in White
10 ¾ x 15 ½ ink and acrylic on paper

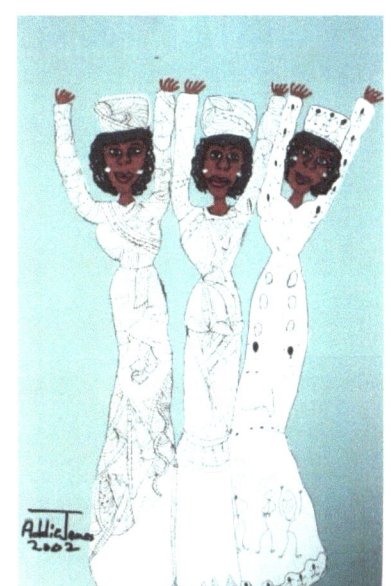

Praise the Lord!

I used to design all my clothes, like in high school, because I worked in a factory where you got material.

They made clothes there. It was in town on South Madison Street. It was called Dillon's factory. Old man Dillon and his son owned that factory, and we used to clean it up at night. They trusted us with the keys.

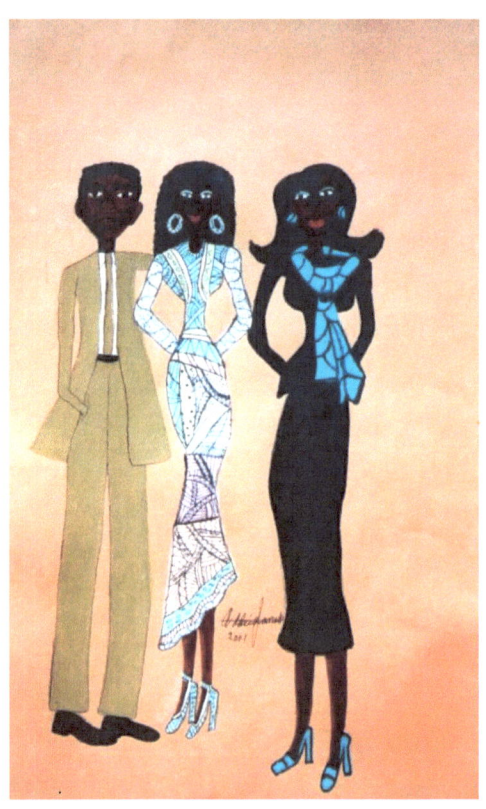

Fashions 12 x 18 acrylic on paper

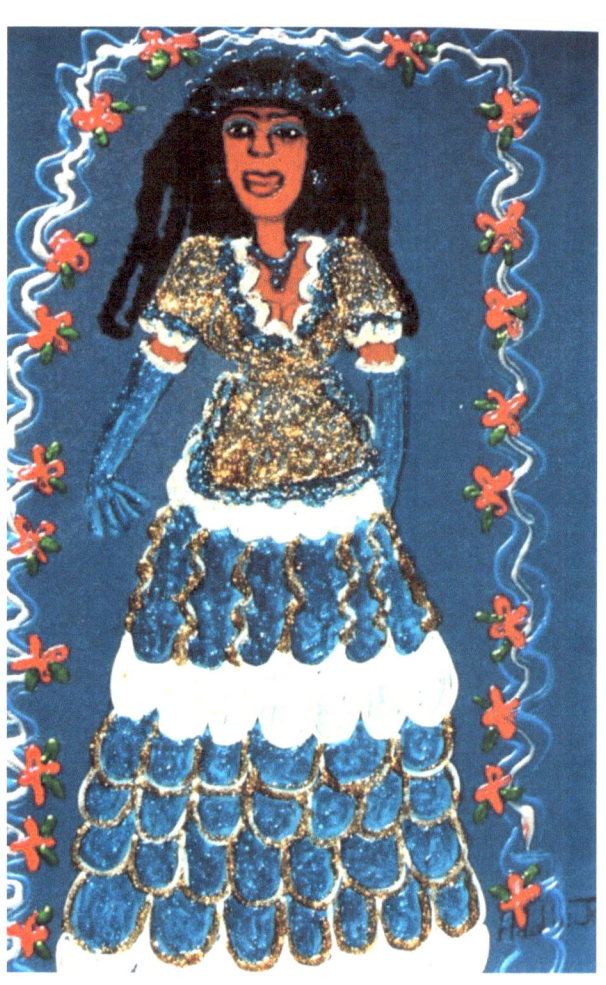

Queen for a Day
8 ½ x 12 mixed media on mat board

Mama and Daddy were both living then, so we would walk to work every day. Every day when Mama and Daddy got off their day work, we would walk up to that factory, through Belmount and uptown.

And I would get scraps of material, you know, that they throw away? And I would make an outfit for the next day.

I learned to cut a collar, a sleeve, without even using a pattern. I could see something, cut it out, and I'd wear it so the home economics teacher would have me modeling every day…

I used to draw fashions and I won a contest, and it was in Washington, DC!
And the man come down here all the way from Washington and brought me this big art kit. I was crazy and young then, and he told me if you finish this art course by the time you finish high school, I will give you a job myself designing clothes. ***Just think…I could have been a great designer!***

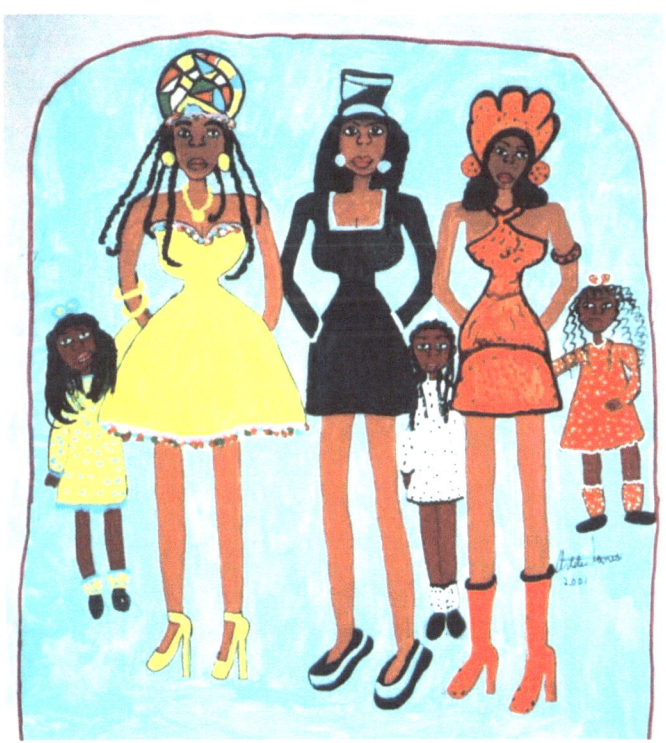

Girls' Day Out, 15 x 16 ½ acrylic on mat board

Mother/daughter outfits were another recurring theme in Miss Addie's art:

Me and my sisters would dress alike, like Mama, you know? We all loved to dress up with everything coordinated, where everything matches…the socks, the shoes…

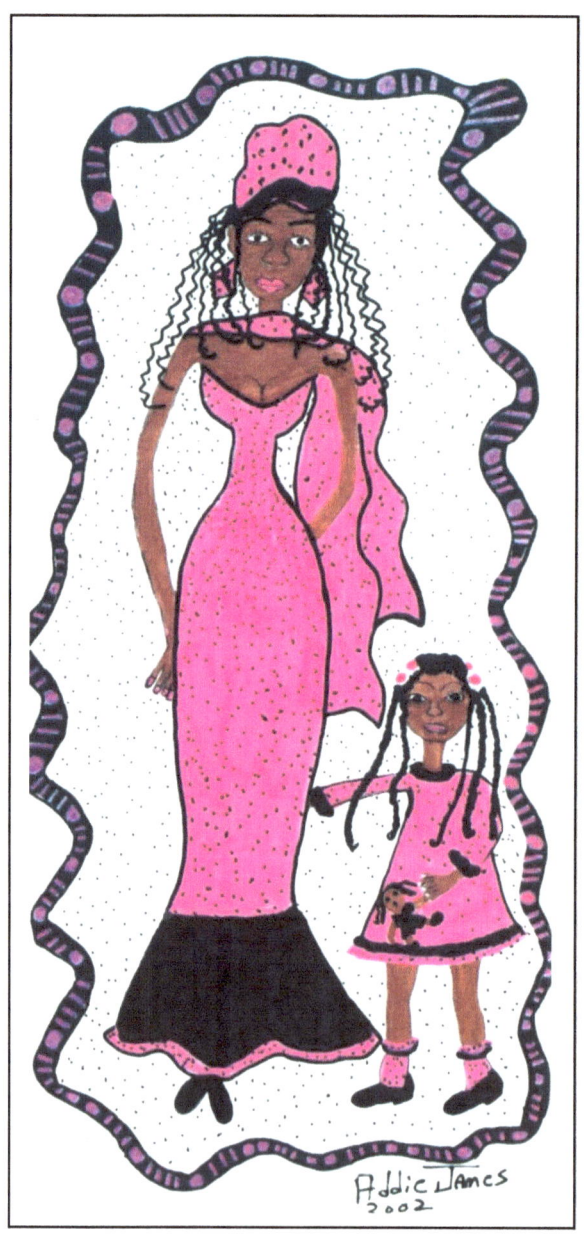

Pink n'Pokadots
9 ½ x 20 acrylic on mat board

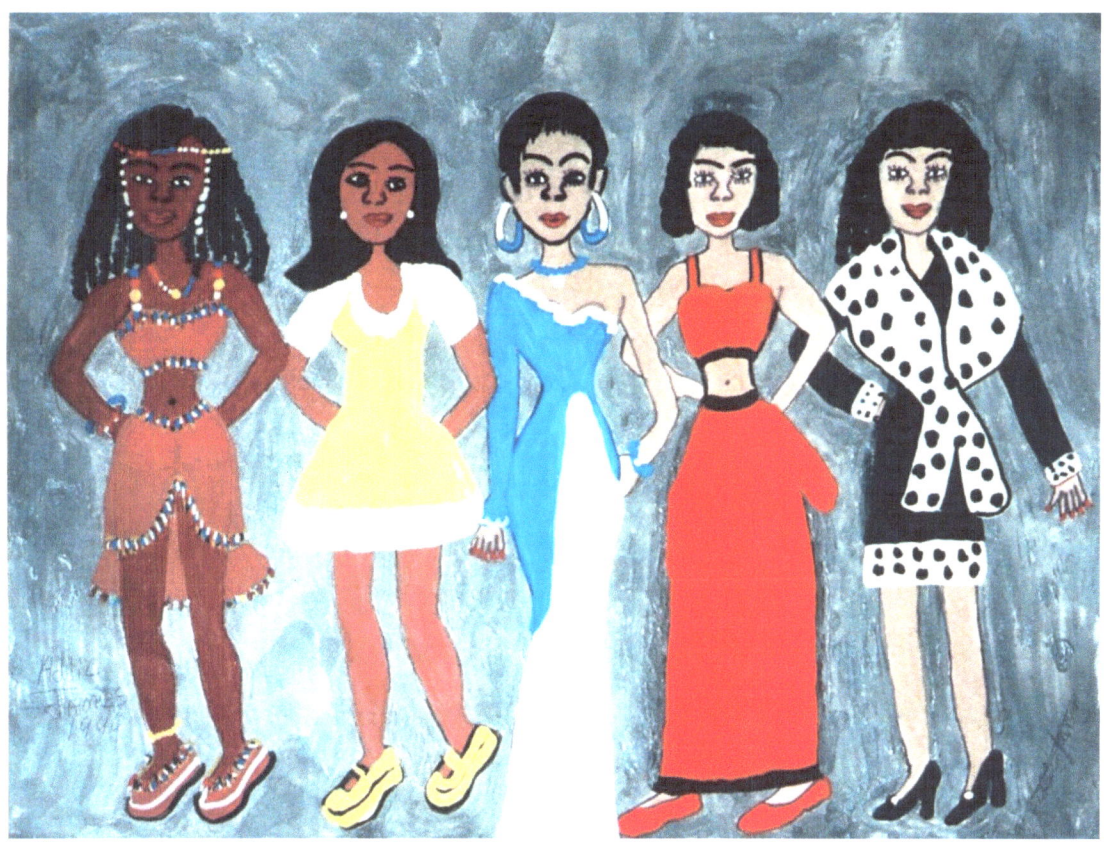

Fashion Show, 10 ½ x 14 acrylic on paper

The favorite dress I ever made was mostly red, but it had some blue with it. It had a crew neck and big sleeves…not too big… and a long tail. It was SO pretty!

Early in 2002, Addie's taste in models broadened to include large people, who then regularly populated her paintings as engaging proponents of what she called *fat fashion.*
When I asked Addie if she missed sewing, she shook her head and said:

You know, I like to draw the clothes, but let somebody else make them.

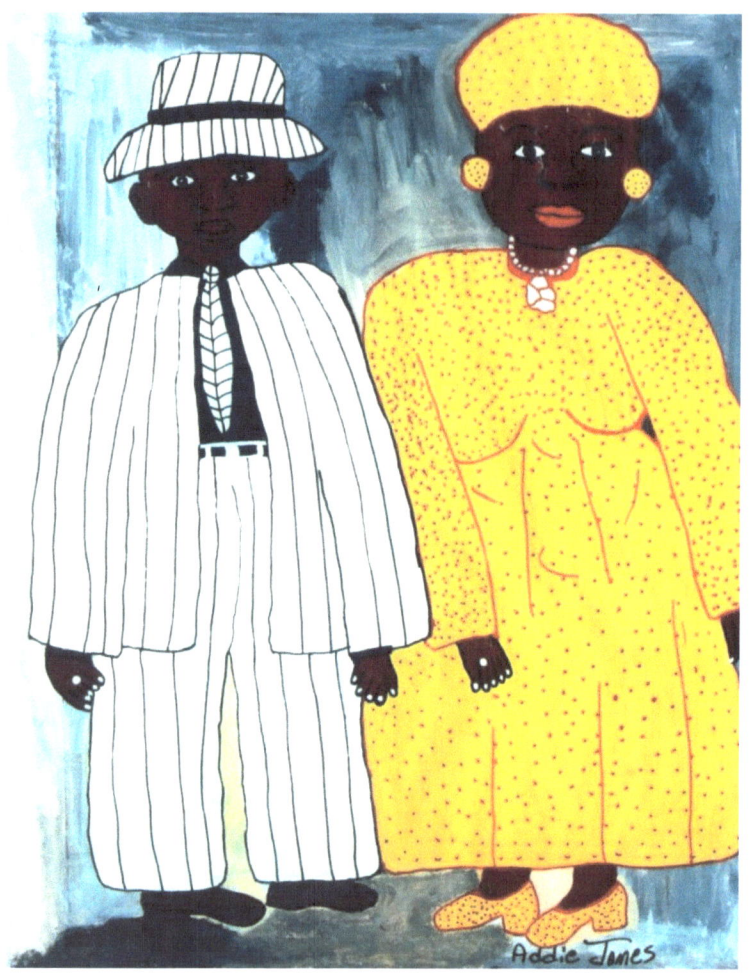

Let's Start Fresh, 22 x 28 acrylic on paper

Come Go with Us, 16 x 20 acrylic on canvas

PASS OUT THE MIRRORS
by Addie James

Take a long look at yourself
Then you wouldn't have the right
To talk about anybody else
Give your glory to God
For He will bid you love and peace
My sisters and brothers,
Thank you for that mirror.

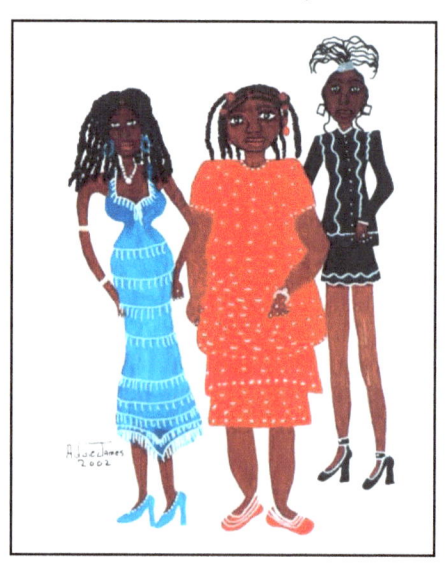

FRIENDS

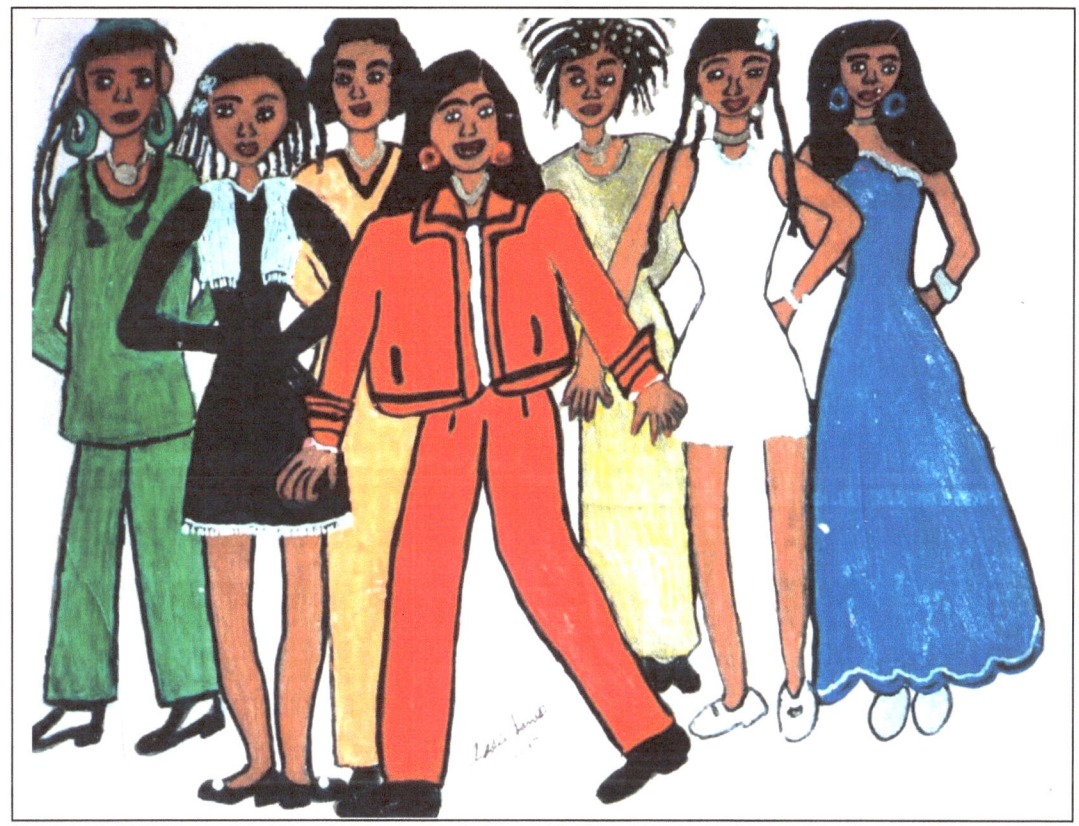

Ladies' Club 11 x 14 acrylic on cardboard

While Addie James created many paintings depicting groups of friends, especially women friends, it was interesting to note that the artist actually preferred a less social lifestyle:

I stay away from crowds. I like to keep to myself, behind the scene. I speak about things from the heart. Where there's lots of people, everyone's running their mouth.

I never went to clubs. I bet I went to nightclubs maybe once in my life.

I maybe had one friend. I didn't trust nobody.

Addie was more comfortable one on one, in intimate situations where more meaningful bonds could be formed. Like many artists, she had an eye for *seeing* relationships, so that in her group studies the body language of her figures told the story.

In "Comforters" *the man in the green suit has lost his wife, and his friends are comforting him. The man in the yellow shirt, he just listens, but the other man…he lays on his hands.*

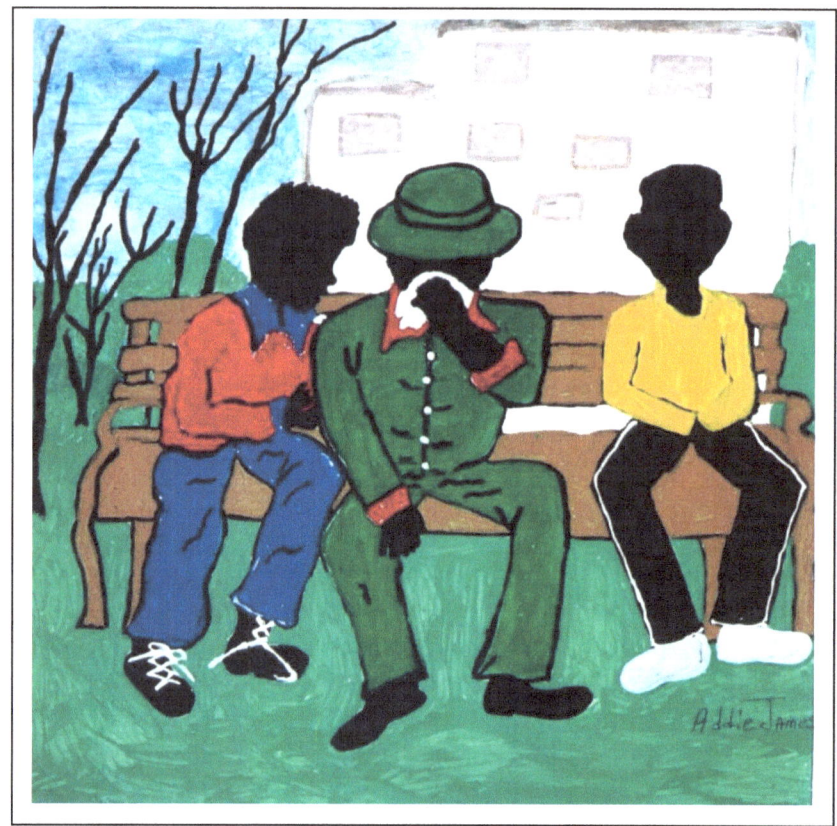

Comforters 11 ¾ x 12 ¼ acrylic on paper

In *New Baby* Addie depicted three women celebrating a new life. The company of other mothers, grandmothers, and, of course, children, were recurring themes in Miss Addie's art, and her life. These were the subjects where she felt most at home.

As a grandmother, Addie absorbed much of her information about the ever-changing world from Christian and Christopher, her twin grandsons, and from Kesha, her teenage granddaughter…all of whom lived with Miss Addie.

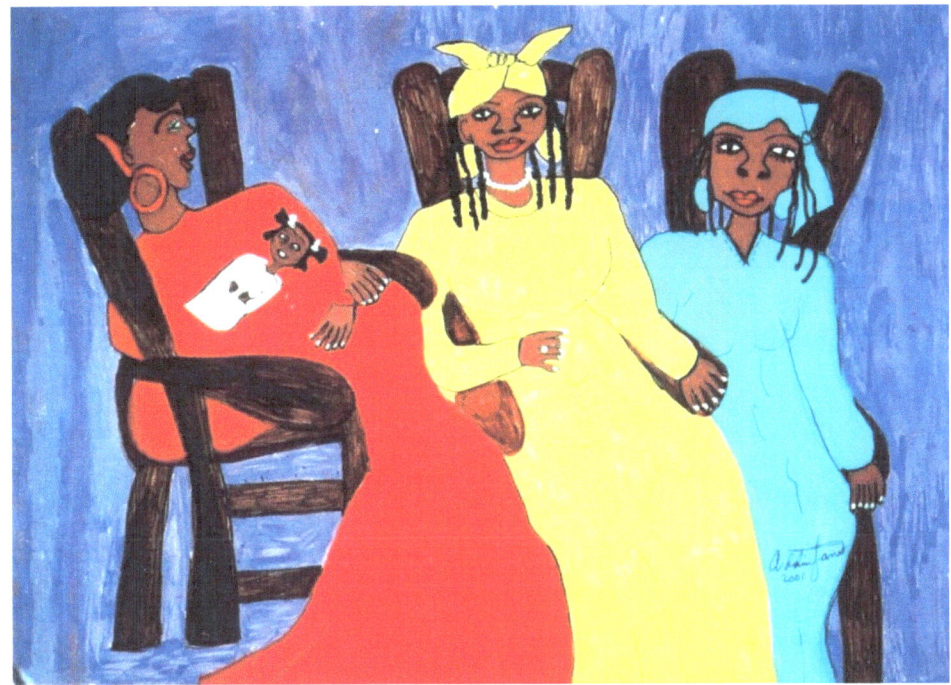

New Baby **12 ½ x 17 acrylic on mat board**

The painting *Boyz* is likely a compellation.   Addie had seen friends of the twins…the way they dressed, *rappers* on TV, and she had watched young men *on the street.*   The children's influence occasionally inspired their grandmother to surprise everyone by painting a portrait of *Tupac Shakur* or *Jam Master Jay.*

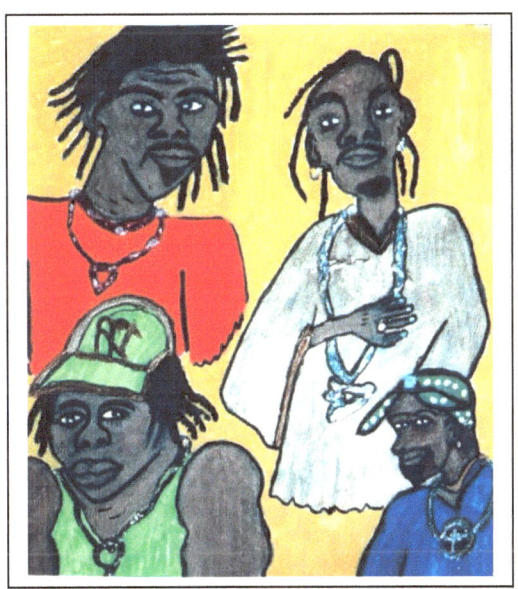

Boyz, 10 x 10 ¾ mixed media on paper

79

Because Addie's paintings often recalled her childhood, harking back to a nostalgic, gentler time, it was easy to loose sight of the fact that Addie James lived in the Twenty-First Century. Don't be fooled, for every now and then she startled and delighted us with a comment about contemporary culture:

about *Talkin' Trash...*

Me and the kids were drawing that day. Puts me in mind of a TV show we was watching: Beavus and Butthead.

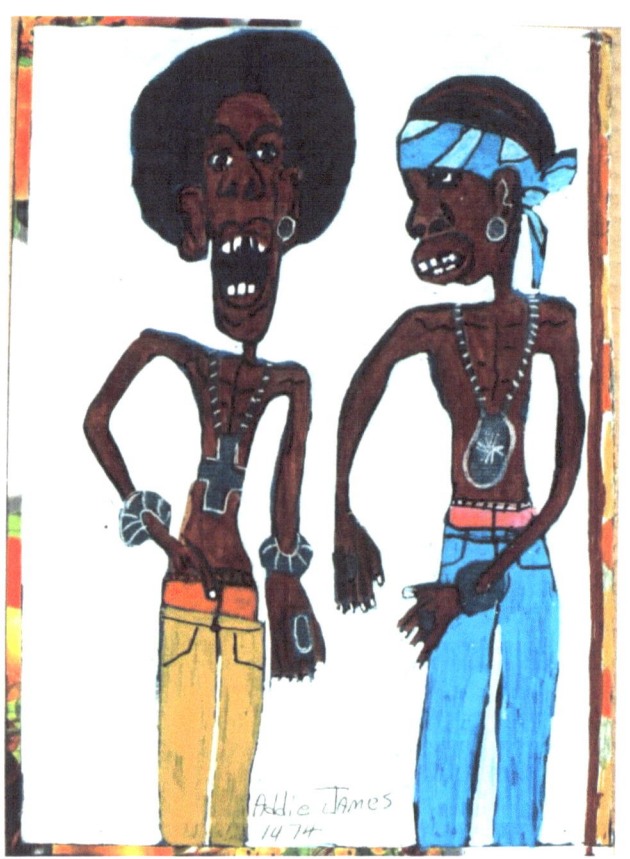

Talkin' Trash, 8 x 10 acrylic on a torn-off book cover

Picture it...a rainy afternoon, the grandchildren captive inside with the television flickering in the corner...

Miss Addie passes out the crayons. She has nothing to paint on but the cover of an old book, but she picks up her brushes and *does her thing.*

When Miss Addie did venture into the wider world, she usually attended an art show. Surrounded by her own works on display, she was never shy. She gave of herself openly, talking and telling stories about her life, and sometimes she took *special requests:*

In Charlotte they was wanting me to do some work for them...those sorority people. They wore red and white, and they even told me what letters to put on there.

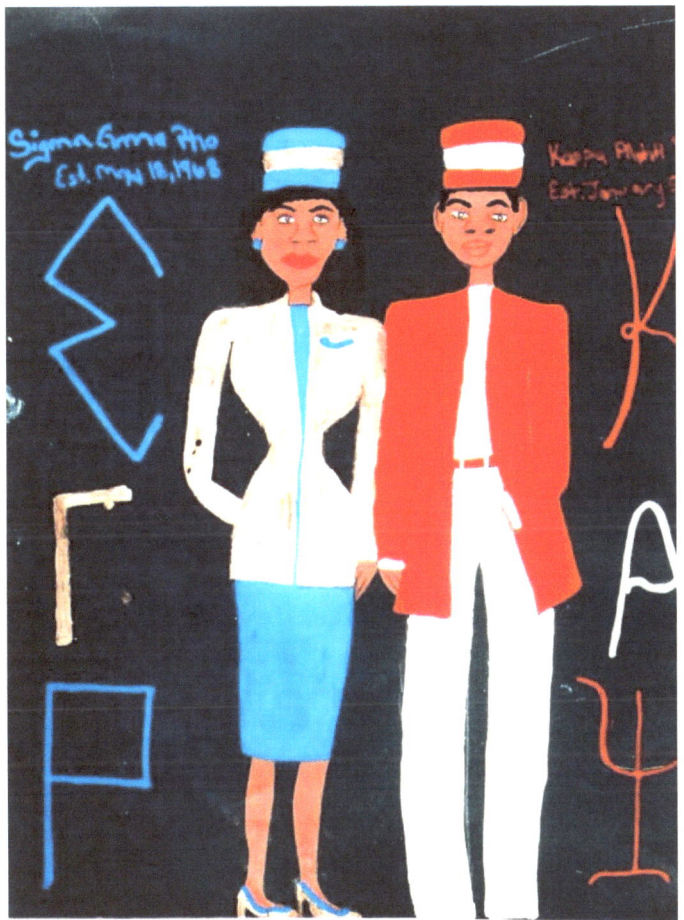

Sorority and Fraternity, 14 x 17 acrylic on paper

I don't care for traveling that much. I'm a homebody, really.
As long as I'm home drawing, get me a little chew of tobacco, I'm satisfied.
But I love to go to art shows,

I've never met a stranger...

Just as Addie James was a citizen of the Twenty-First Century, she was also a woman with romantic interests.

Her grandmotherly demeanor may have easily distracted from the truth that she had enjoyed a rich love life. *Lovers at the Window,* with its nurturing organic design and its passionate *red* intimacy reminds us that hot blood coursed through Addie's veins.

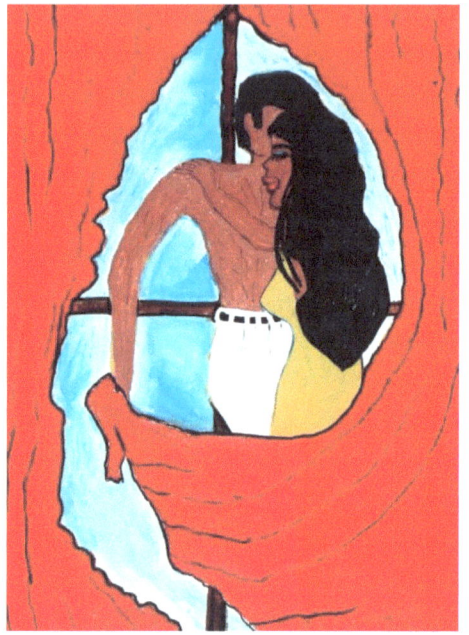

Lovers at the Window, 9 x 12 acrylic on paper

The romantic relationships in Addie's work often evoked tenderness and innocence:

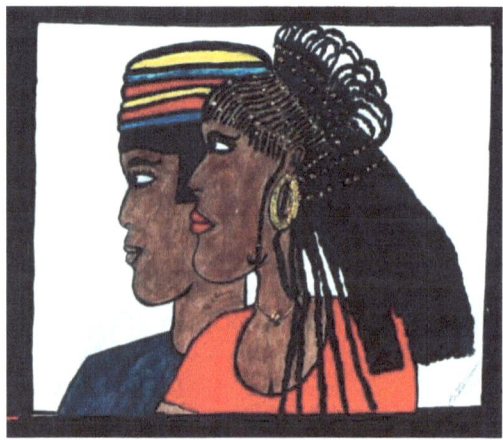

The Faces of Love, 12 x 14 mixed media on paper

Addie said of *"We Got the Blues"* *they been drinking and having a good time, but they are sad.*

This painting was unique because Addie gave these figures exaggerated, oversized heads. The perspective, shooting up from a low vantage point, was also unusual for Addie. The effect, intentional or not, lent the couple an engaging, wide-eyed vulnerability.

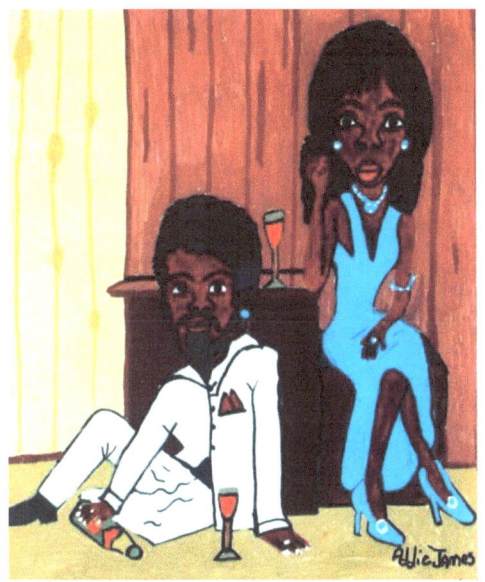

We Got the Blues, 8 ½ x 11acrylic on paper

She said of *"Saturday Night in the City:"* *This is what men do in the big city on Saturday night. They dress up fine, play cards. Oh, they have a GOOD time!*

Saturday Night in the City
13 x 18 ¼
acrylic on mat board

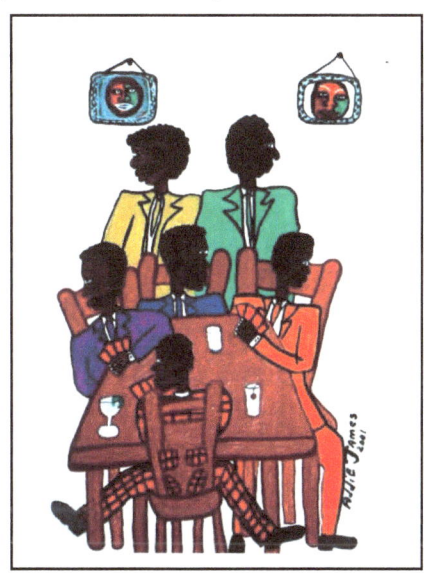

In fact, Addie James had little experience of *big city* ways. Only once had she ventured far beyond her Statesville home:

My brother, Clifford, died in New York. And I went to New York, and I never want to go back there again. I was so afraid going across that water. I was so afraid!

We went together in a van, and I was the only one had the nerve to get up and speak at my brother's funeral. But I NEVER want to go back to New York again.

MY LITTLE ROOM
by Addie James

When I want to get away from the world
I go to my little room.
It gives me a sense of peace.
I meditate and pray.
I can feel the spirit
Of God around me.
I pray for my family and friends.
Also for peace in the world.
I'm not rich, but it's not about money.
I thank God for my little room,
For God's holy spirit.
It keeps me safe and sound.

I don't have to look for Him
I know he's around.
I try to be kind to everybody,
Even to those who do not like me.
When someone talks about me,
I talk to God about them,
On my knees.
I know that's what God wants me to do
It keeps Him pleased.
I thank God for this beautiful afternoon
In my little room.

FAMILY

While no one in Addie's family played an instrument, music was very important in their lives. Her twin grandsons, Christian and Christopher, performed dance routines throughout the region, while Addie herself wrote numerous songs.

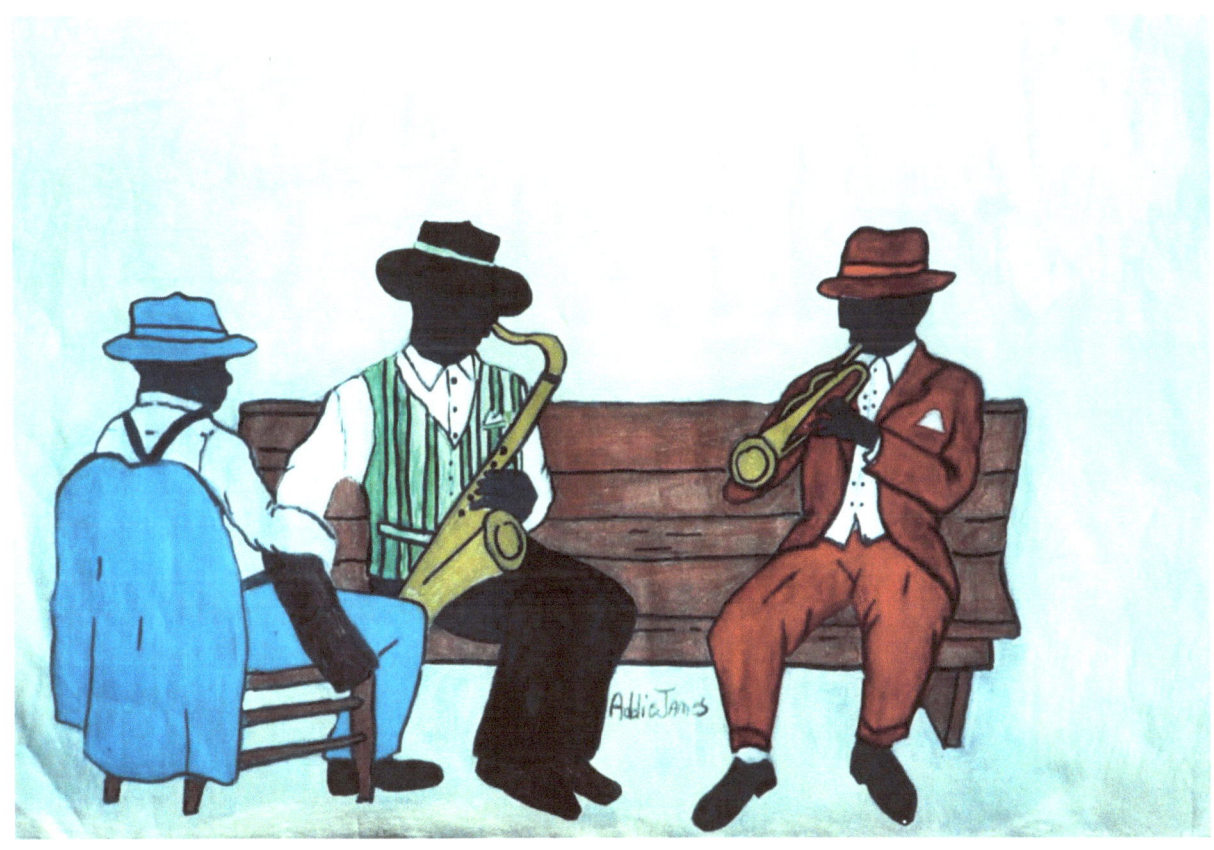

Jammin', 12 x 18 acrylic on paper

In the chapter *I've Been Through the Struggle* we explored Addie James' biography and learned details about her family: she was one of seven children who had lived her entire life in Statesville, North Carolina. She was the mother of five children and grandmother to six. We already knew that a close-knit family unit was the cornerstone of Miss Addie's life.

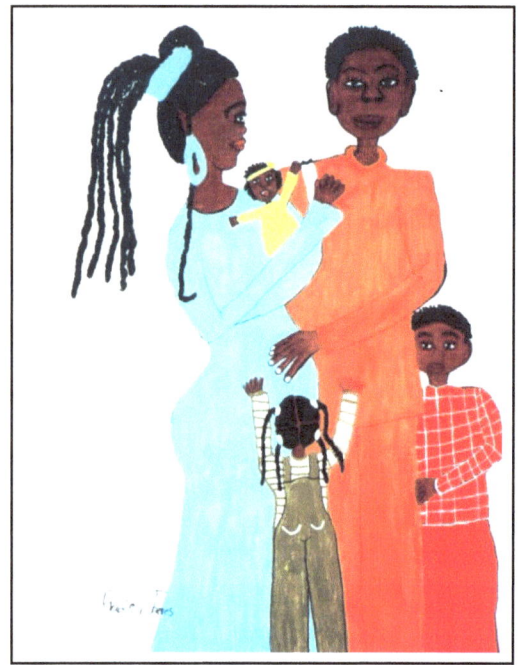

Family of Five, 10 ½ x 13 ½ acrylic on paper

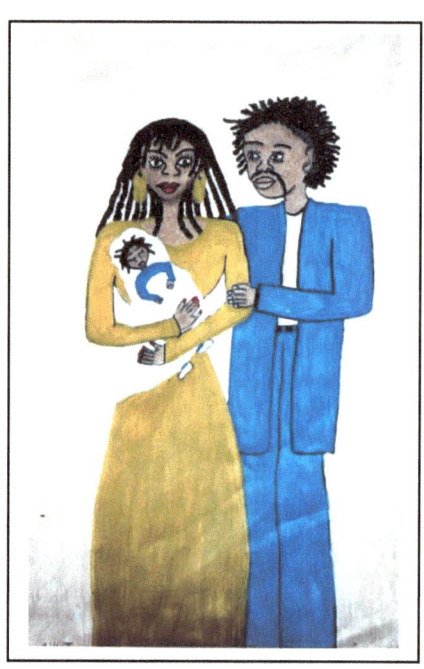

Our Child, 12 x 18 acrylic on paper

In **Family of Five** Addie may have been recalling herself as a child, or herself as a mother, or even reflecting upon her families of grandchildren. One thing was certain, whenever Addie talked about family, her stories radiated warmth and togetherness, so that any chapter about *family* is best told in her own words.

Her sister, Janie, whom Addie called *Dot*, was her best playmate:

My sister and me...*she had a side of land, and I had a side of land. We used to take out little buckets and we'd go on my land first picking blueberries, chicken berries...all that kind of stuff.*

  We'd eat wild onions, sassafras tea...ooh, that was GOOD, the best tea in the world. You used to boil the sticks and then you strain it. It was the best tea. We used to put peppermint in it...my mama ground peppermint, and it was the best tea in the world!

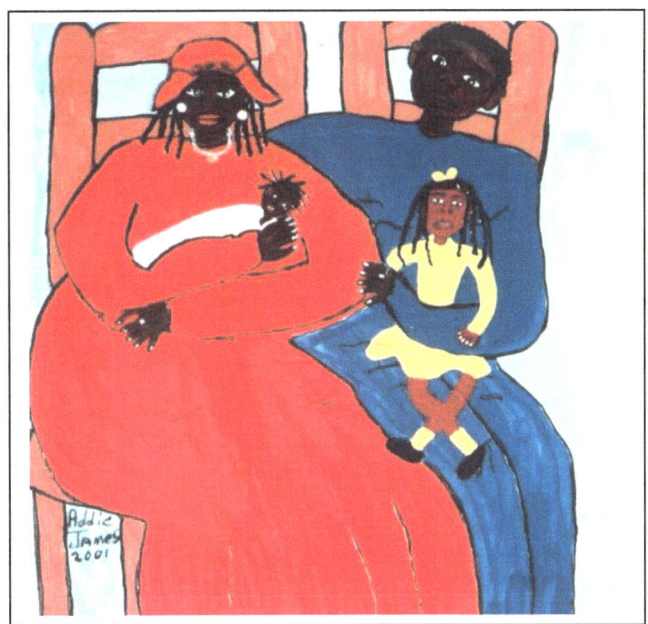

Mama's Family, 15 ¾ x 15 ¾ acrylic on mat board

But of course, Mama was the nurturing figure in little Addie's life:

And we ate poke salad, and Mama would catch a chicken. She'd pull a chicken up and clean it…called cleaning it out, feeding it nothing but grain and corn, and then she'd kill that chicken. She'd pick poke salad out of the garden, and OH BOY!

We'd come home and she'd be making a dishpan of teacakes. I've tried and tried to make teacakes, but I just can't do it. They're kind of thin biscuits, kind of sweet, but I've never been able to make them…never been able to capture the teacake.

And my mama used to can sausage. If I could have just one more sausage ball out of that jar, oh, that was SO GOOD! She made liver mush; she made sow's meat…I mean EVERYTHING was homemade, and it was delicious!

She made all kind of fruitcake. Oh, we had chickens, and cows, and pigs, and oh, it was so much fun when **pig killin'** *time come! We'd play with that bladder…blow up the bladder.*

In the wintertime, that's when we kill pigs. Certain time in the winter, certain time of the MOON, or the meat wouldn't be right. The meat skin wouldn't do right. Great big meat skins, my goodness!

While Mama fed and nurtured her children, Willy Snow Maddox, **Addie's father**, was a strong man and dependable provider, who served as Addie's role model:

My father was a big part of the family. *He would drink a little, but he was a big part of my life.* ***He was an artist.*** *He could just sit down and draw a little something. But he made this airplane and a white man got a hold of it and took it away. Daddy drawed it out before he carved it out.*
My parents knew I was a great artist, *because I was trying to do what Daddy was doing, and I just caught on, you know?*

Yeah, and we had this old Studebaker car, and Daddy loved that car. And I'll tell you that story…
One day we were going to the grocery store and the car stopped right on the railroad track. And Daddy threw everybody out…the cushions…everything. Everybody got out of the car, though, and the train come along and took the front of the car off.
I was sick for two weeks.

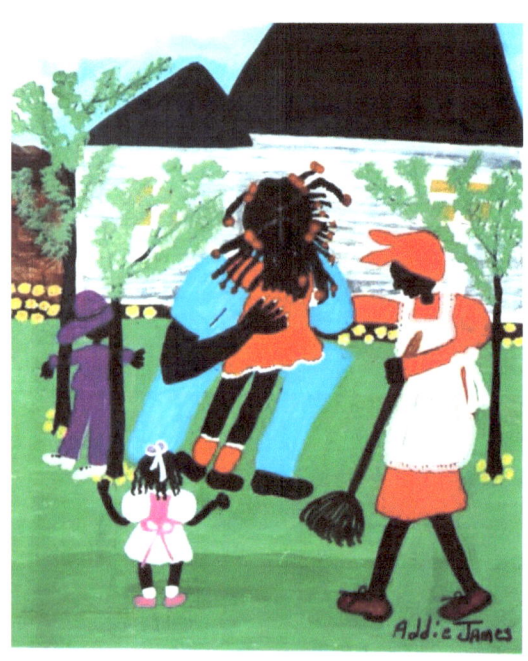

Daddy's Girl, 12 x 13 ¼ acrylic on paper

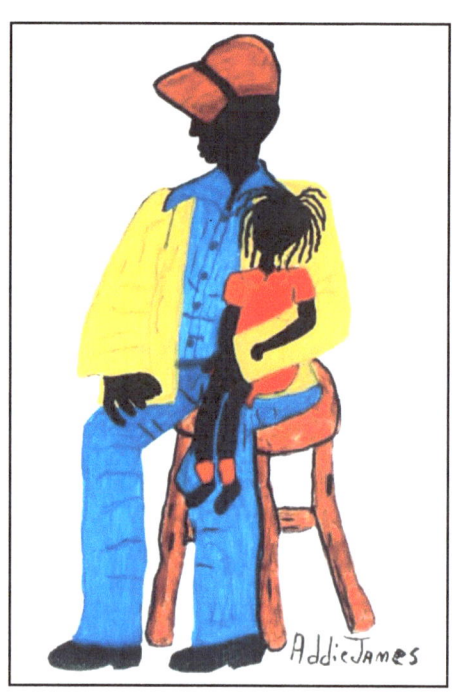

Father and Daughter, 7 ½ x 12 acrylic on paper

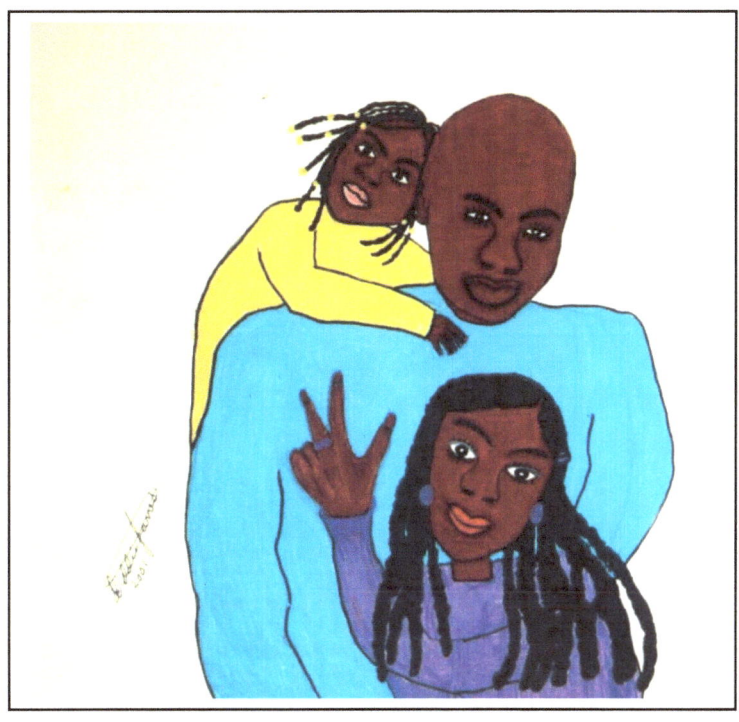

Family Time, 14 x 14 acrylic on mat board

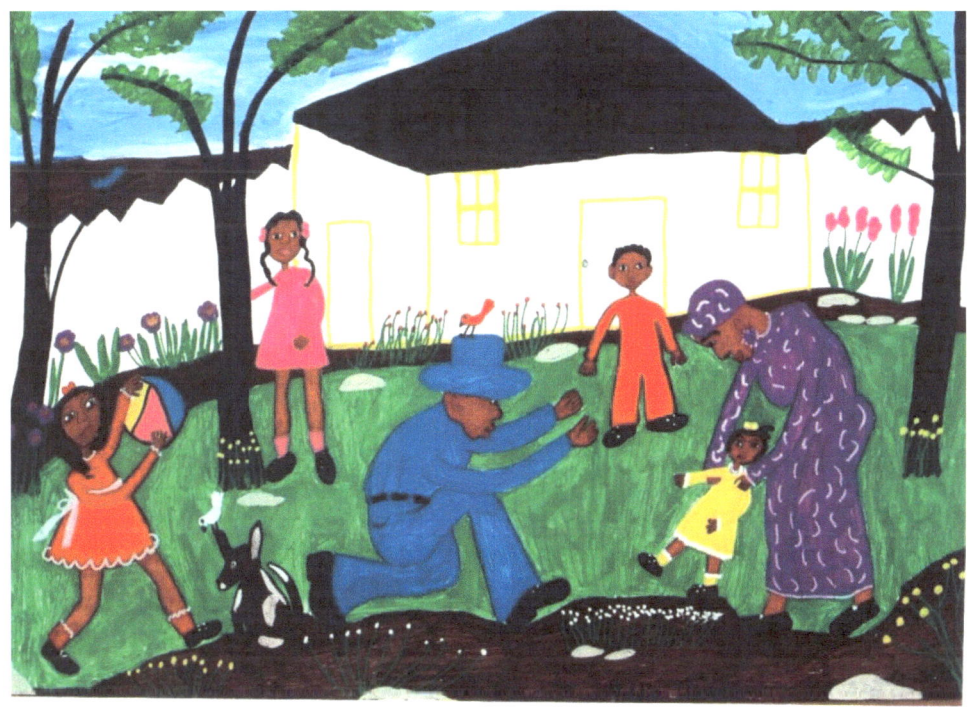

First Steps, 16 ½ x 24 acrylic on mat board

Addie, along with her brothers and sisters, was raised with a strict moral code.

In *Family Life,* the husband has his arm around his wife, while the other woman is his married sister.

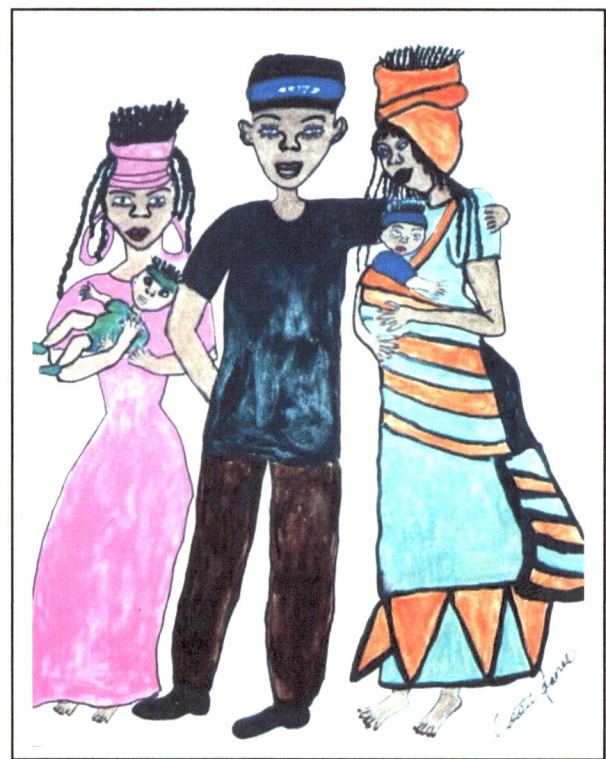

Family Life, 12 x 14 ½ acrylic on paper

The lessons in living Addie learned as a child served her well, and she tried to instill these values in her own children and grandchildren, and yet, she worried about kids today:

You know the kids today have peer pressure. We thought nothing about no "peer pressure" when we was growing up. WE had things to do, like when Mama used to get us a big pasteboard box, and we would make so many things out of it. We'd lug a big box all the way home when we seen one along the side of the road, down the railroad track, just to play with.

You know kids today go out of their yard to worry other people...we didn't do that. We would never cuss, but my sister and me would go in the toilet, and she would say "shit" and I would say "shit," and oh, we thought that was SO BAD!

I thought playing cards was actual sin. I didn't ever learn how to play cards. Now I don't feel that way. My grandchildren be sitting there playing cards, and I feel so dumb...don't know how to play cards.

Children don't know how to have fun now. Back then we'd make hoppy toad houses. We'd put our hands down on the ground and take dirt and put it over our hands and make big hoppy toad houses. It was SO MUCH FUN!

We found something to do every minute of the hour.

And kids today are BORED. I don't know where that comes from. That's a NEW thing. They don't know how to make things, INVENT things. I don't remember saying the word "bored

These modern days, I don't see how a child could get bored... all the things they have... I try to get kids to write a book, or paint a painting... I tell them to just INVENT something, and use their minds...

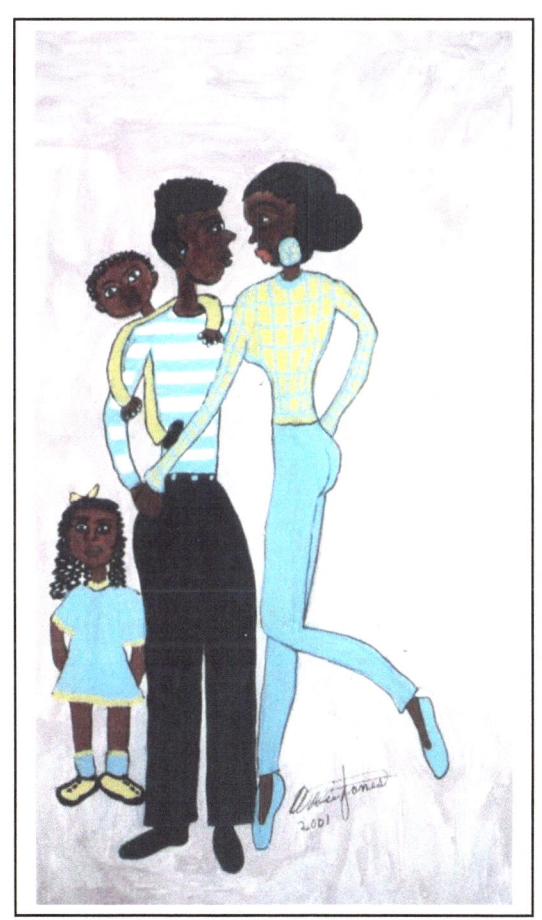

Family, 10 ½ x 13 ½ acrylic on mat board

I tell the kids: You can do it!

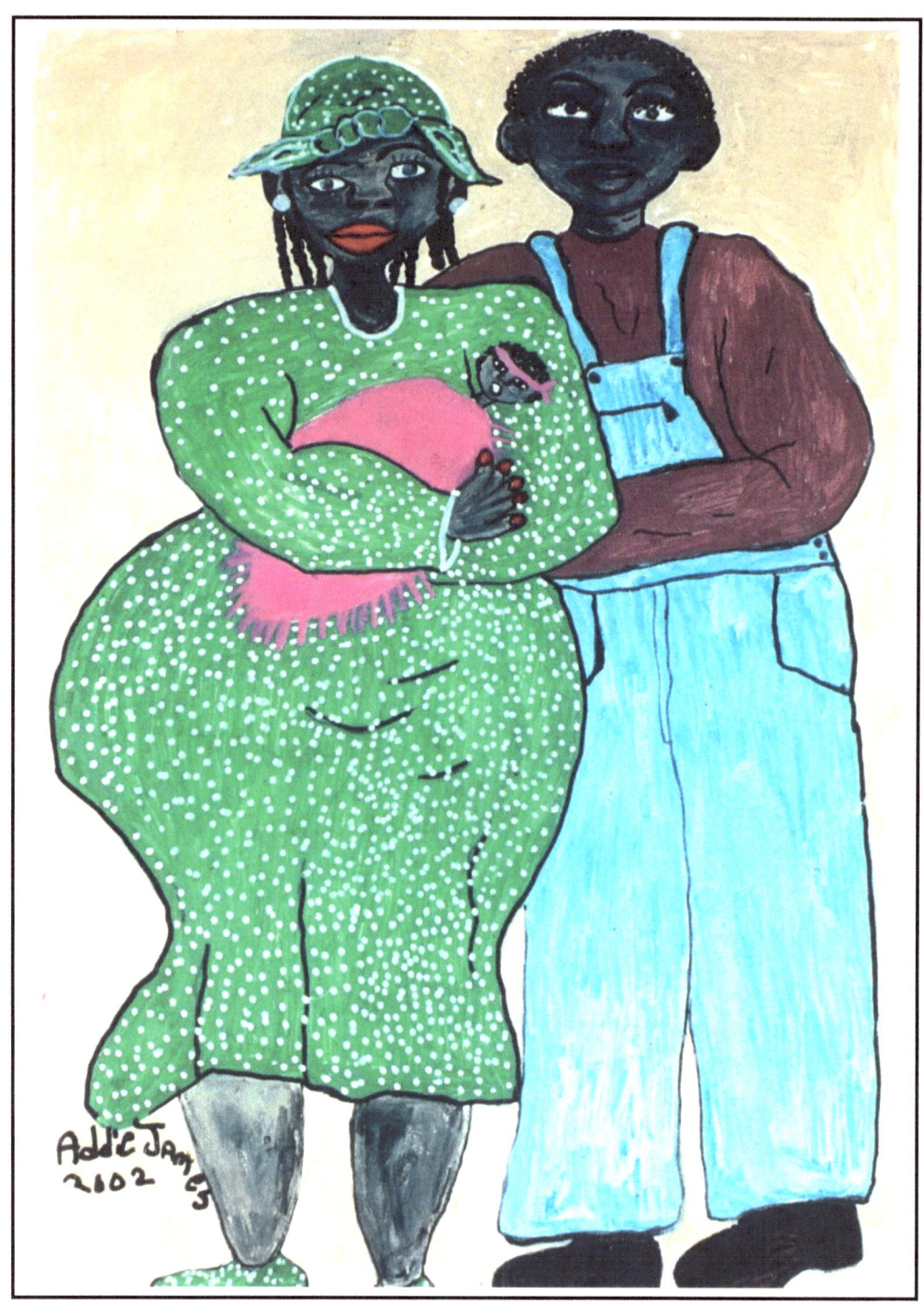

We Finally Got Our Baby, 10 ¾ x 15 acrylic on mat board

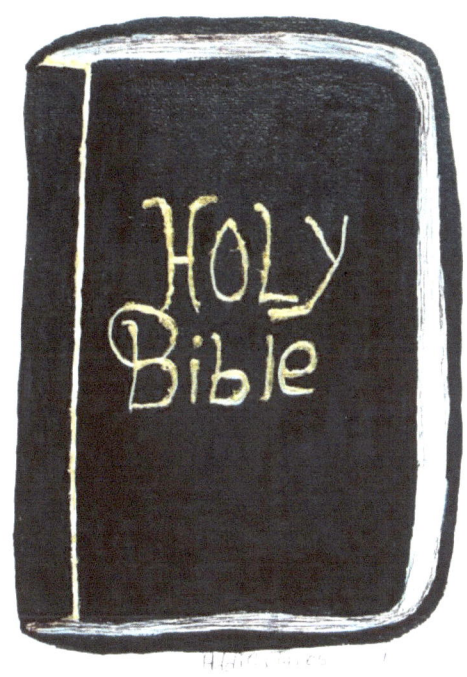

Holy Bible, 11 x 13 #/4 acrylic on mat board

FAITH

If family was the cornerstone of Addie's life, then faith was the mortar that bound it all together. From earliest childhood, Addie attended church and read the Bible. Her faith sustained her through poverty. It comforted her when she lost her parents, her brother, her husband, and a beloved son.

Going to Church, 24 x 30 acrylic on mat board

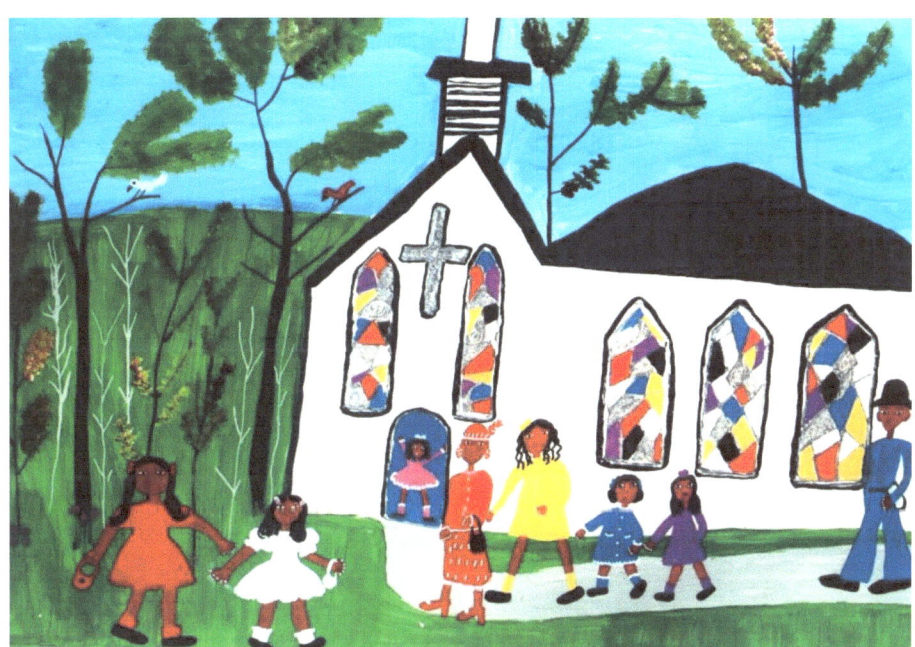

Oh yes, we went to church EVERY Sunday. We went to the Holiness Church, and they used to pray over us and do what they call "tarrin'," rubbing it all over your head. I never liked that. Rubbing it all over your head to get the Holy Ghost. I never did like that. I wanted to hit them so bad, I didn't know what to do!

While Miss Addie continued to attend church, she believed that organized religion was not the only path to God:

You don't have to go to church to be good people. *Some of the baddest people of all are in the church. If you don't even go to church, if you do your part in the world, you all right.*
Some of the very people be up there preaching aren't the best people.

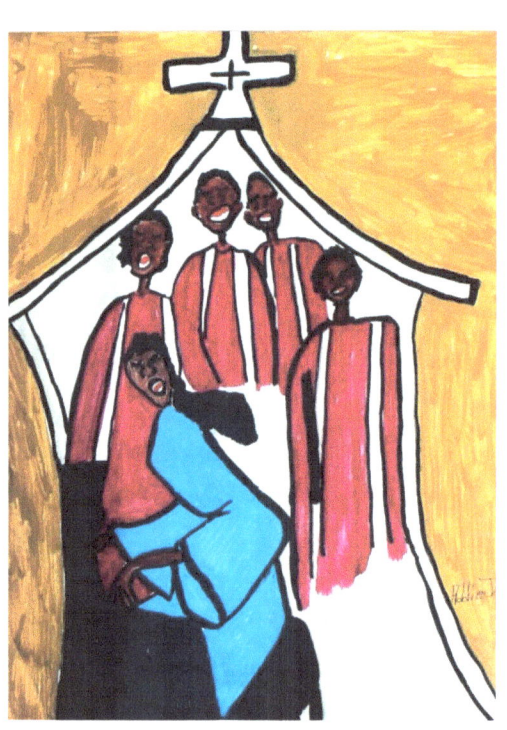

Gospel Singing 9 x 12 acrylic on paper

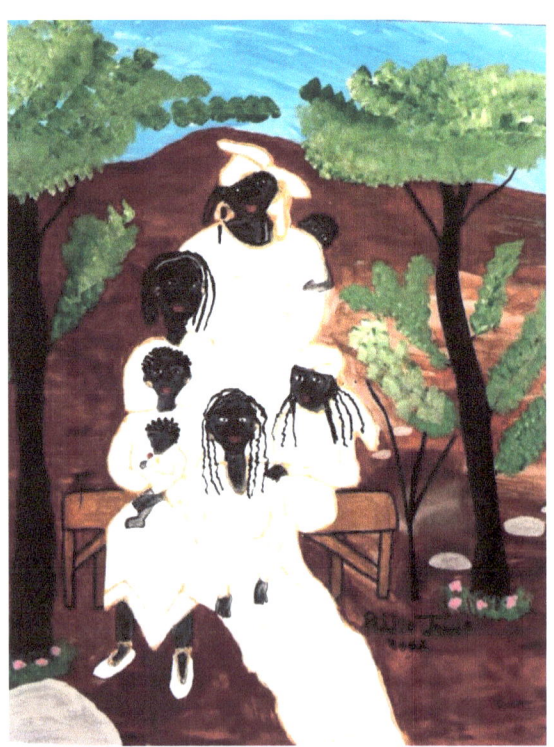

People, 16 x 20 acrylic on mat board

94

Oh yes! And you can talk to the trees. I love nature. I can just go out there and find a pretty rock, and I'll just treasure that more than anything…

I know my brother was having a lot of trouble, and I had a pretty rock, and I give this rock to him, and I say: "You just keep this rock, and God will bless you. He still got that rock, and he carries it in his pocket.

There is so much blessing out there in the world of nature. I've found Indian arrow heads when they was working down here in the field. I took the kids down there, and I've got those Indian arrow heads now.

That's where God is, because maybe you come across a child or somebody that needs help and you help them. I don't care how much I got, if you come to my house and I'm cooking, you can EAT. I'm cooking…you can eat.

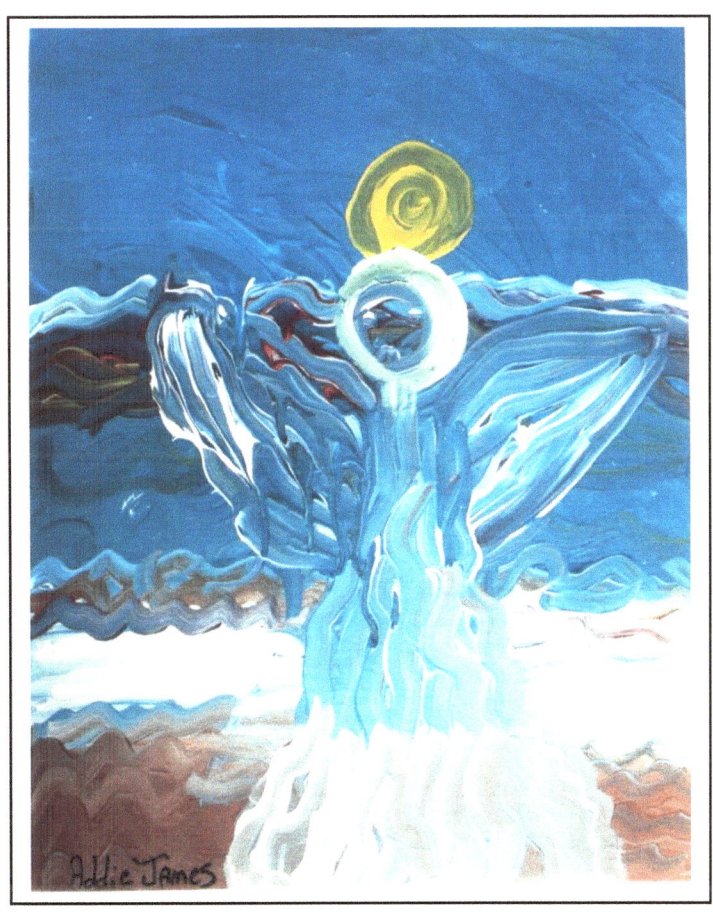

Spirit of the Angel, 16 x 20 acrylic on canvas board

Addie James' faith inspired her art. In turn, her religious subject matter often prompted others to purchase these painting to be displayed in a public venue as an inspiration to others.

An anonymous donor presented a painting to Miss Addie's church, while one of the artist's angels brought comfort to residents at The Brian Center, a nursing home in Statesville.

Have You Tried Jesus?
by Addie James

Hey there, little Sally Jane,
Why you look so tired and weary?
Come on, child, sit down here.
Tell me about it.
You tell me you have been to the psychologist?
To talk to your doctor/preacher/sister/brother?
Sally Jane, what I want to know is
Have you talked to Jesus?
He the one will set you free.
You know He died on the cross, for you and me.
And let me tell you something, Sally Jane,
Stop running around like you crazy
Being stressed out and so run down.
Go home in your prayer closet
And tell Jesus all about it.
Be patient, understanding, and have faith
That's all you have to do
Thank Jesus, yes.

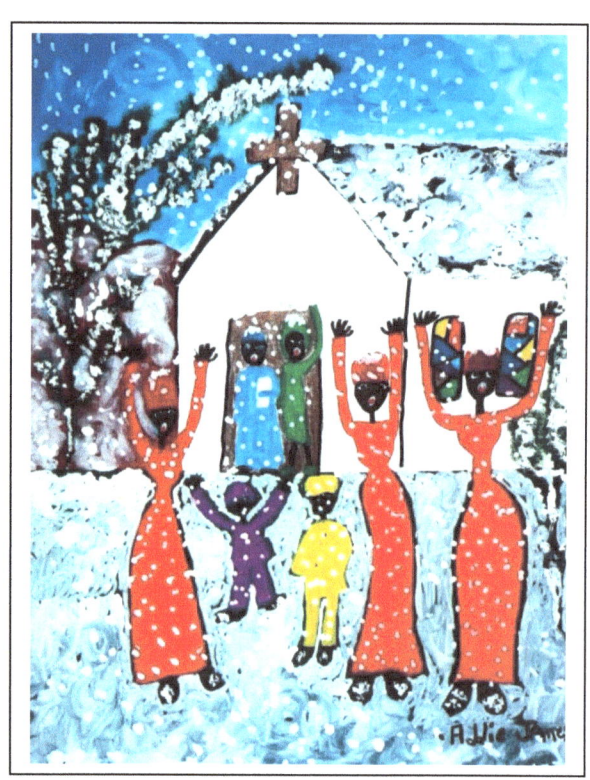

Hallelujah, It's Snowing
14 x 18 acrylic on paper

Addie James' faith seems to have endowed her with **unique psychic skills.** As she told her stories, I glimpsed the **mystical aspect of her religion:**

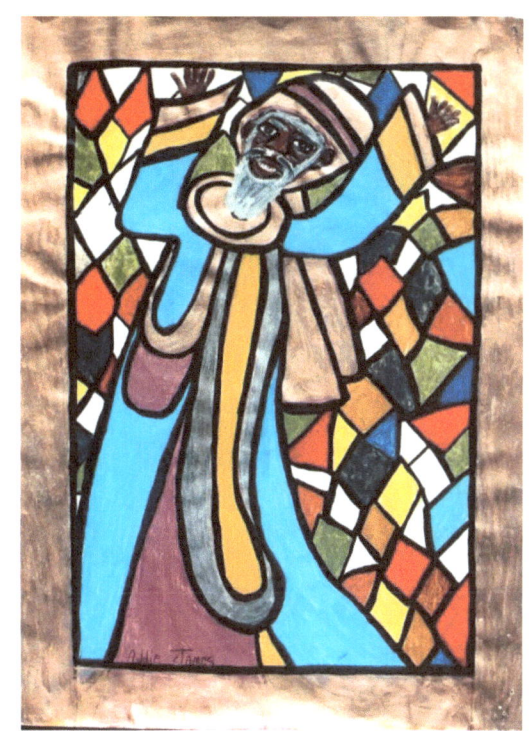

Spirit with Stained Glass, 10 ½ x 14 mixed media

My husband and I liked to ride around, and one day we went to the airport. And we were sitting there and this old man come around. He could hardly walk, and he said: "Will somebody please help me find my locker?"

And everyone just turned away. And I told my husband, "why don'tnobody help that old man find his locker? I'm going to help him!"

And he said, "Are you crazy?"

But I got up and said, "I GOT to help that man. I don't care what people think, I'm going to help that man!"

And I got up, and the man could hardly walk. I don't know where he thinks his locker is, but he took me to his locker.

And while I was opening the locker, I was just talking, and before I got into the locker, he stopped me and turned me around, and he looked at me.

*He said, "**You know what? God is going to bless you.**"*

Then I opened the locker for him...wasn't nothing in it. And when I turned around, that man was gone. Completely gone.

*I walked around in the airport, and I never seen him. **And it was an angel...nothing but an angel.** It was a test from an angel from God. God wanted to tell me He was going to bless me.*

God Got a Plan for You
by Addie James

God has got a plan for you.
If you listen closely
He will tell you what to do.
Listen, listen, He will tell you what to do.

Bow down your head in prayer.
So let us pray to our Heavenly Father.
It doesn't matter where you are at,
bow down your head, it's time to pray.

God has got a plan for you.
Listen, listen, listen
He will tell you what to do.

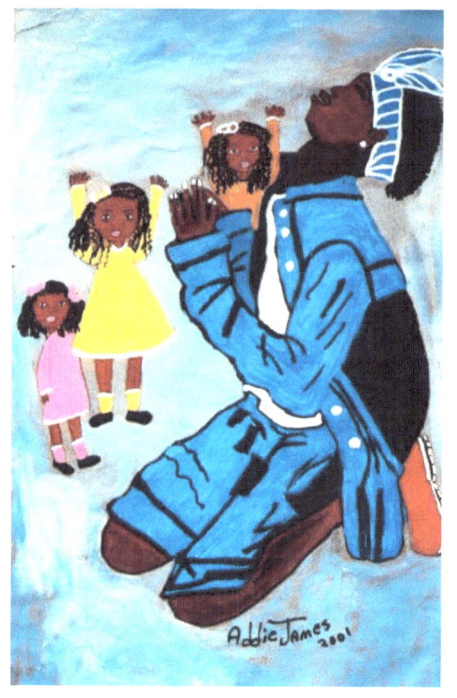

Praying Time, 9 ¼ x 13 ¾ acrylic on paper

Part of God's plan for Addie James was to find her a job in a factory, where she helped to manufacture medical furniture. It was here she discovered a **magical ability to hear voices:**

One time I was sitting upstairs at the window in the furniture factory. I was looking down, and I seen these two white men talking, and even though they was far away, I could hear them just like I was standing there, and that's the truth.

And one was saying to the other, "We gonna get time off!"

And when they come up to me, I say, "Oooh, we gonna get time off!"

And they just look at me and say, "How you know that?"

And I say, "Just kidding."

Among the voices Addie heard were those of her twin grandsons singing to the dance routines they performed throughout the region. Most of these routines were *Pray-sings* to the Lord. They established the twins as artists in their own right as they continued their grandmother's tradition of **giving thanks through art.**

As for Addie, she believed **the Lord will provide:**

One day I went to work, and you have to go by the water fountain to come in.
And I said, "Lord have mercy!" because I didn't have nothing to eat that day.
No money, or nothing. I said, "Lord have mercy!"
I was just standing there and I honestly don't know how I got across the room
to the water fountain and back again, but when I come back
I had ten dollars, and I picked it up at the water fountain.
Now I can't tell you where it come from,
but in the flick of a minute
it appeared

Who Broke the Chains?...God
8 x 10 mixed media on paper

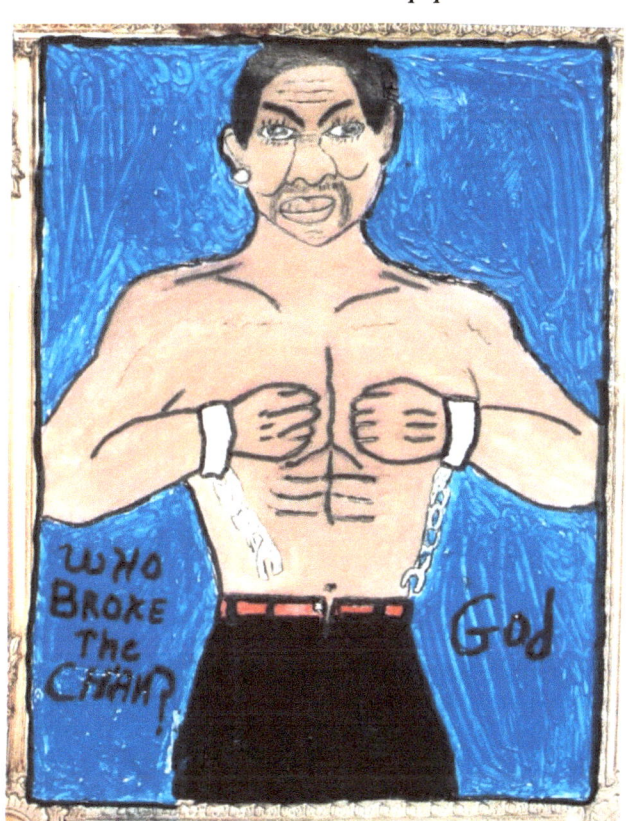

Addie said God provides, but He was also a vengeful God, who righted wrongs and punished the wicked. She believed this on a very personal level as revealed by two more stories from the furniture factory:

And then one day I came to work and there was this man named Charles. He run a bad house and sold whiskey and what not. I just looked at him and I said to myself, "Oh my God, you gonna get raided this week and go to prison!"

I was trying to debate all day whether to tell him or not. I told my sister-in-law, Jackie, but she said thinking that way would make me crazy, and sure enough, I never did tell him. And that week he got raided and went to prison. I'm just psychic. I can't help it.

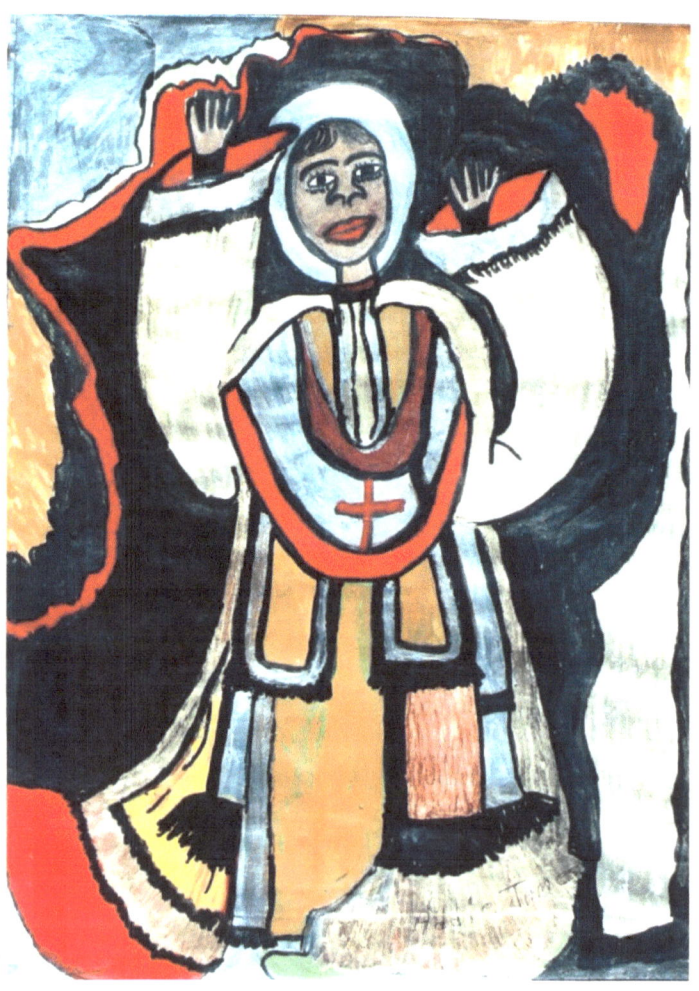

Spirit in the Wilderness, 9 x 12 mixed media on paper

100

Don't cross Miss Addie!

The boss man's girlfriend wanted my job. I put the little stripe things on all the furniture. I could do it so fast! That was my job. And the girlfriend wanted my job, and the boss man come and put me on something else, and I was so mad, I cussed him out.

And I told him, I put my finger in his face, "You know what? Something BAD is going to happen to you." I told him those words.

And the other boss man, he was white, and they were together in this thing. I told myself, "You think you're so smart, but one Person is smarter than y'all..."

I say, "You can have the girlfriend, but what you want to take me off my job for?" And I said, "Something's going to happen to you, and it won't be very long, you just wait and see..."

And that weekend the man fell out of a tree and broke his neck.

SISTER
by Addie James

A sister so kind and giving
She always takes time to talk to you
Or say a little prayer for you
No matter what the problem is
She's always there
Who is she? Where is she?
She is...SISTER PASTOR

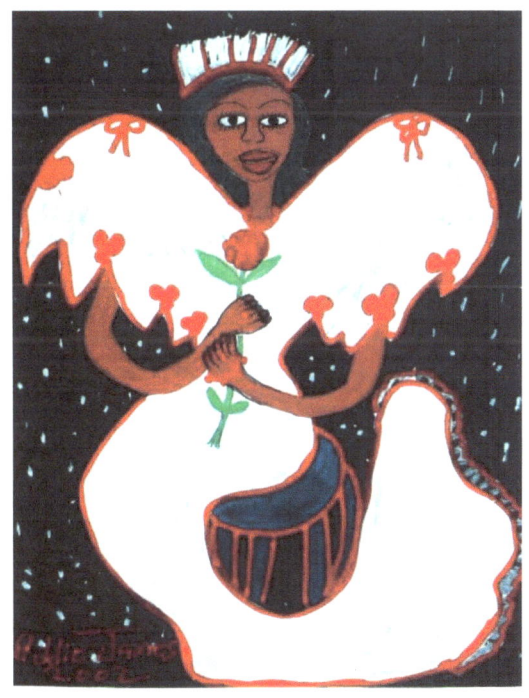

Angel with a Red Rose
7 ½ x 9 ½
acrylic on mat board

Before my mama died, I dreamt it. Everybody was so real. I went up to the kitchen to take my pills, and the spirit knocked me over two times, just like that. And I knew Mama was dead. I know things before they happen, and it's scary sometimes.

In Addie's life God provided, punished, but most of all, **God healed the sick.**

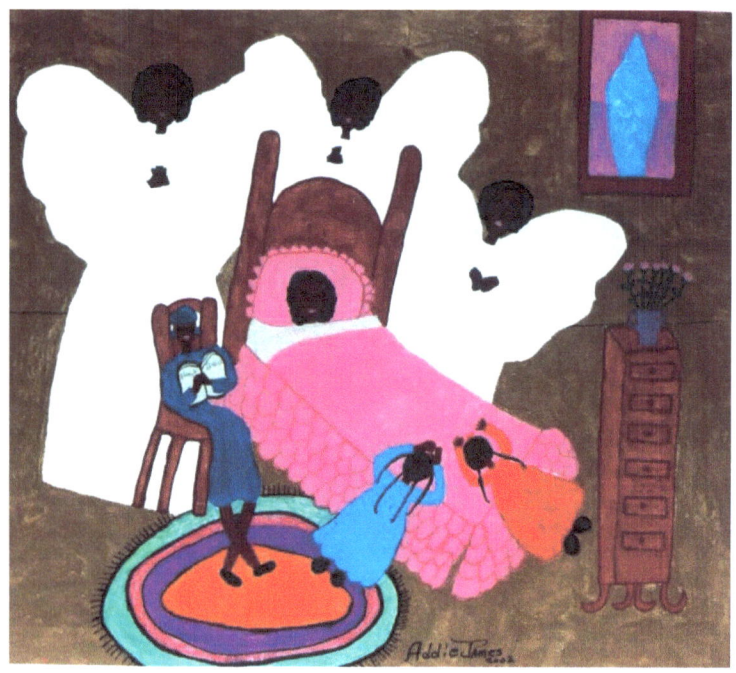

Mary Alice's Angels, 25 ½ x 29 ½ acrylic on mat board

I believe in God so deeply. *The doctor told me I was bigger than I should be, and my knees just hurt so bad! The doctor said he was going to take cartilage out and my knees needed operating on. I used to lay up on the couch all the time, and I was here by myself, and my knees kept hurting.*

Then one day the Lord said, "Get up," and I walked over to the door and I fell on my face and prayed. And when I went back to the doctor, he said, "Addie, your knees are better, and that's the truth!"

PRAISE THE LORD!

I believe in God! *And I went into the hospital one time to have a gallstone operation; my gallstones were so bad. And they said, "Addie, how in the world did you make it? Your body is so worn out. We going to work on you a little bit, build you up so you can last the operation." And I say, "Okay."*

And when everybody got out of my room, I fell down on my knees, and I asked God to HEAL, and I got up the next morning and swung my legs out of bed and walked around. And the doctor said, "Addie, how in the world did you get well overnight?"

And I said, "God."

And he said, "Well, we gonna go ahead and operate on you. And when you wake up you're going to be in intensive care, and the nurse gonna be there for everything you need...even if you go to the bathroom, you'll need help."

But when it was over, I stood up, walked to the bathroom, washed my face, and the doctor said, "Addie, what kind of person are you?"

And I said, "It ain't me, it's God."

Face in the Church Window
8 x 10
acrylic on mat board

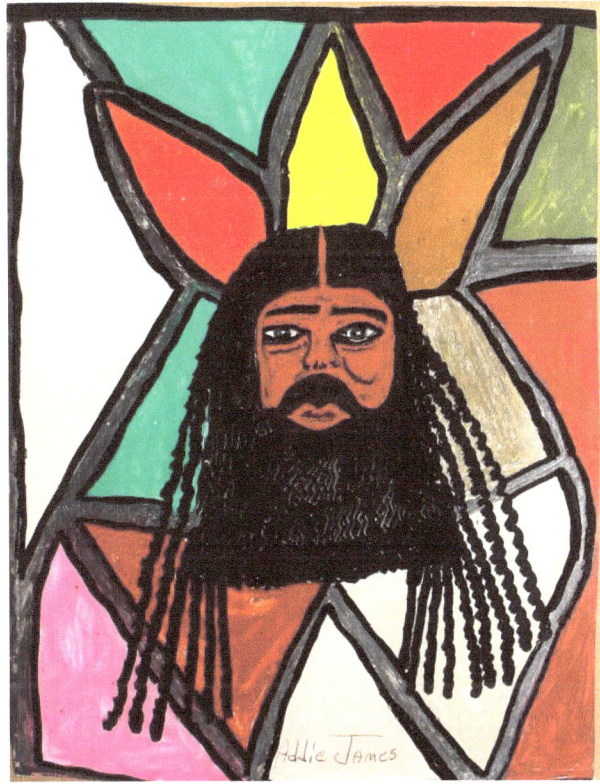

Miss Addie believed God's healing power was a blessed gift. It was a gift she hoped to pass on to others by presenting small angel paintings to patients in the hospital. An article in the Statesville paper described Addie's generosity:

"She knocks on doors of people she doesn't know and stops people in the halls. Male, female, young, and old, James says she has never met a person who doesn't want an angel."[12]

A Guidepost article also quoted Addie:

"Whenever I see people with sad faces because their lives don't seem too pretty to them, I know what to do. I pull some black paper out of my bag and make little angel pictures. The bright colors I use just light right up on black paper! When I finish, I pray God someone will use it to find peace and beauty.[13]

And Addie described the angels to me:

When I go to the hospital with my little angels, I know which room to go to, because God is guiding me, and they NEED an angel. And I have to give them an angel. You know, that makes me feel so good.

The last time I was over at Davis Hospital and I went to the children's department, about twelve children were there, and I give every one of them…black or white…a little angel.

I give a rich woman one. You can always tell a rich person, they have the best of everything. And she was really sick, and she was thinking she wasn't going to make it. And she used to travel all around the world…to Asia, Africa, and everywhere.

And I went up to her room and she said, "Come on inside, now."

And I said, "I got something for you." She was just lying there all by herself, and I said, "Lord, you are going to be all right. You know God's got things He wants you to do." I give her an angel, and she give me a great big hug. I said, "Just keep your angel here beside you and God will take care of you."

---

[12] From "Touched by an Angel; Statesville Woman Gives Others the Gift of Hope." Carla Froedge, *STATESVILLE LANDMARK AND RECORD,* September 23, 2002
[13] From "Painting Life Beautiful," Addie James, prepared by Karen Barber for *Angels on Earth, a GUIDEPOST publication, March-April, 2003*

Addie believed the forces of good always prevailed, but she also acknowledged evil in the world. When I first saw Addie's paintings of **Heebie-jeebies**, I assumed they were sinister beings, but I was wrong.

Indeed, Addie did not believe in voodoo or witchcraft, and her *Heebie-Jeebie* was, in fact, the hero of a comic book she always wanted to write. He rescued children from drugs and other dangers on the street.

I meant to write the book. He was going to be the good guy, and he could do things other people could not do.

I know there's a Devil. *Oh yeah, there's a force for evil. When you say your prayers you have to ask God to keep a shield around you, and then keep the blood on your home, on your children, and on you. When the famine comes back in the Bible days, good things come to the house that was protected.*

Heebie-jeebie
11 ¾ x 17
Mixed media on paper

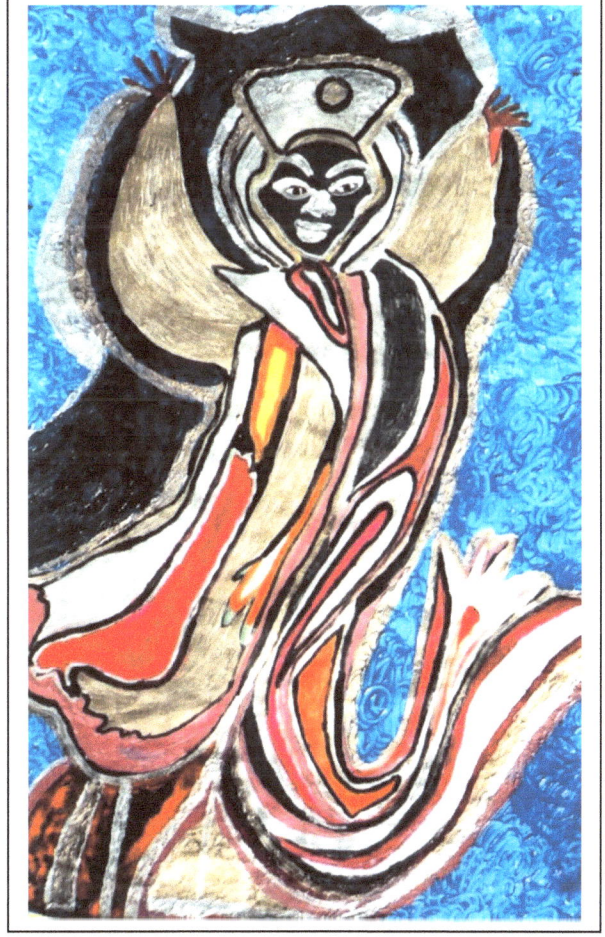

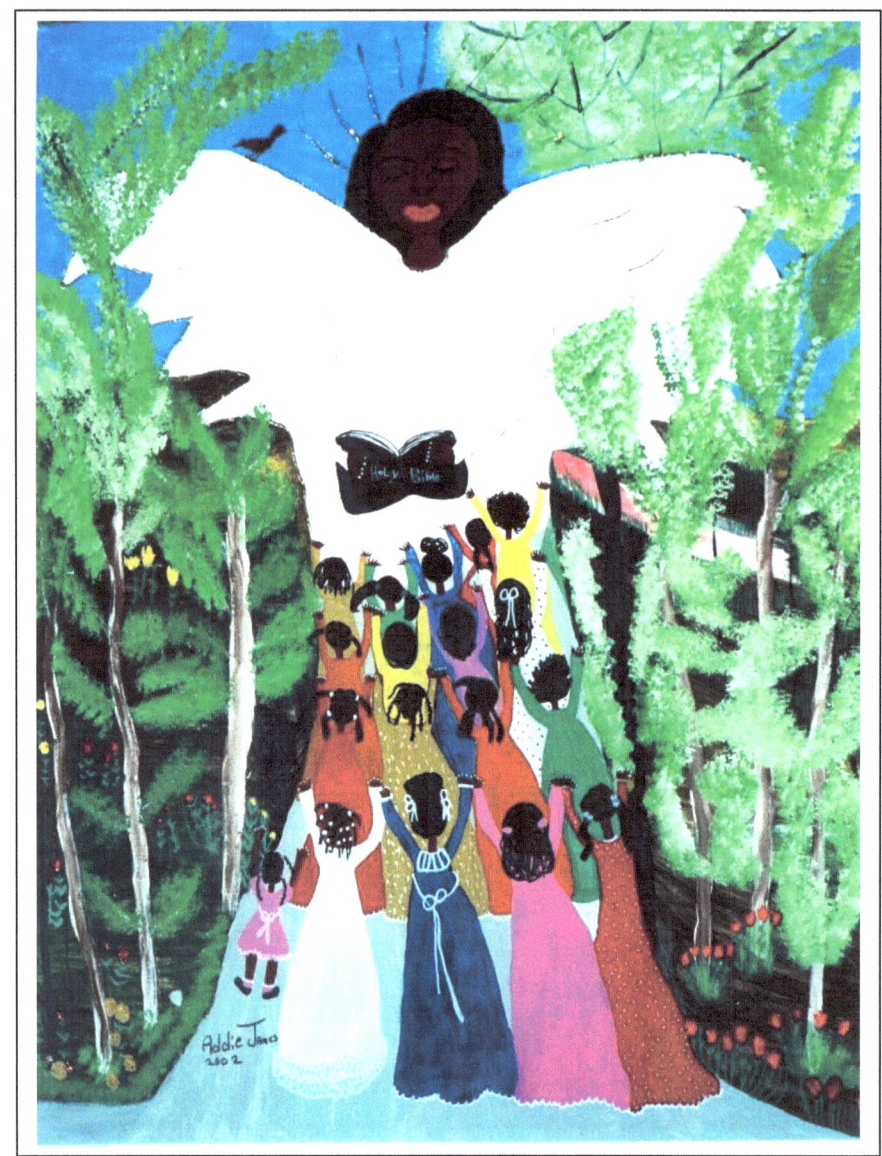

Angel at the Crossroads
36 x 48
acrylic on canvas

These are poor children and they're at the end of their rope. They are hungry and they need to eat, and they are walking a long road into the woods.

And this angel is there to help them.

HALLELUJAH, it's CHRISTMAS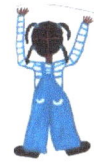

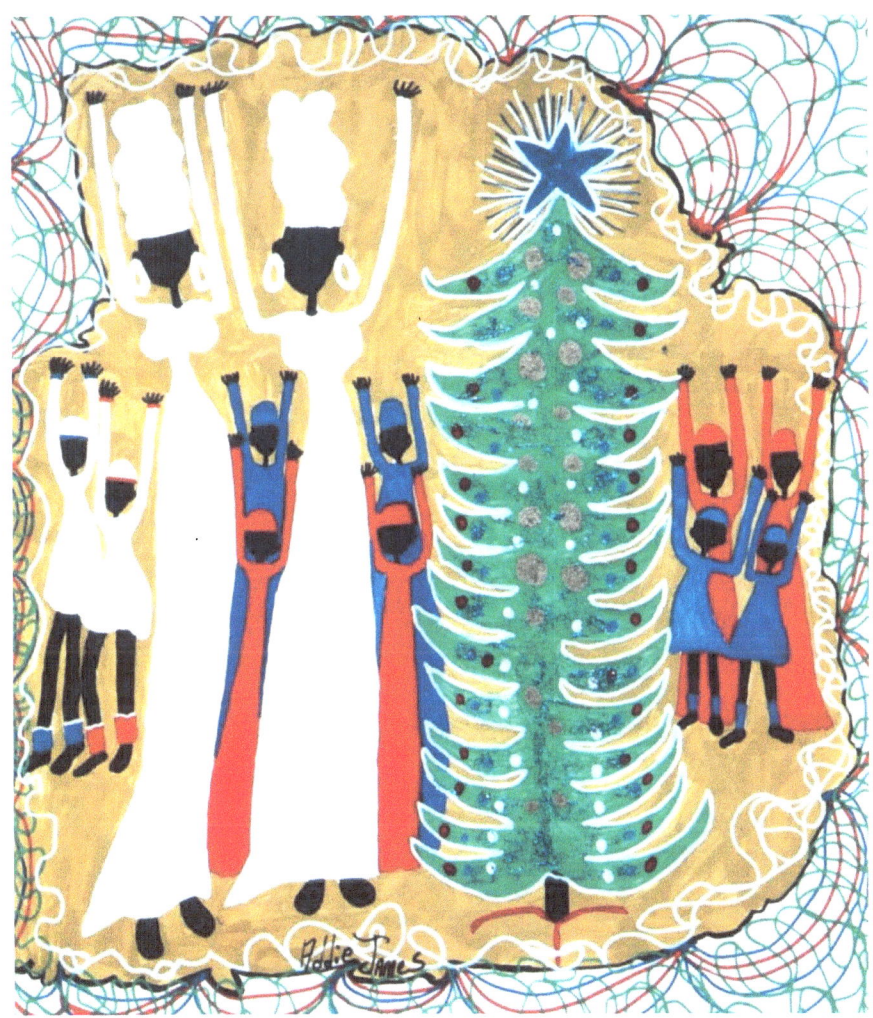

Hallelujah, it's Christmas, 14 x 18 mixed media on mat board

The small trees around Addie's house had lost their leaves. Their naked branches were stark against a steel gray sky, and a frigid wind bent the dried grass surrounding her old deck as I entered the house to record yet another session for this book.

It was right before the holidays, November 2002, and we had been meeting like this for more than a year. Addie had been ill, with a stay in the hospital late in the summer, but as always, her spirits were high, she was producing volumes of marvelous art, and she welcomed me into her cozy little room like an old friend.

By then we had a system. We would settle side by side on Addie's sagging couch, where she did all her painting, and first we would look at her new work. As always, I would resist nothing and would buy everything for the gallery. Next we would turn on the twins' karaoke machine, which served as our tape recorder, and find a place on the cluttered coffee table to set the big, glittering microphone. And Addie would begin to talk about her life...

That day, Madaron, Addie's daughter, was baking sweet potato pies. A tantalizing aroma drifted from the tiny kitchen, and I said a secret prayer that one slice would be reserved for me. And in keeping with the season, our conversation turned to Christmas:

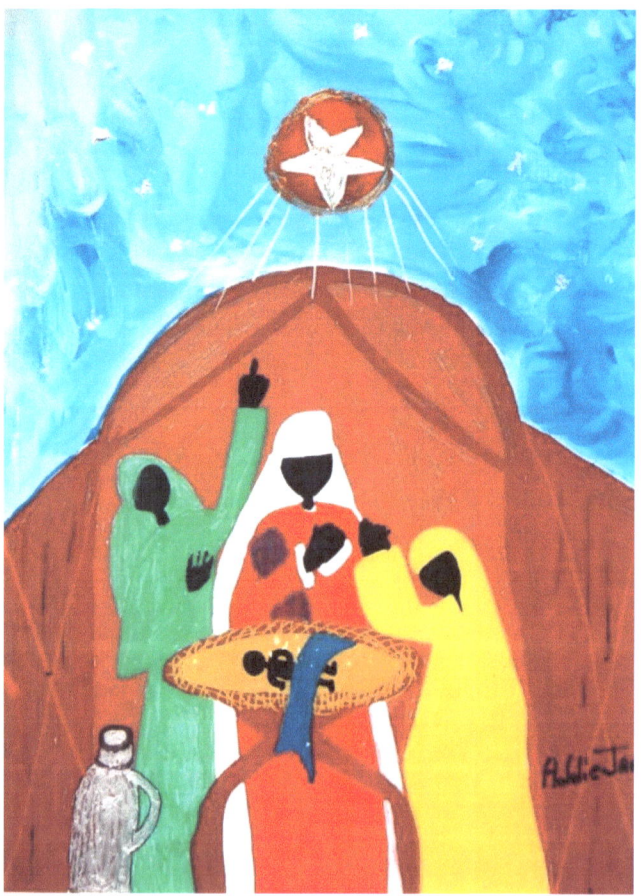

Christ Child, 12 x 16
acrylic on paper

Christmas was always great. Always. Homemade blackberry wine...that was the BOMB! I know how to make it myself. And wine made of nanas and lopers (bananas and cantaloupes) That was SO good!

Miss Addie's Christmas art alternated between religious and secular subject matter. Her nativity scenes were both joyous and reverent, usually including the three wise men and the star of Bethlehem.

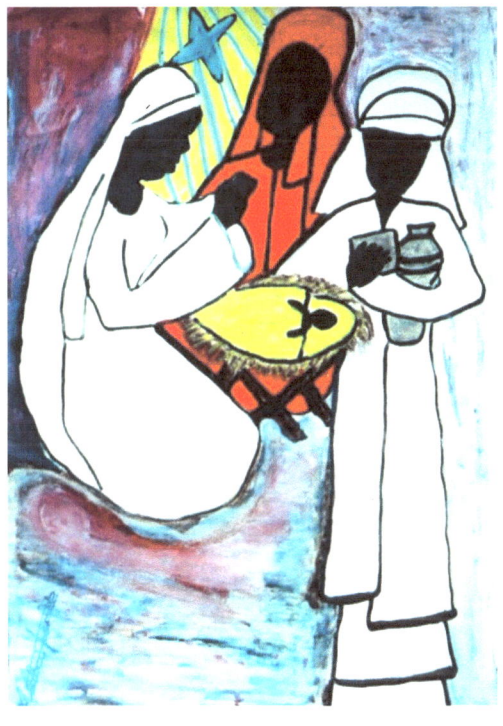

Gifts for the Christ Child
7 ¾ x 11 acrylic on paper

The figures, including the Holy Family, were always black, and the Christ child was a tiny, stick-like doll. He was both vulnerable and adored, lending a sweet naiveté to these works.

We always cut a tree out of the woods. Lord, that's a tradition. And I love to see that every child gets something for Christmas. I remember one Christmas the children from down the street came by, so we gave things to those children too. They ate with us too, breakfast, dinner, and supper.

I always have the whole family. I always bake cakes. We have about thirteen cakes. We cook a turkey, a ham, and a hen. And one year I had deer meat.

I had rabbit. You get a rabbit, wash it good, boil it and cut it up. You boil it until it's tender and then salt the pieces. You boil it in WINE. Then you take it out and flour it, and then you fry it.

I love to eat wild stuff. My daddy and my brothers used to hunt, and I would know how to clean all that stuff. Like a rabbit, you skin it and get all the fur off it, and cut those little feet off and keep them for good luck charms.

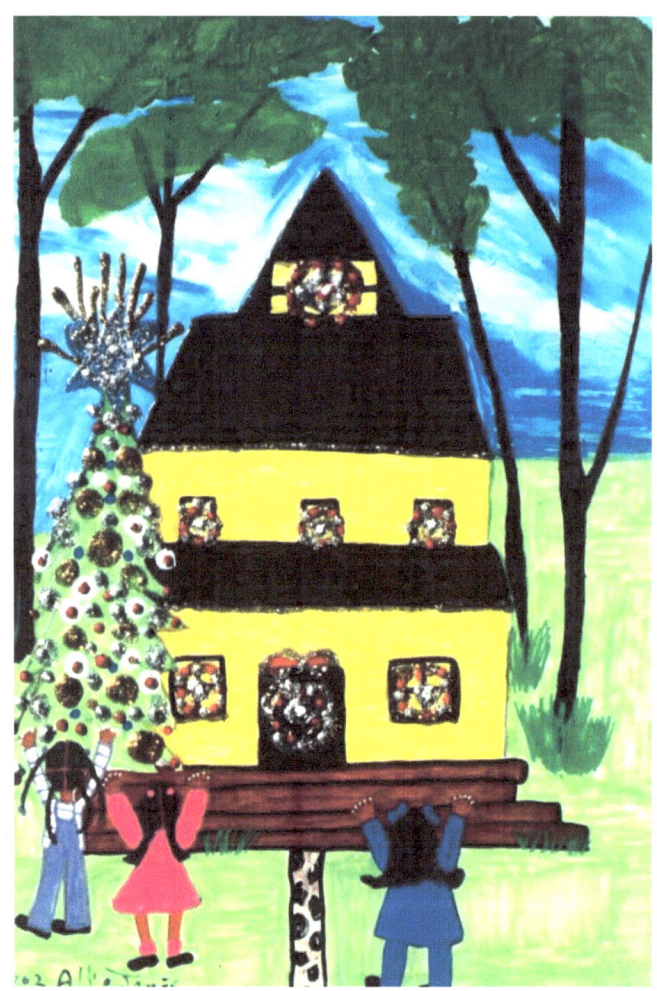

Christmastime at the Yellow House
12 ½ x 15 ½ mixed media on mat board

Family, fun, and food were
the rule in an Addie James Christmas.
Although the family had little to spend
on gifts, an abundance of good will more
than compensated for any lack of
material gain.

This **abundance of spirit**
permeates Addie's Christmas paintings,
which are filled with glittering texture,
glued-on sparkles, a celebration in 3-D.

Addie made an *electric Christmas
Tree*:
*When I drawed out that Christmas
tree, I said "I've just got to get me
some lights on that. So I got the lights
at the drugstore. I had to poke little
holes in that thing with an ice pick,
then pushed them through
and plugged it in from behind.*

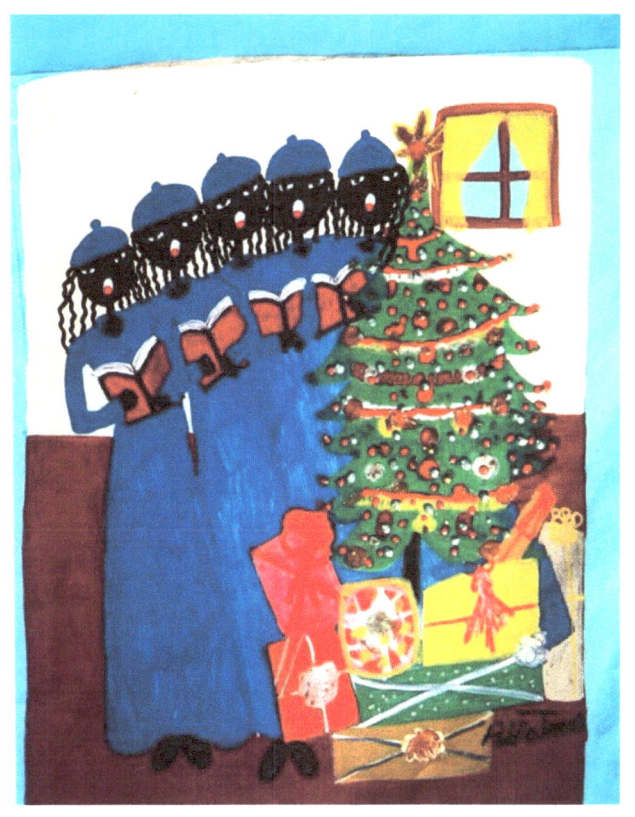

Christmas Carols
12 x 16 mixed media on paper

*Oh boy, Christmas was the BOMB! You know them big paper grocery bags? Mama
would fix us a big grocery bag of nuts and candy and apples and oranges. We didn't
get but maybe one thing for Christmas, but that big bag of candy and nuts made up for
it.*

*And we had playhouses. Mama would even put those little bags in our playhouses.
And she would make five, six, seven, eight cakes...fudge cakes. And people would
come from all around just to get a taste of her cake. She made all kinds...coconut,
pineapple fruitcake was her specialty, and chocolate cake. We ALWAYS had a lot of
cakes, and they were the best!*

In keeping with her tradition of making the best of the least, Miss Addie began creating **ghetto Christmas trees:**

In the ghetto, all folks can find is a branch fallen off some old tree. They take that branch and they stick it in a trashcan, and they decorate it up so pretty...they have a GOOD time, boy, a real Christmas.

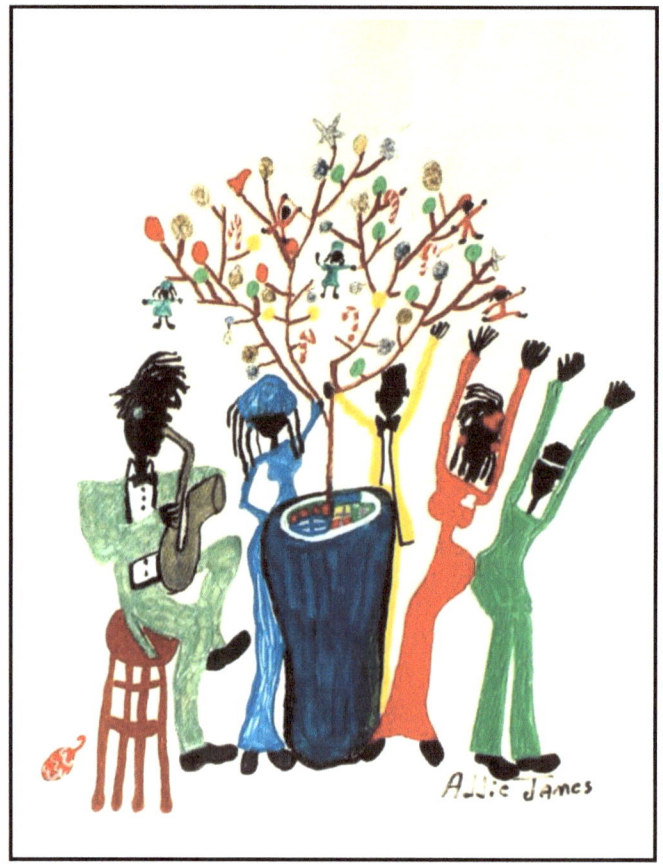

People Sing at the Ghetto Tree
11 x 15 mixed media on paper

Anybody that comes by...a little child...and I'll fix him a bag of nuts and apples and cakes and give him a meal. And I'll make them corn stuffing and that's the BOMB.

Well, you can make corn bread, nice and brown, boil you some eggs, dice your celery and all that stuff...and you get you a turkey gizzard and pieces of turkey all chopped up and put in herbs and spices, especially sage. Put all that in a pan and stir it up and put it in the oven and let it brown.

And I like a brown giblet gravy, cook it in the pan until it's thick and brown...cranberries and cake...do everything from scratch. And I love to cook my turkey with champagne; that makes it tender.

After Christmas is over, you take that turkey, chip it up or grind it up real good, put some eggs and some onions in there, and fry it into croquettes; it's SO GOOD! **OH, LORD, I'M HUNGRY!**

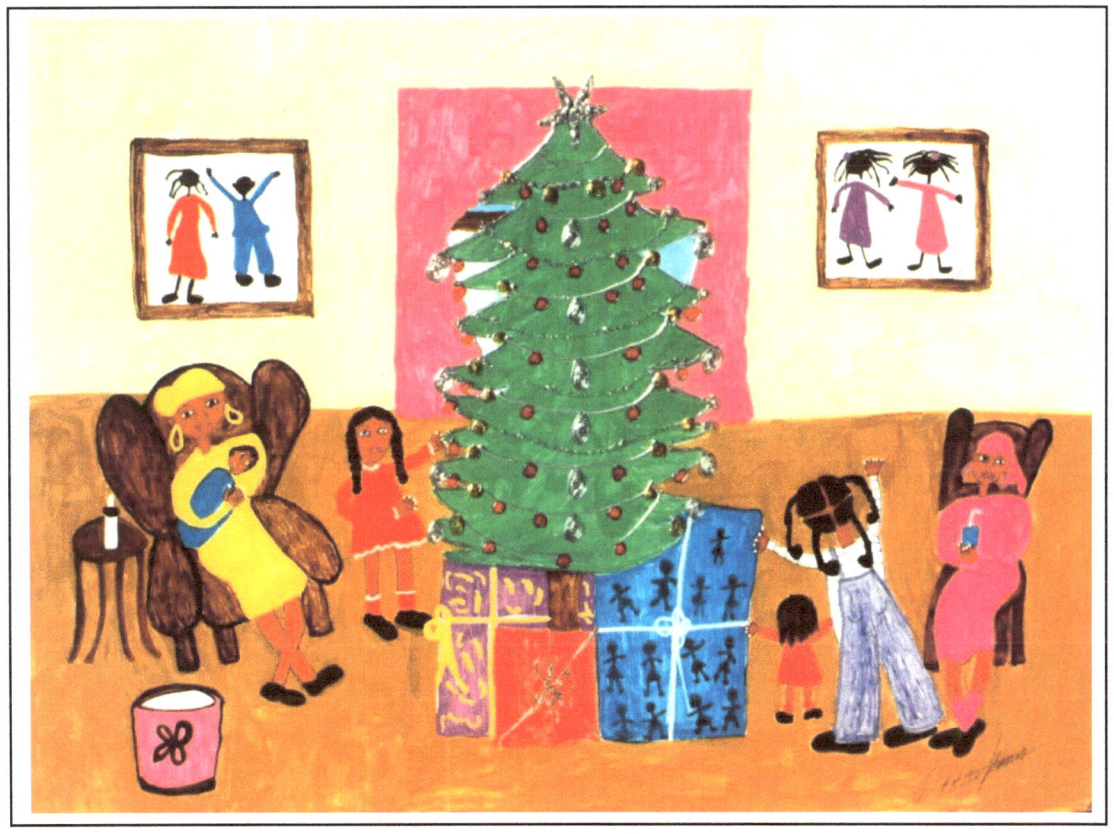

The gifts, 21 x 23 mixed media on mat board

I was hungry too, Miss Addie. On that cold November day my stomach was growling, my mouth was watering, and Addie's stories had whipped me up for a feeding frenzy. Luckily, Madaron brought us both a piece of hot sweet potato pie, fresh from the oven. **Thank you, Jesus,** and thank *you,* Madaron.

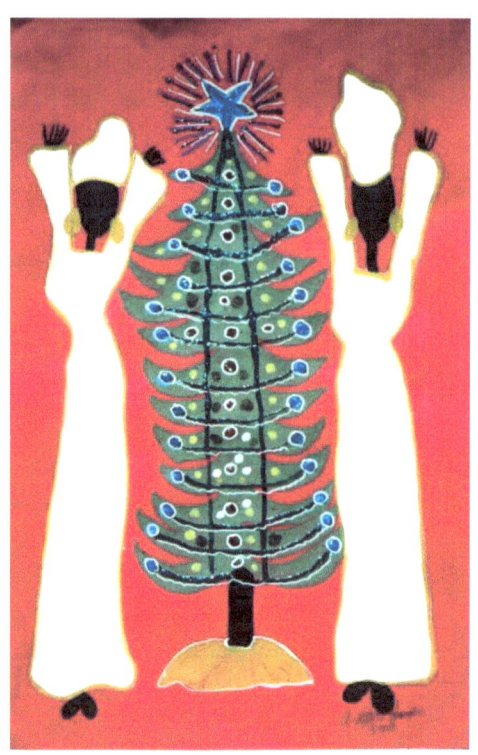

The Star, 12 x 18
Mixed media on paper

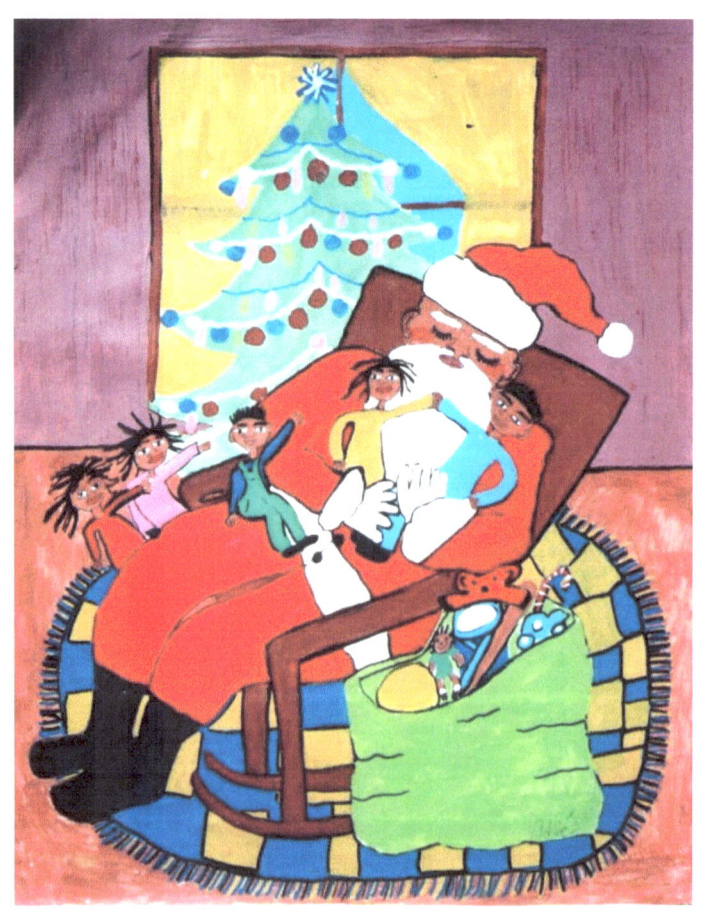

Santa Claus, 11 x 13 ½
Acrylic on mat board

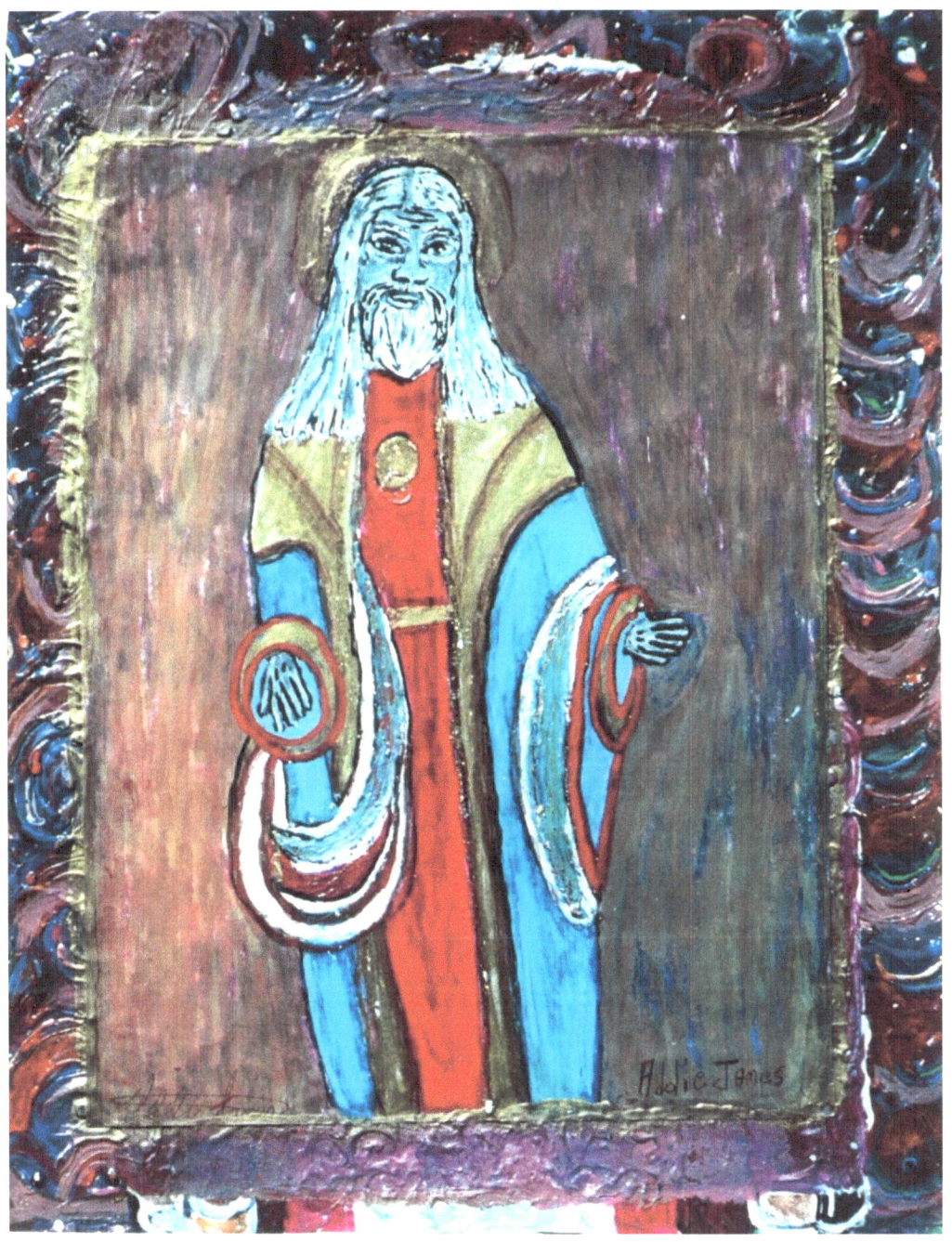

The Savior, 10 ¾ x 13 ¾ mixed media on paper

HALLELUJAH, it's a PARTY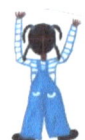

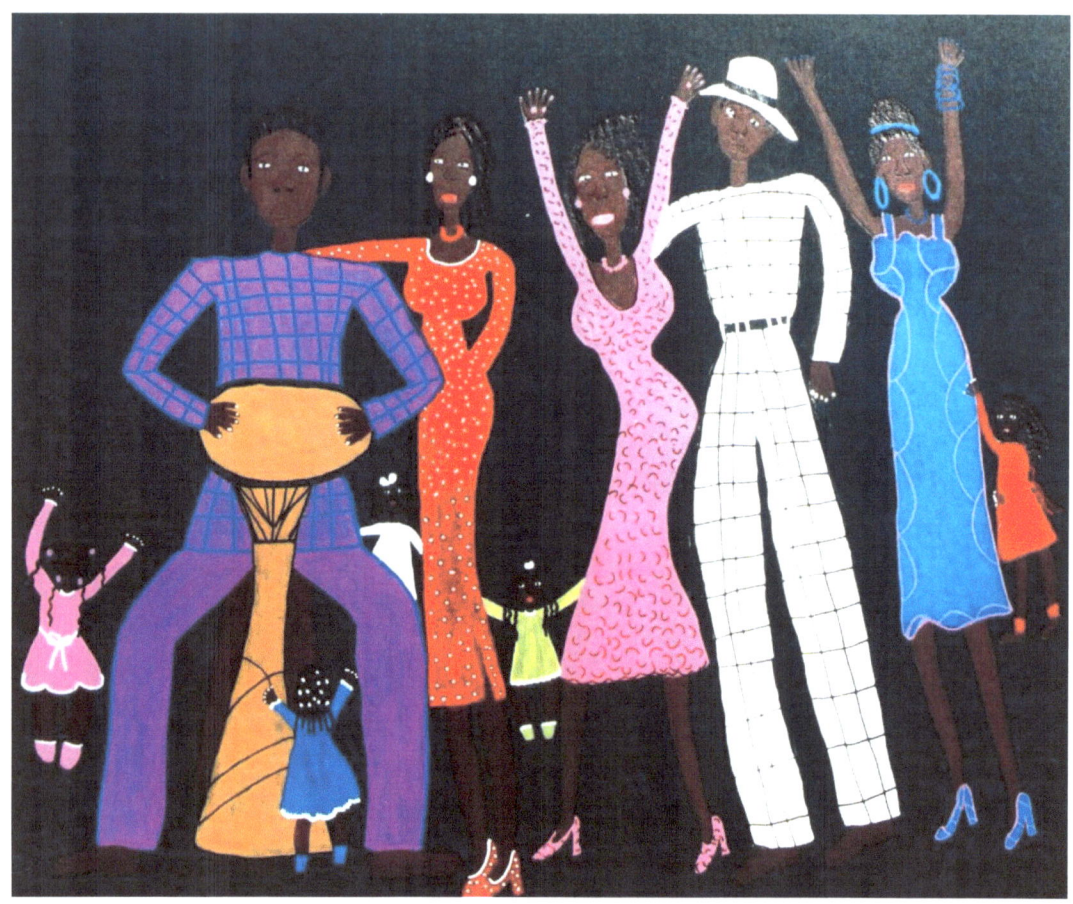

Party, 32 x 37 acrylic on mat board

Addie James admitted she preferred an insular life at home in the company of her family to the hubbub of clubs and the society of revelers. Still she produced many rollicking paintings depicting the bright lights, music, and dancing of the party life. Along with the fertile harvest of her imagination, Miss Addie gathered much inspiration from what she saw on television and from accompanying her twin grandsons to their lively dance performances.

Yet in many of these party paintings a family theme prevailed. In *Party,* where brilliant color vibrates off a black sheet of mat board, Addie created a masterful composition, which clearly expressed the relationship of two couples attached to their respective children. The little girl in a green dress, suspended in the center between the two mamas, implied a relationship between the women; perhaps they were sisters?

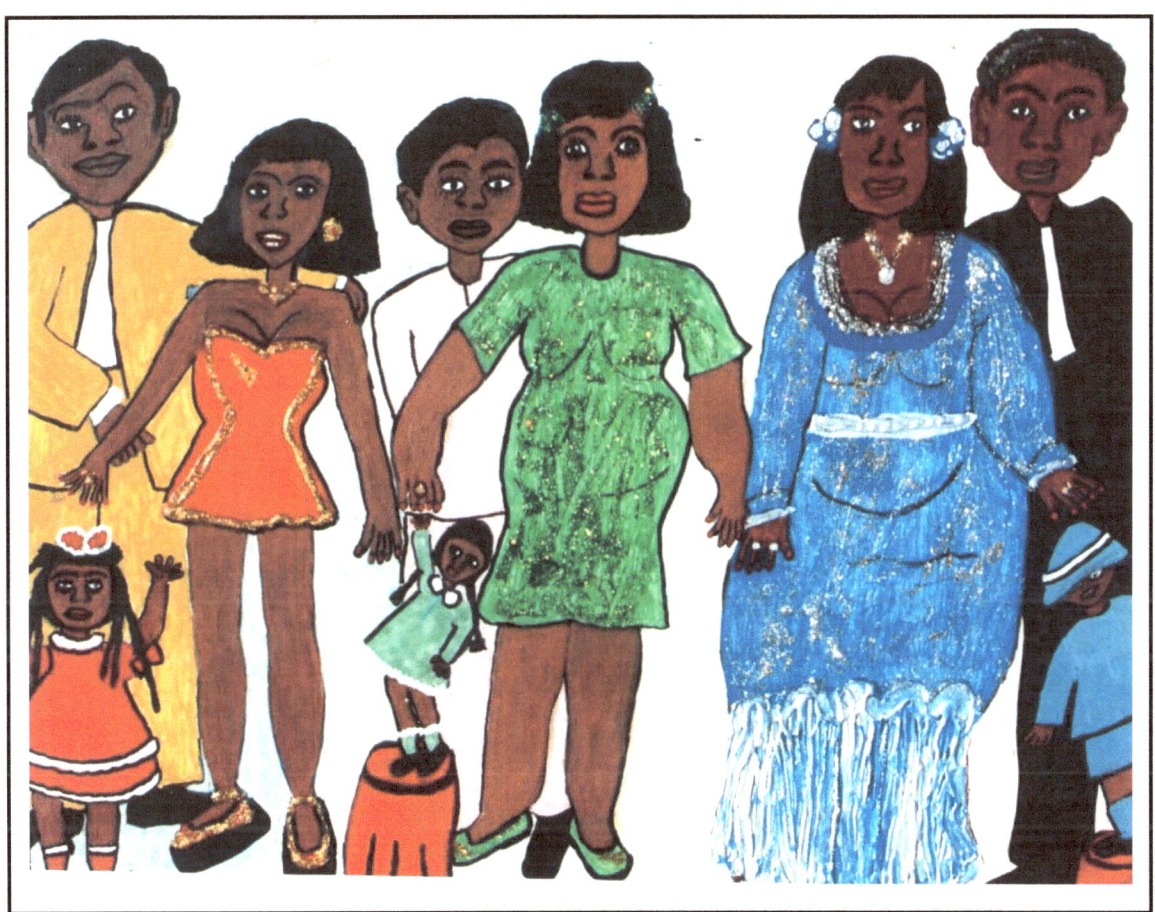

Family Celebration, 14 x 17 ½ mixed media on cardboard

In *Family Celebration* Addie again brought her powerful understanding of composition to bear by conjoining the figures. Mothers and their children were dressed in matching colors, and their subtle touching…arm to hand to arm…indicated this family's solidarity as they stepped out into a wider world.

117

Whether Addie's astonishing skill in composing relationships was deliberate or intuitive was unclear. It was certain, however, that in her party paintings she consistently revealed a graphic sophistication usually associated with years of art school training.

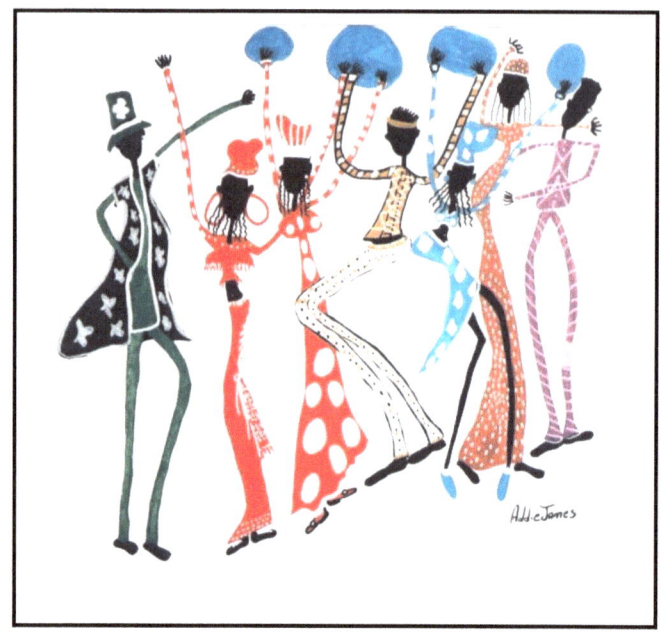

Strike a Pose, 17 ¾ x 19 acrylic on paper

In *Strike a Pose,* Addie's use of black silhouette faces and liquid, undulating line coupled with the joyous *hallelujah gesture,* both excites and convinces even the most critical viewer.

Songs come to me
 just like someone
 was telling them to me.
Poerty comes the same way
 and I just write it down.

 If I don't write it down,
 then I forget it.

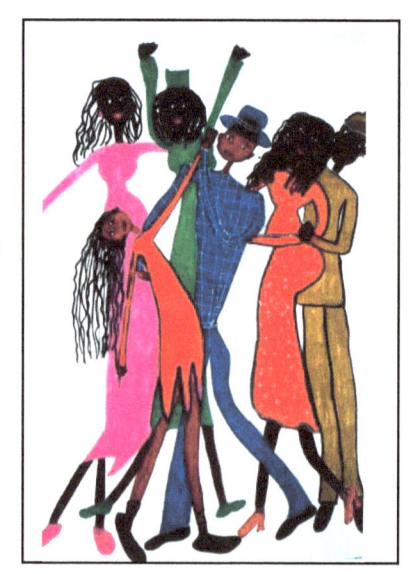

Dance, 10 ¾ x 16 1/2
Acrylic on paper

118

RHYTHMS
by Addie James

My blood raced strong.
I want to dance, dance to that rhythm.
There is no limitation to my rhythm.
It is my treasure.
Rhythm has no boundary.
Rhythm is in my heart,
Sharp like pain.
Every day I thank God for my rhythm.
When I hear that rhythm,
I clap my hands, tap my feet.
Thank you God
For that rhythm beat.

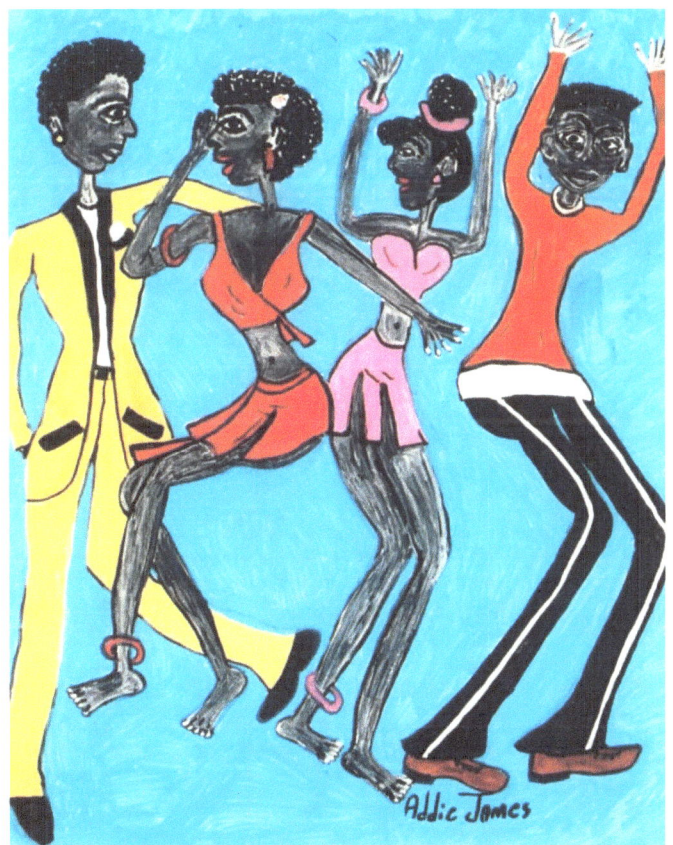

Hip Hop, 11 x 14acrylic on mat board

Occasionally Addie created a piece like *Singing the Blues,*
which imparted a hint of pathos…of opportunities lost.

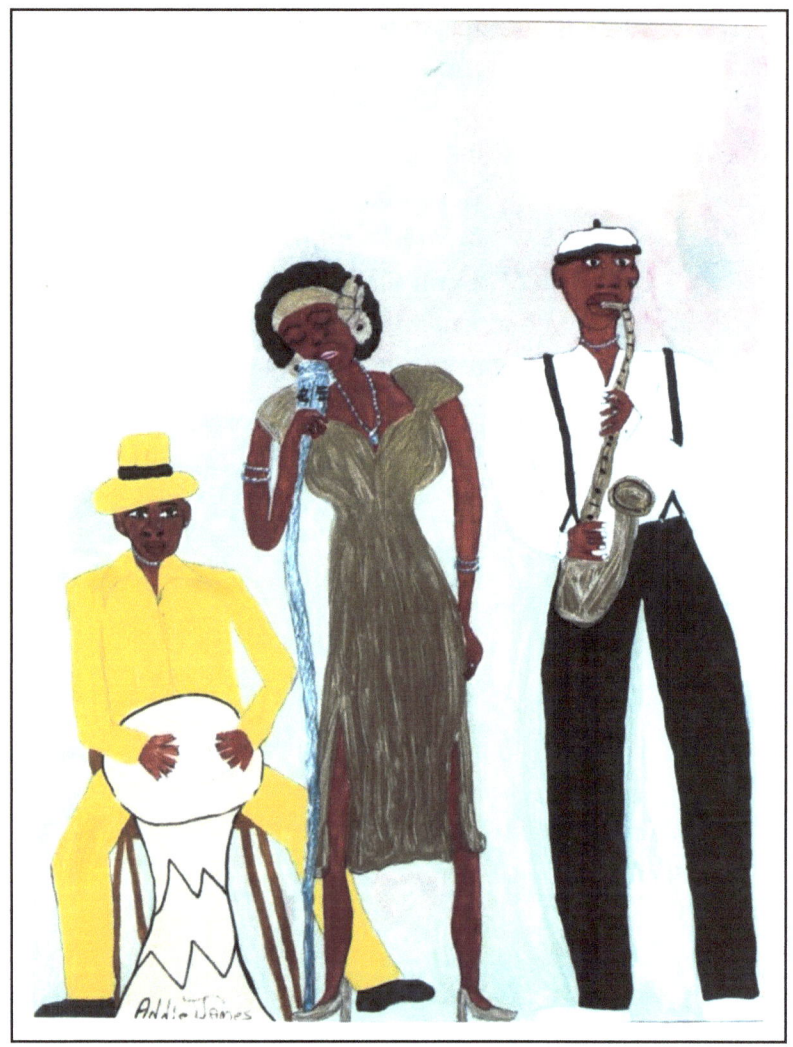

Singing the Blues, 24 x 30 acrylic on canvas

Well, I never had much of a love life. *I never went with a lot of men. There was this one man I liked. He was a schoolteacher, and he actually came to see me.*

The way I got men to like me? *Like we'd go in an eating place and all the girls would be carrying on over this good looking dude, and I said "You go in there and turn your back on him, and he's going to pay attention to you."*

I had so much fun doing that. You never go into a place and act like you want a dude, want to talk to him. I made them want ME.

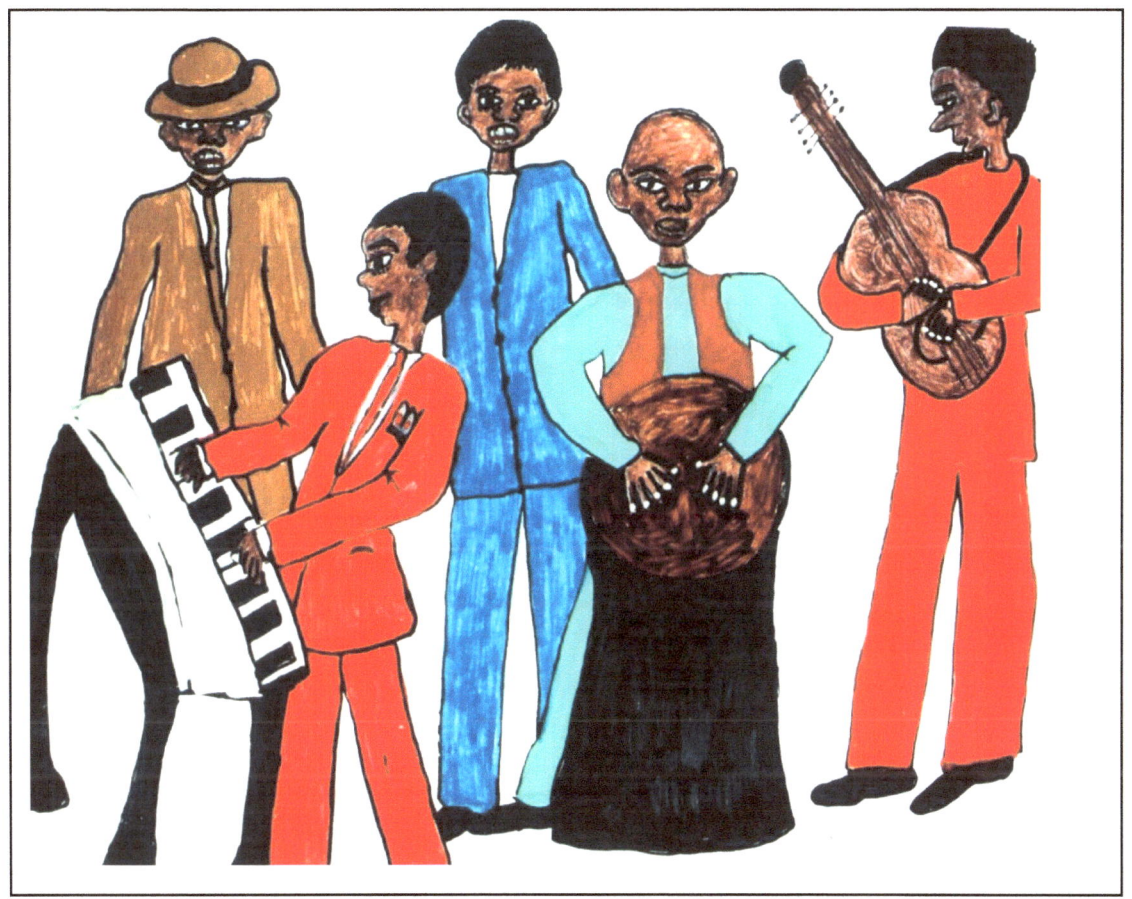

Makin' Music, 11 ¼ x 14 acrylic on paper

On the subject of *lost opportunities*, Addie often recalled two incidents: when she rejected an offer to enter the fashion industry (see *Fashion* chapter) and when she walked away from a career writing songs. While Miss Addie's poetry had always been an important outlet for her emotions, writing musical lyrics was an almost visceral need.

*I used to write poems and songs, and I would sing my songs, and **Music City Song Crafters offered me a contract.** And they made all my songs. They used all my songs, changed around the names, but the words were the same.*

I've heard every last one of my songs. And I never would sign one of them contracts, because you had to have money, and I didn't have the money.

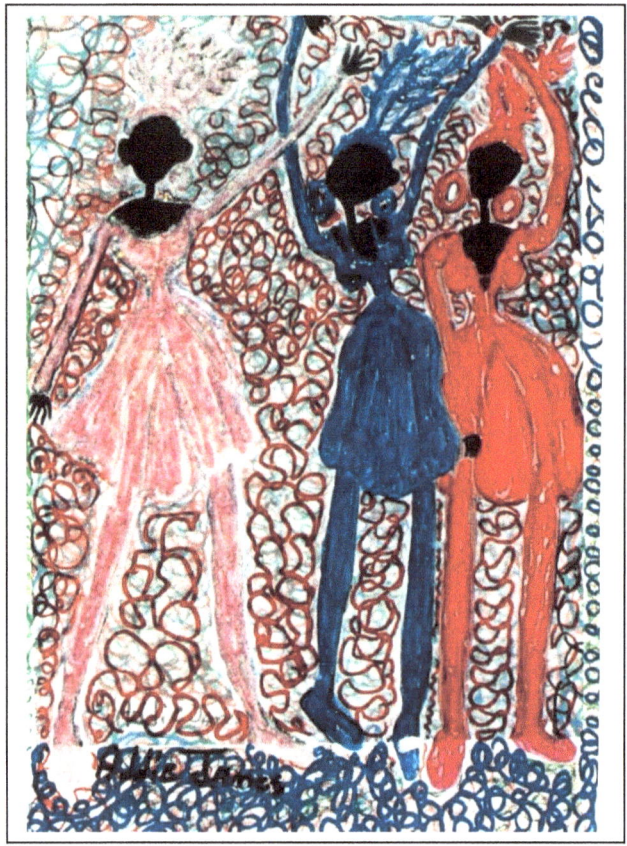

New Year's Party, 8 ½ x 12 mixed media on paper

While Miss Addie regretted her *roads not taken,* we can be thankful she channeled her creative energies into the visual arts.

The influences of writing poetry and lyrics, even her preferences in singers and movie stars…these all combined to enrich her paintings, which will always be her greatest legacy.

I used to like Marvin Gaye, Stevie Wonder, Michael Jackson, Gladys Knight, and The Supremes.

I used to like Charlton Heston. He used to play those Bible roles and he was very good. And Elvis Presley...I used to like him too. And Diana Ross, Diahnn Carroll, and Sammy Davis Junior.

I used to love TRUE LOVE stories. I read all kinds of stories, but those TRUE LOVE stories, I would just get into them. I was one of the characters. They're great!

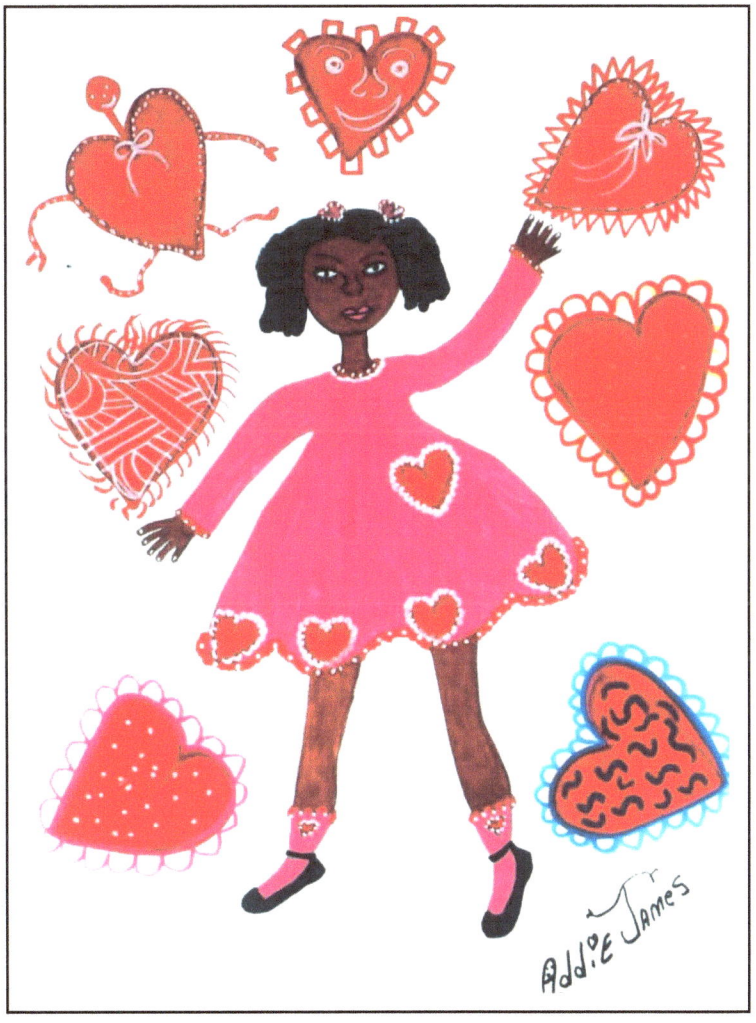

Dressed up for Valentine's Day
10 ¾ x 14 ½ acrylic on mat board

My birthday is August 11, 1943. Oh boy, we'd always have a party and a big cake. I always said, "It's a very special day. I am next to the President." I said. "Mama, today the flag should be flown and the carpet should be rolled out, because today is my birthday!"

Birthday Party, 20 24 acrylic on canvas

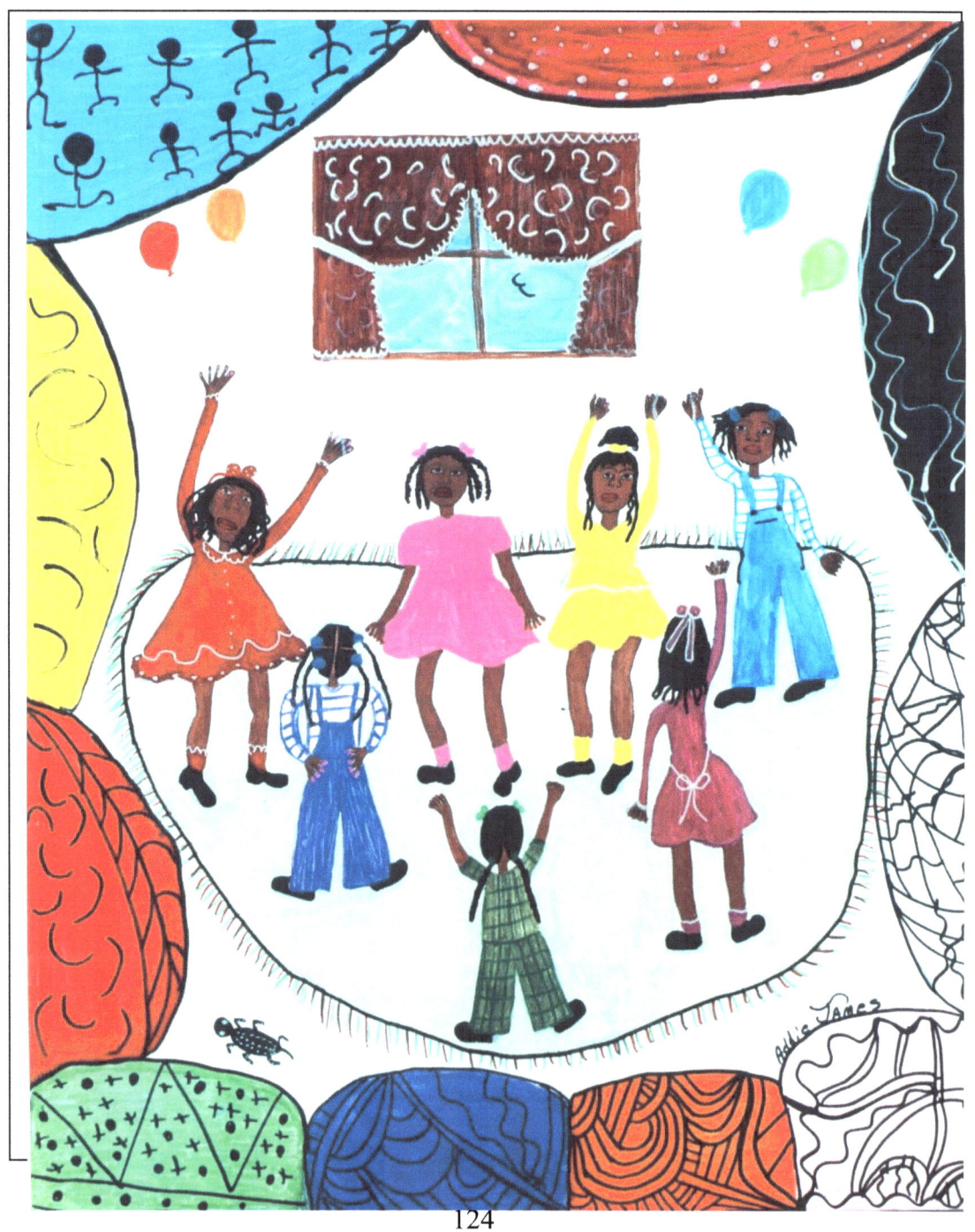

THE SHADOW PEOPLE
Thinking Outside the Box

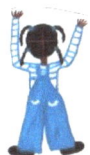

In January, 2002, we began giving Addie packages of acid-free mat board, the *doughnut holes* that fall out when a framer cuts a mat opening. We hoped she would paint on these as well as the scraps of cardboard, wood, or other available materials she tended to use.

It wasn't that we did not appreciate the unique, folksy effect of Addie's paintings on found objects; we simply did not want her magnificent body of work to self-destruct some years down the line. Some of her chosen surfaces, charming as they are, contain acids which will eventually disintegrate, taking the paintings along with them to oblivion.

Happily, Miss Addie took to the mat board immediately, and we breathed a sigh of relief knowing that these works on museum rag mat would be preserved for posterity.

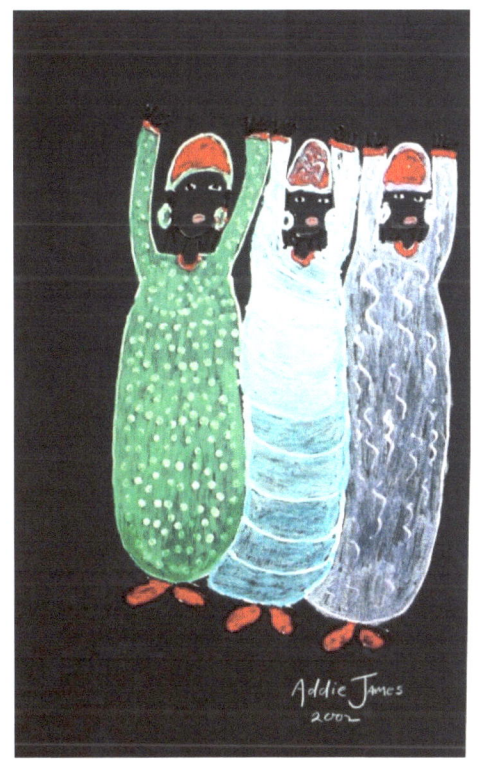

Addie took a special shine to the
black mat boards, on which her vibrant
colors seemed to *jump off the page.*

At first we teased her, saying
now she was like the much maligned
black velvet artists. In fact, the impulse
to paint on black may be far more universal
than we realized.

Hallelujah Women, 9 ¾ x15 ¾ acrylic on mat board

Regardless of an artist's
talent, whether he sells his art from an
abandoned dirt lot beside a defunct gas
station, or in a posh Madison Avenue
gallery, a black surface never fails to
pop color and create extreme drama.

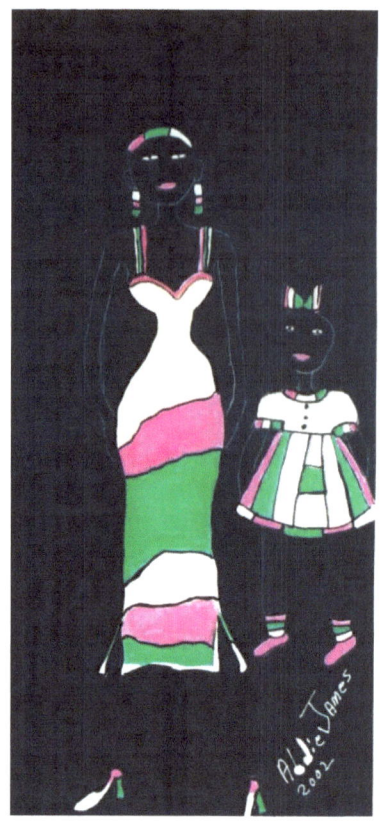

Look Alike Day, 9 x 20 acrylic on mat board

In Addie's case, using black mat board inspired a new body of work called ***shadow people***, and Addie's shadow people betrayed a level of sophistication not previously seen in her work.

Here Miss Addie chose to use the black surface as her figures' skin. Using a thin pencil line to indicate the contours of a face, a hand, a leg…she demonstrated her **mastery of negative space**, from which the eyes, lips, and fashions floated freely in the composition.

Again, whether these decisions were practiced or intuitive is unknown. They *were* inspired, but if you asked Addie:

It's nothing special. It just come to me one day. I put down my pencil and started drawing…

Miss Addie called all her experimental art ***abstracts.*** She had never heard this term until an art professor from Mitchell Community College saw her work and called them *abstract.*

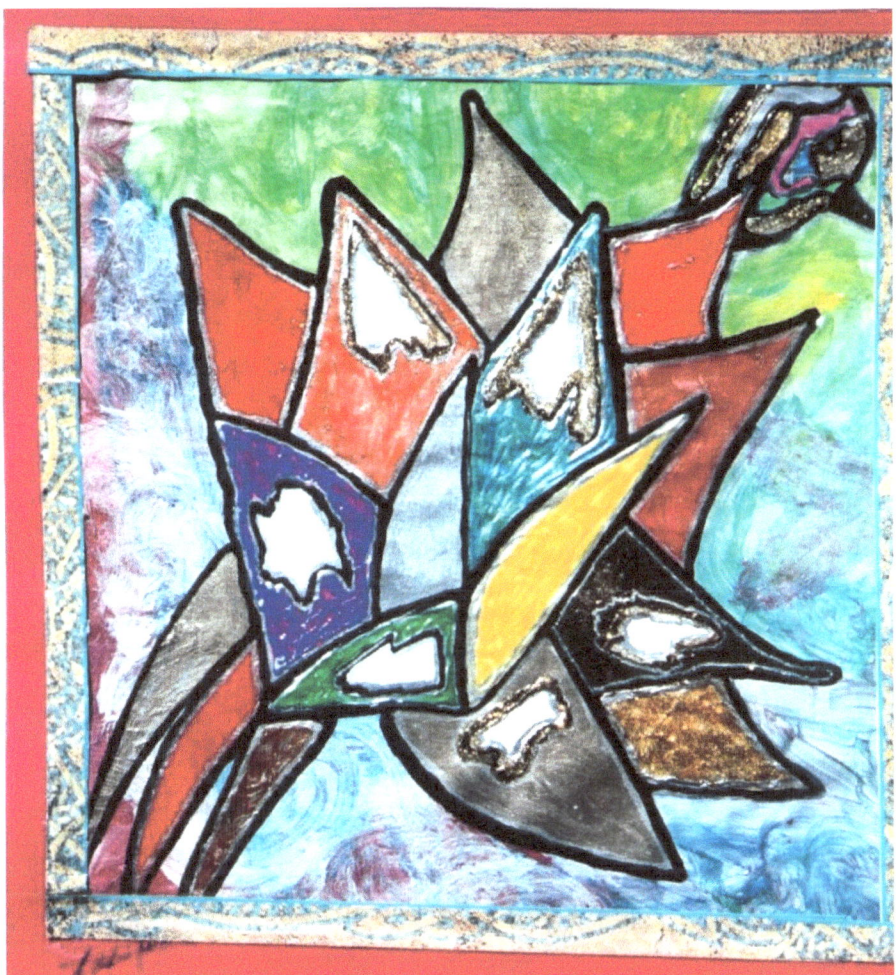

Bird of Time, 11 x 11 mixed media on paper

Bird of Time is a complex collage of cut paper borders, watercolor, and enamel texture. Addie said maybe it's a Bird of Paradise, but mostly it reminded her of the flowers she made when she worked at the furniture factory:

Whenever I went to the bathroom, I would make paper tissue flowers and I'd stick them in a little crevice anywhere. I would always do that. Everywhere I worked I would do that. I still do it.

I like to do abstracts.
I like to do them my way.

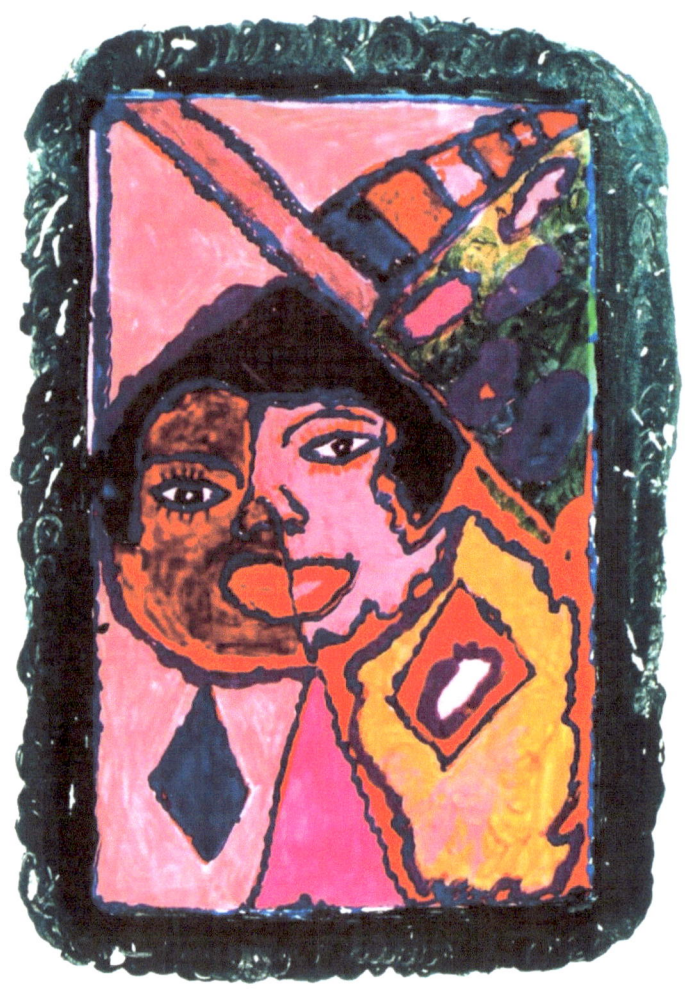

Color My World, 7 x10
acrylic and pink cellophane on paper

I have to do it for ME, not because of something YOU want. That's what's wrong with kids today. They do things for other people. I say to them: "I bet when you put on your clothes, you thinking about what other people be thinking about it." I say, "You put on your clothes and think what YOU be thinking about it. You can't be dressing up for other people."

Oh boy, I was something back then, I declare. I think I was living in a different millennium.

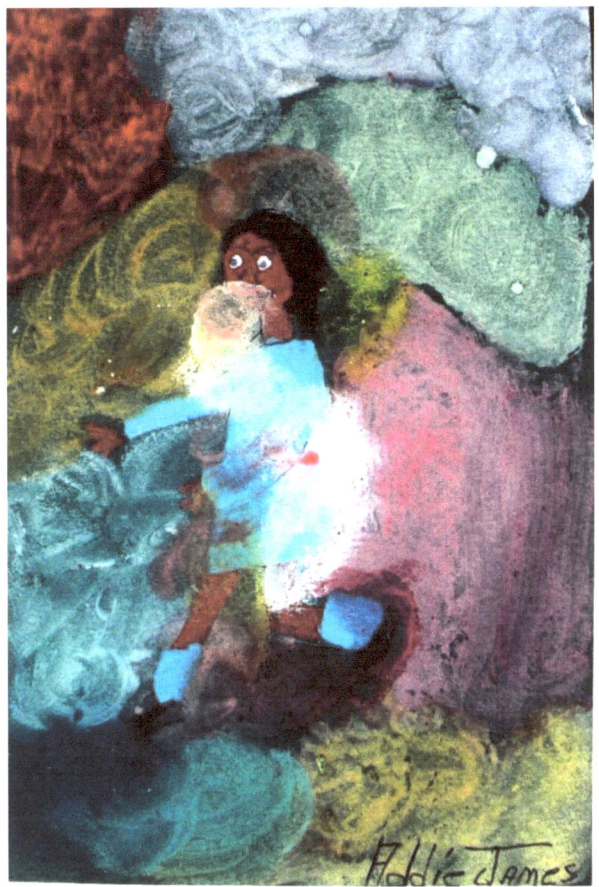

Lost Child, 8 x10 mixed media on paper

Lost Child was one of several paintings in which Addie created figures emerging from turbulent modulated clouds of color, thereby evoking an atmosphere of mystery, fear and confusion.

OUR CHILDREN
by Addie James

What about our children…
Sex, drugs, alcohol and aids…?
Or understanding, peace, and love
For one another and God?
It sums up to a few things,
Let's take action and pray,
Ladies and gentlemen.
Our children

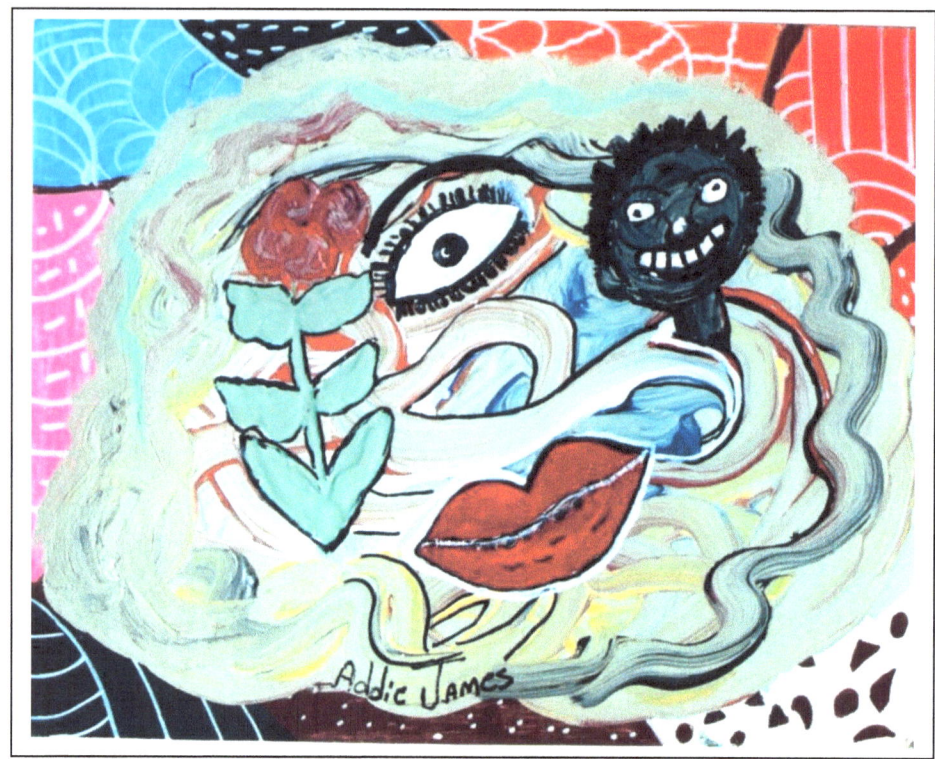

Smiling Abstract, 11 x 14 acrylic on mat board

All the elements of Addie James' talent…figures, patterns, creatures, colors, and symbolism…came together in her abstracts, exerting themselves in a violent, musical cacophony.

Lost and Found
11 x 14
Acrylic on canvas

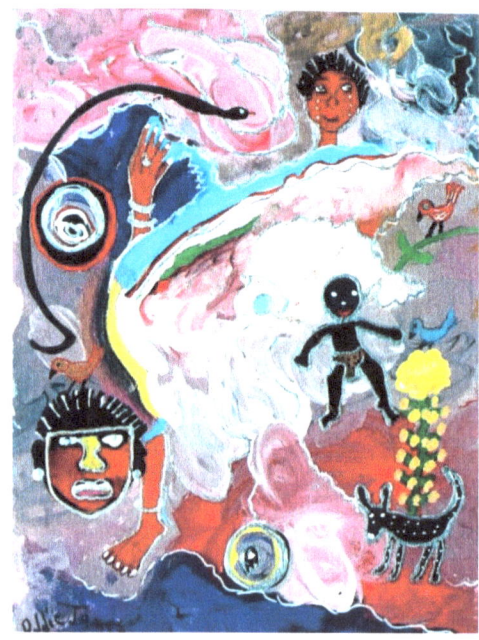

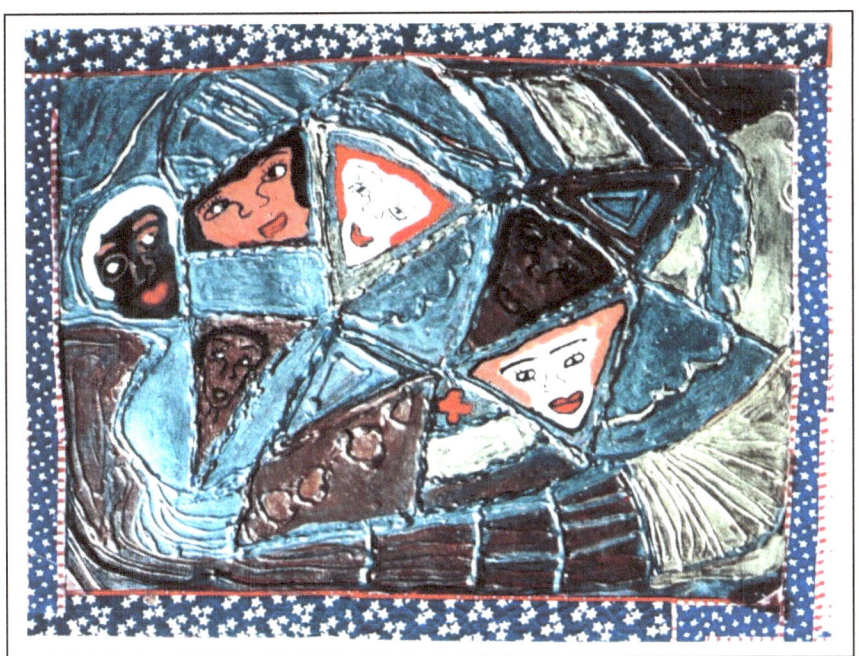

Faces, 10 x 13 mixed media on paper

Often Miss Addie's abstracts offered a social statement, like the issue of cultural diversity in *Faces* or the racial harmony in *Through the Eyes of People.* When Addie intended to use symbolism, usually she would express it through abstraction.

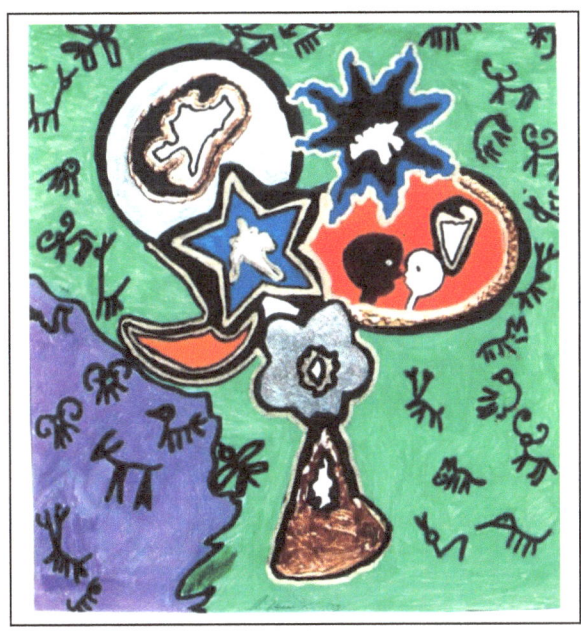

Through the Eyes of People
10 ½ x 11 ½ acrylic on mat board

131

These miniature paintings
are anchored by an intricate spider
web of pen and ink pattern.
God's Critters echoes the playfulness
of Miro, while *Apple of My Eye*
offers a witty play on words.

**Make no mistake,
behind Miss Addie's calm façade
beat the heart of a comedian
with a rapier-sharp wit.**

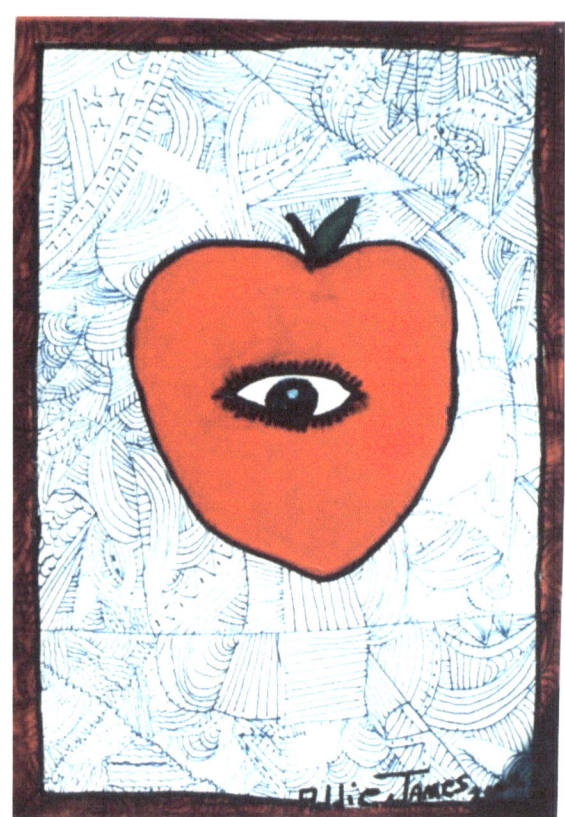

Apple of My Eye, pen and acrylic on mat board

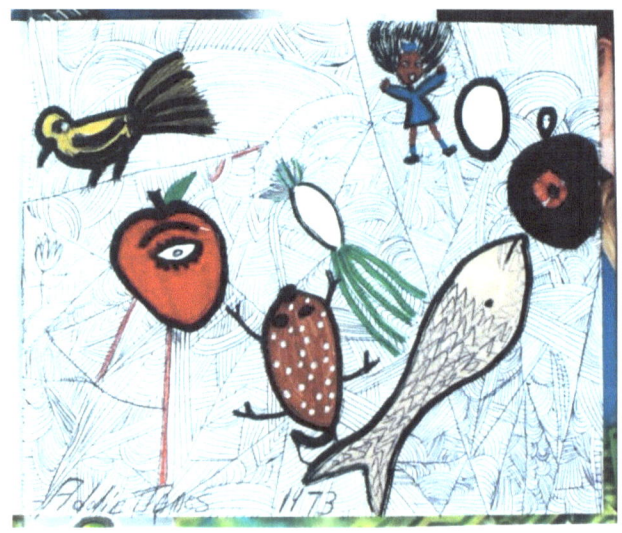

God's Critters, 5 x 7 pen and acrylic on mat board

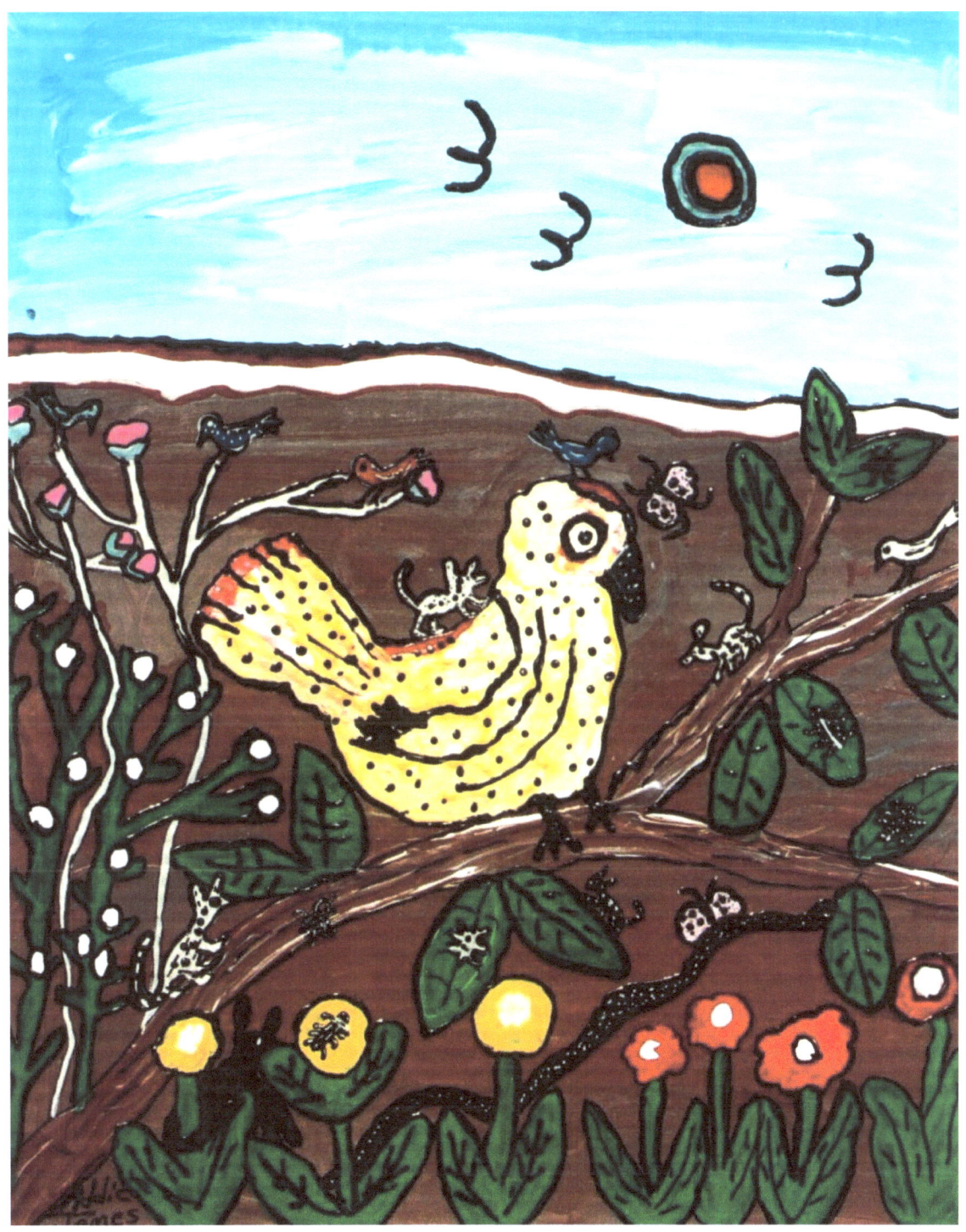

All God's Creatures, 16 x 20 acrylic on cardboard

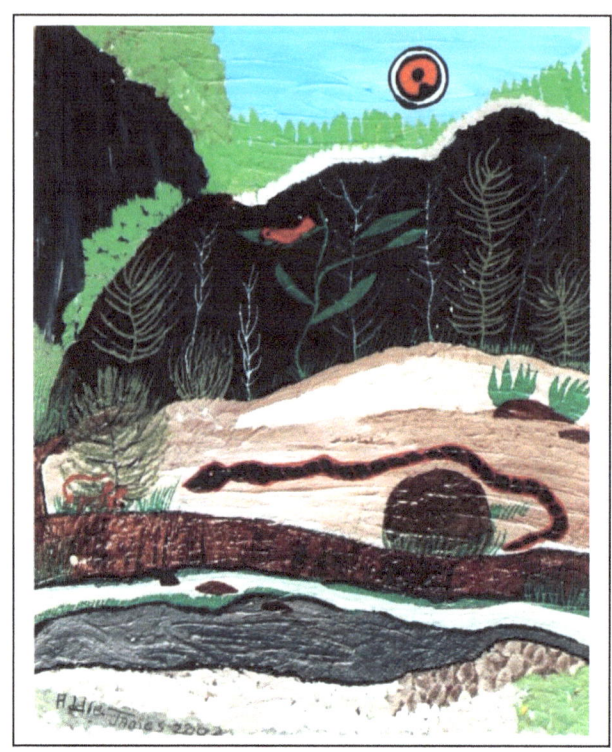

Creatures of the Earth, 16 x 20 acrylic on cardboard

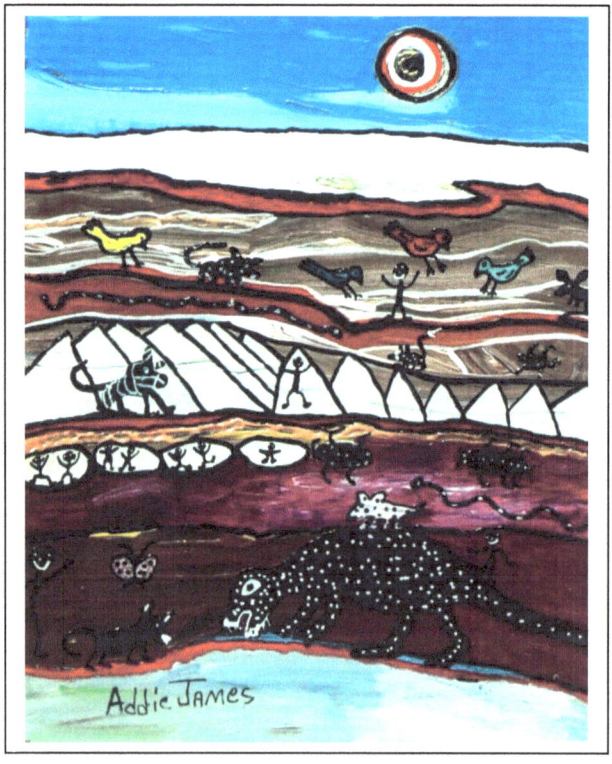

Creatures of the Earth, Sea, Sky, 16 x 20 acrylic on cardboard

AFRICA

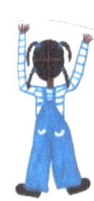

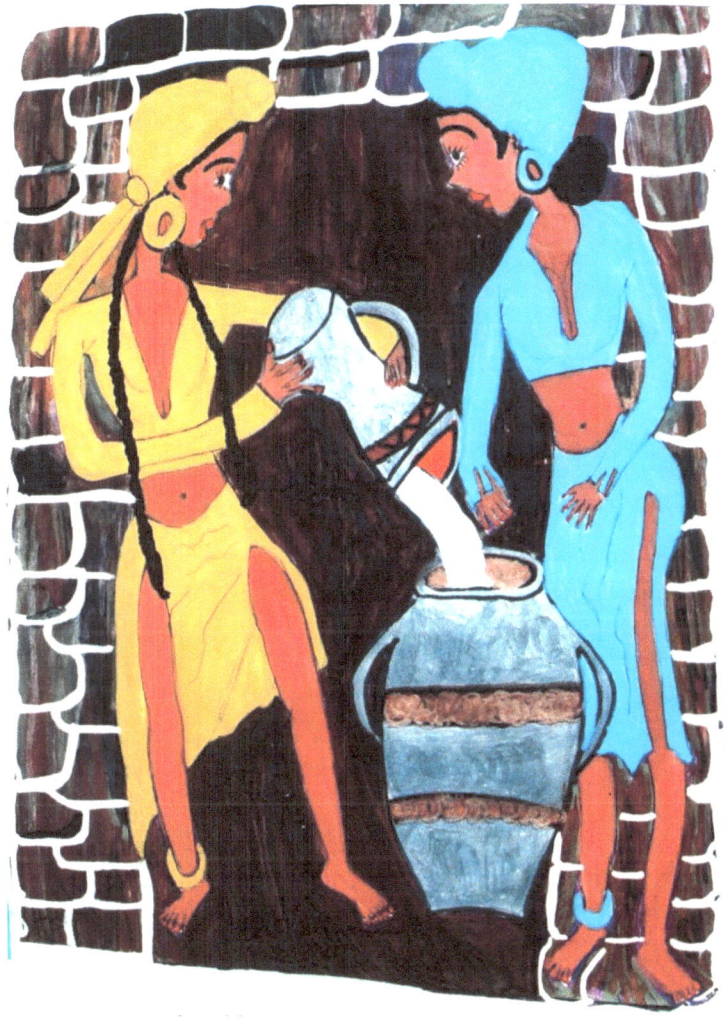

Maidens Bringing Water, 10 x 14 acrylic on paper

Many African American painters are inspired to paint Africa.

Addie painted Africa *sooner* than *later,* so that most of her earliest surviving works included African subject matter. Exploring these early paintings (1970-1990; most were never dated) one can trace the evolution of the stylistic elements which dominated her work

Many of Addie's early pieces depicted *water bearers,* an image which was etched in the mind of those of us who were children in the 1950's.

We all gazed at images from *Life* and *Look* magazines, and of course, *National Geographic.* It was here we formed our early impressions of Africa, including the idea of women bearing water. Addie also reaped inspiration from the Bible and its illustrations. In *Maidens Bringing Water* Addie's use of pattern emerges in the stone wall and her use of bright color in the dresses. But the use of brown, as in the background, is seldom seen today.

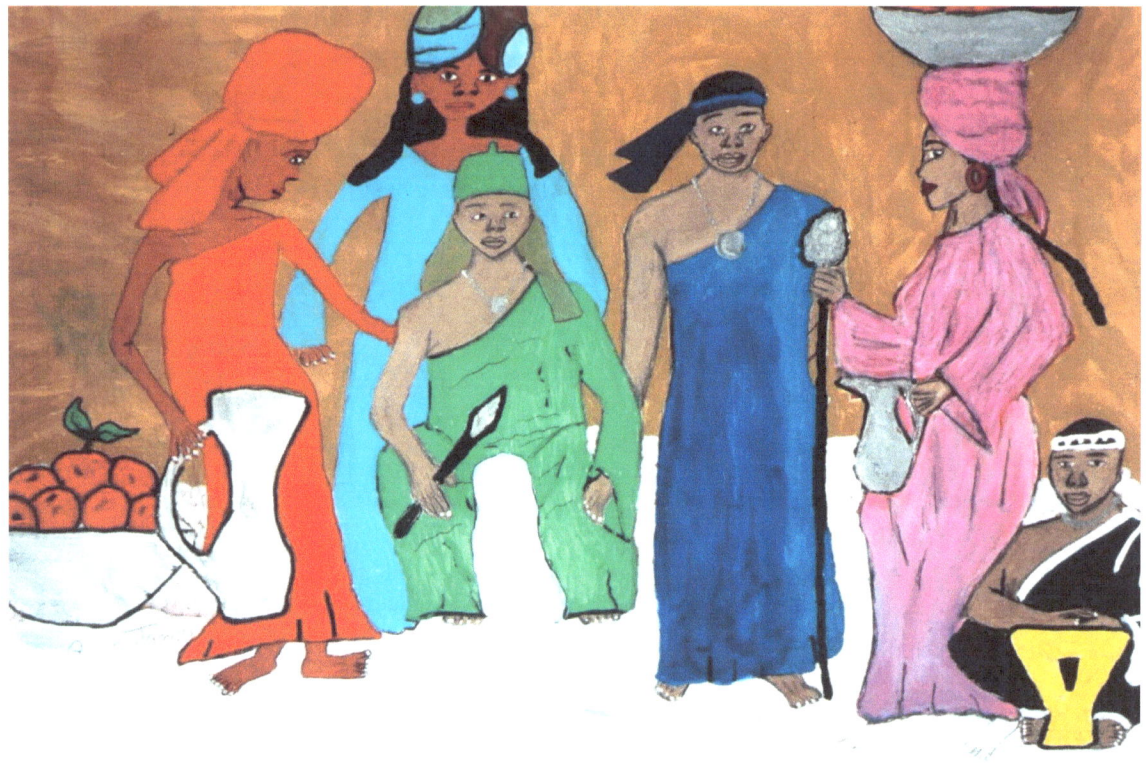

Tribal Feast, 12 ½ x 17 acrylic on paper

Tribal Feast, another early work, has a Picasso-like appeal with its linear, cubistic bowl of apples, white pitcher and carving stone. The men's faces have a primitive quality, while the women's are more stylized and defined, as in Addie's later work.

In *Woman with Jug*, Addie's keen fashion sense and the addition of three-dimensional silver glitter added to the woman's jewelry mark a clear transition to later styles.

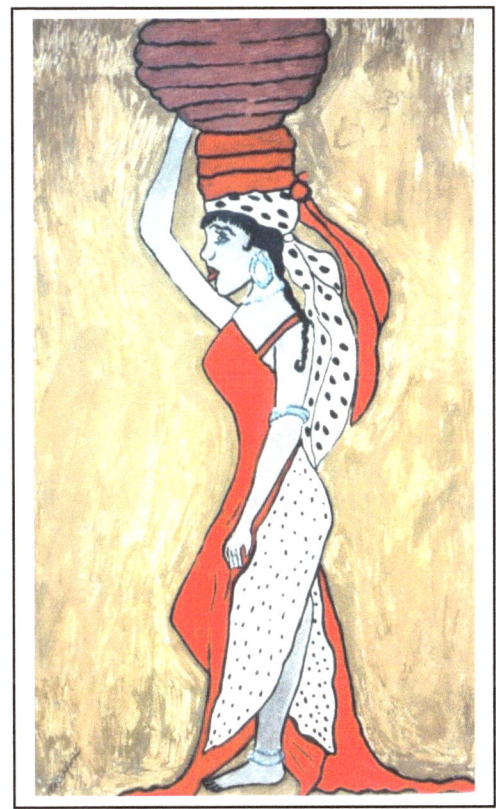

Woman with a Jug, 10 ½ x 19 mixed media on paper

The exuberance of *Rhythm* epitomizes the joyous abandon and freedom associated with the African beat. Paying little attention to anatomical correctness, Addie's abstract musician captures the energy and spirit of the moment with effortless success.

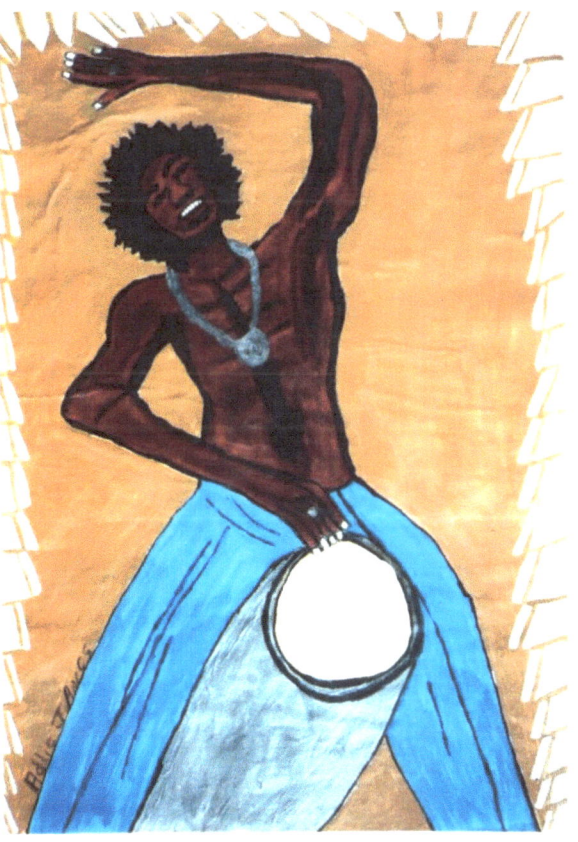

Rhythm, 9 ¾ x 13 ¼ acrylic on paper

Addie purchased several imported African figurines at a yard sale. These little ebony sculptures inspired her to paint *African Trio*. Note the early use of the *hallelujah gesture,* a little touch of American Revivalist religion superimposed on these jungle celebrants.

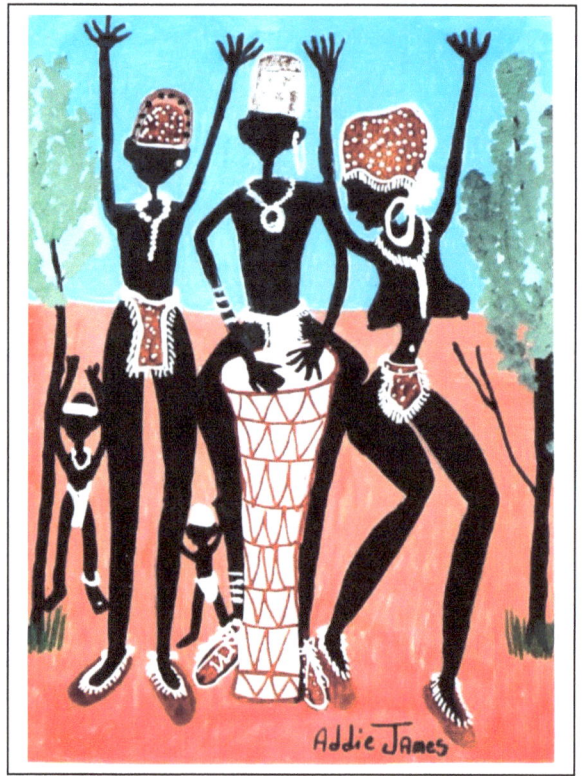

African Trio, 12 x 16 acrylic on paper

By the time Miss Addie painted *Rejoice* and *African Beauties* in the late 1990's, all the elements of her mature style were evident.

Rejoice, 8 ½ x 12 acrylic on paper

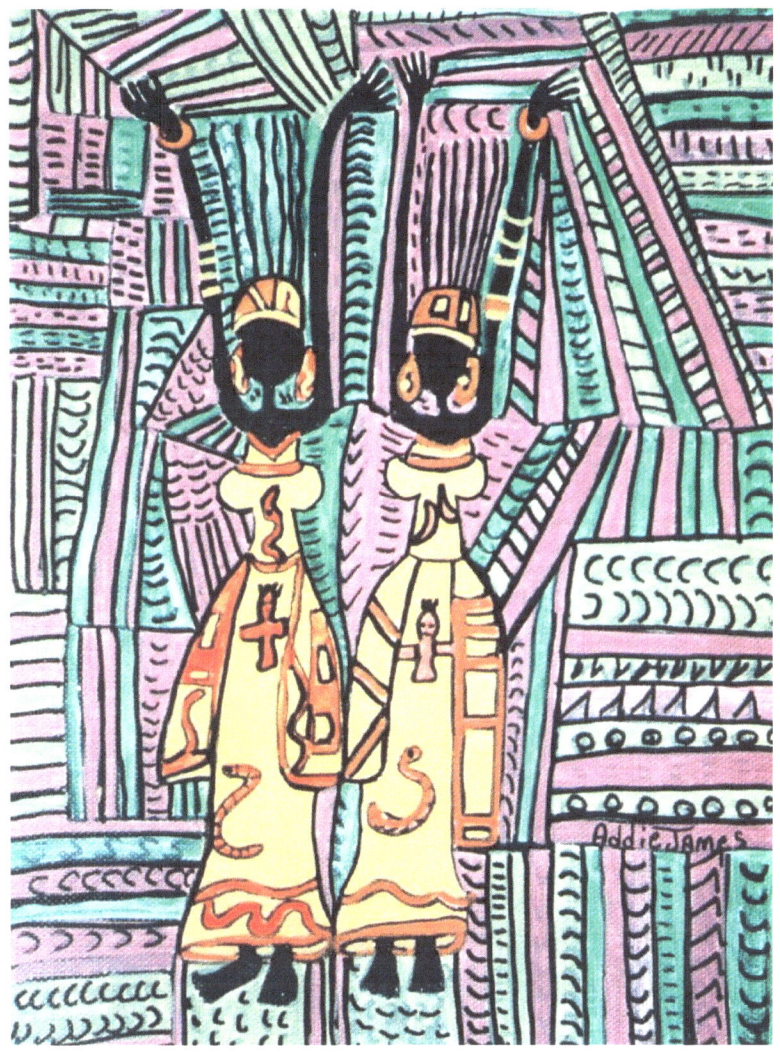

African Beauties, 9 x 12 acrylic on canvas paper

And while Addie enjoyed painting Africa, the concept was not an important issue in her everyday life. Unlike many of her fellow black painters, **Miss Addie was not overly concerned with her cultural heritage:**

I keep thinking about Africa. It's all imaginary. I've never been to Africa. I don't celebrate Kwanzaa and I'm not into that ROOTS thing. I celebrate CHRISTMAS.

We're all Americans…what's the difference?

AFRICA
by Addie James

That's not my home!
Talking about sending ME back there?
Why, I want to know?
I don't know anything about Africa.
I was born right here in Statesville, N.C.
This is my home, don't you see?
I know I got a right to be here
The same as you…the same as me.

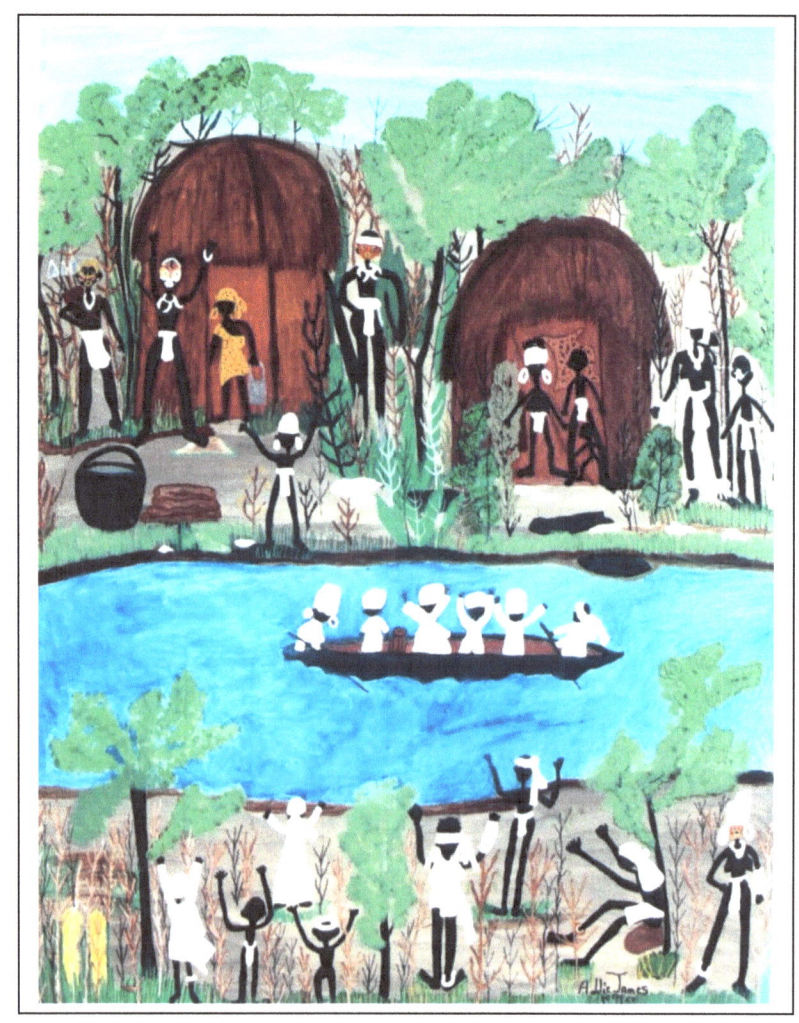

Village People, 35 x 45 acrylic on canvas

Fortunately Addie James had always been able to see beyond the ugly issues of racism to a vision of international harmony. In the beautiful painting, *Dove of Peace,* the elegant African's worried expression is balanced by hope. The giant white dove perched on his head, coupled with Addie's intensely happy colors, helps us believe in her message of peace.

Dove of Peace, 20 x 30 acrylic on mat board

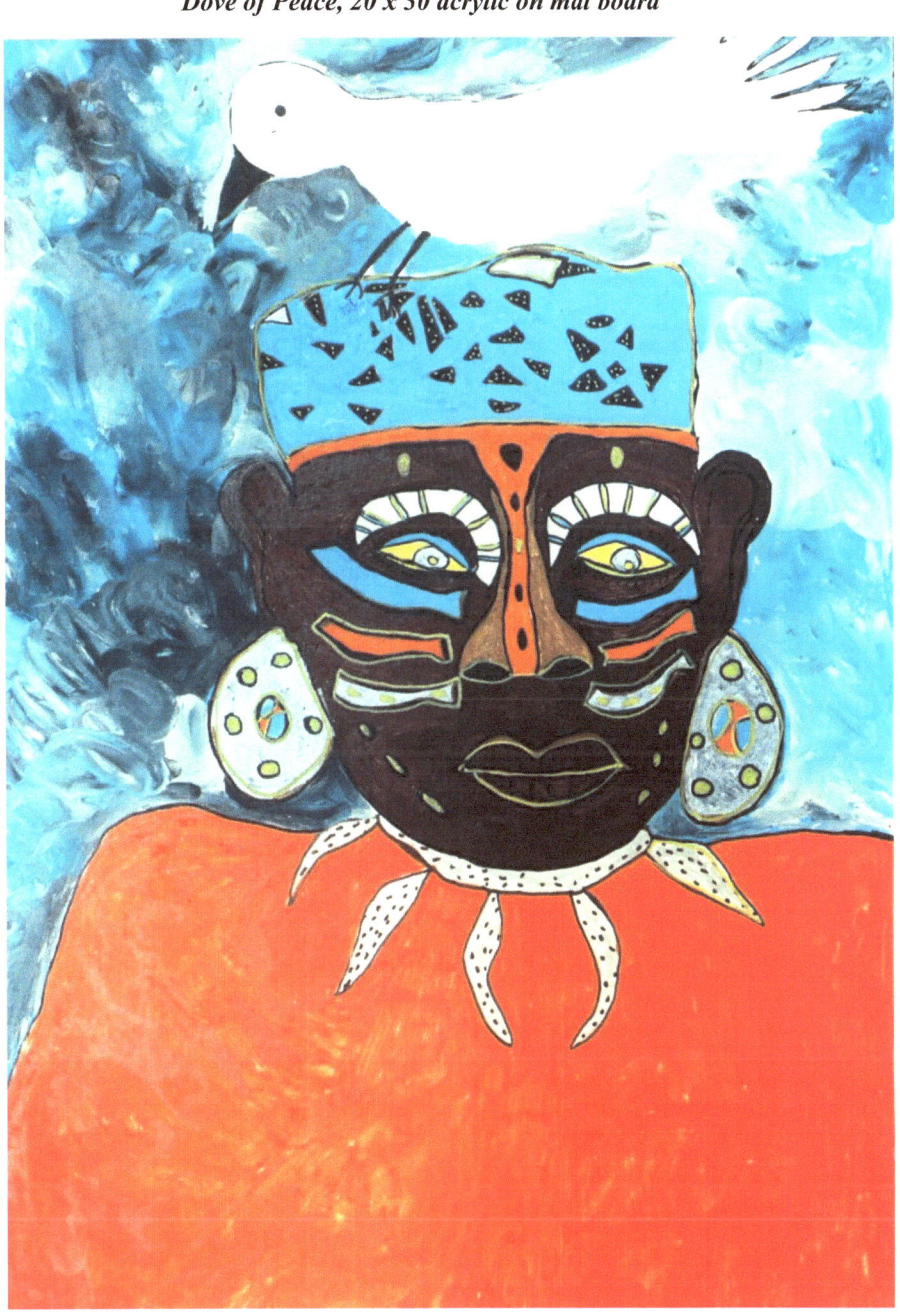

THE QUILT THAT CAME TO LIFE

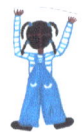

Like most folk artists, Addie James painted on virtually everything and anything she could lay her hands on:

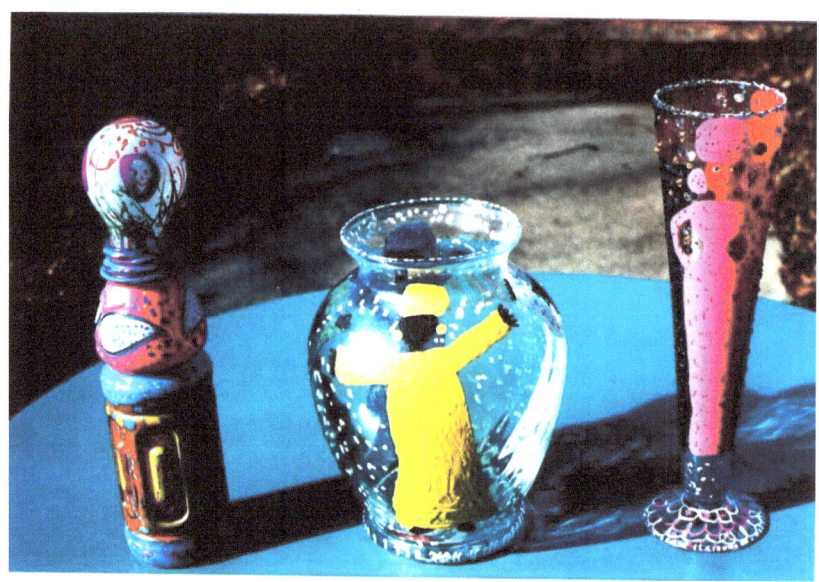

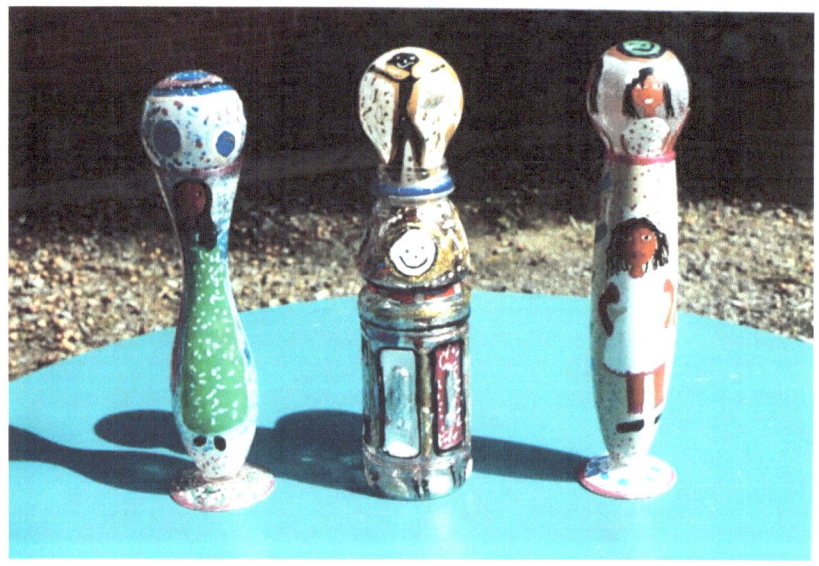

Painted light bulbs acted as stoppers in painted plastic soda bottles or bud vases, while fashion ladies danced in a snowstorm on a plastic bowl and adorned a fluted champagne glass…

Cardboard cut-out masks, rigged with head wires, showcased Miss Addie's playful nature and tongue-in-cheek humor. Who else would give birth to *Comedy/Tragedy Cool Cats*?

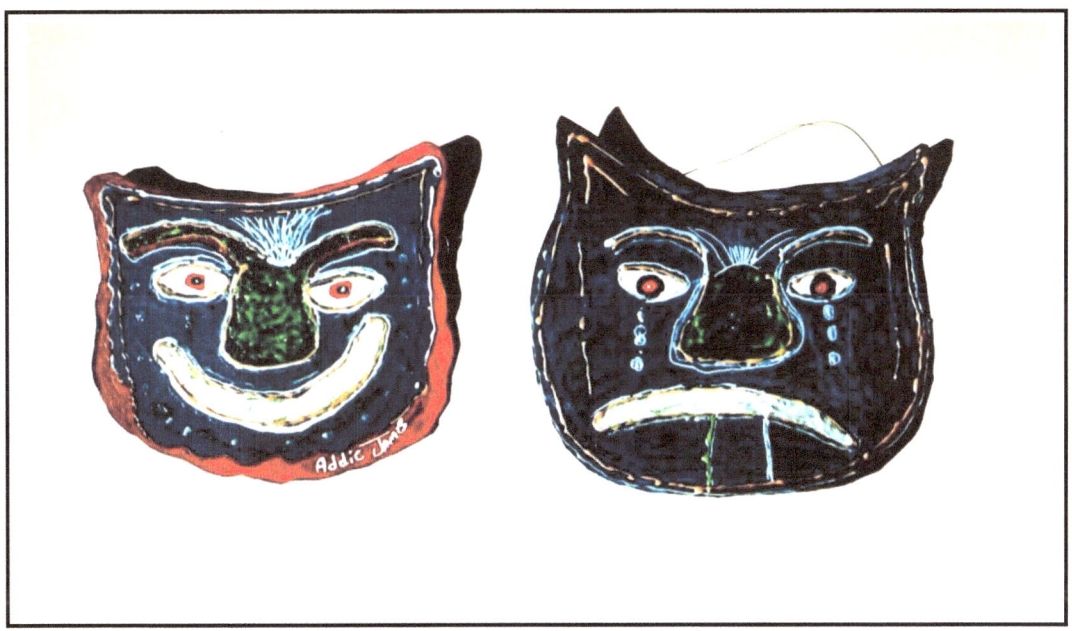

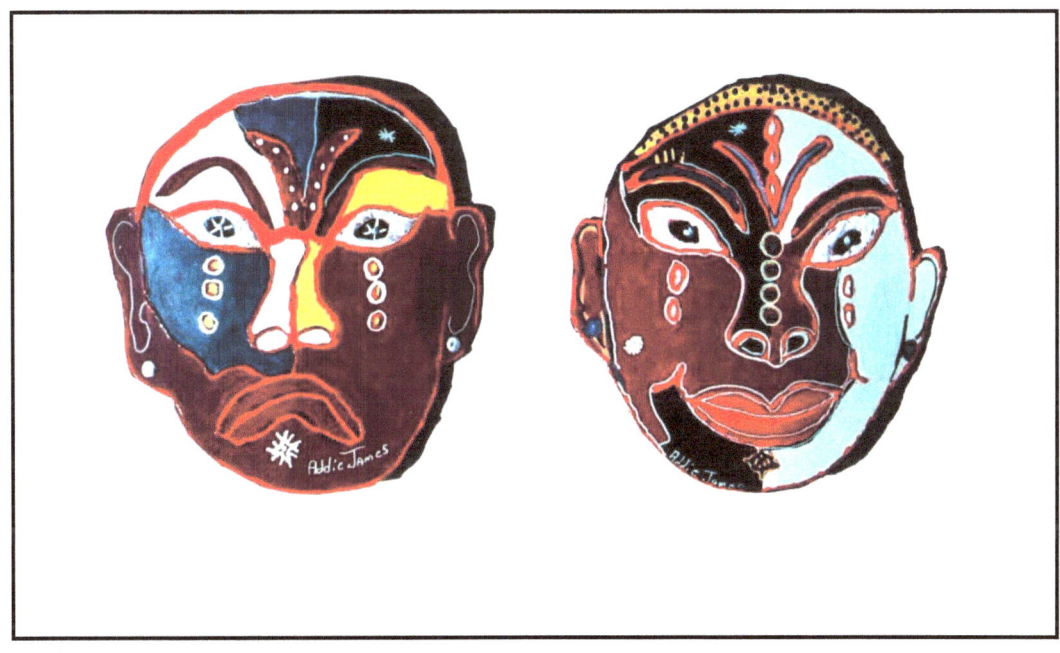

Deer bones were the strangest things I ever painted on…but I'll take anything I can get…

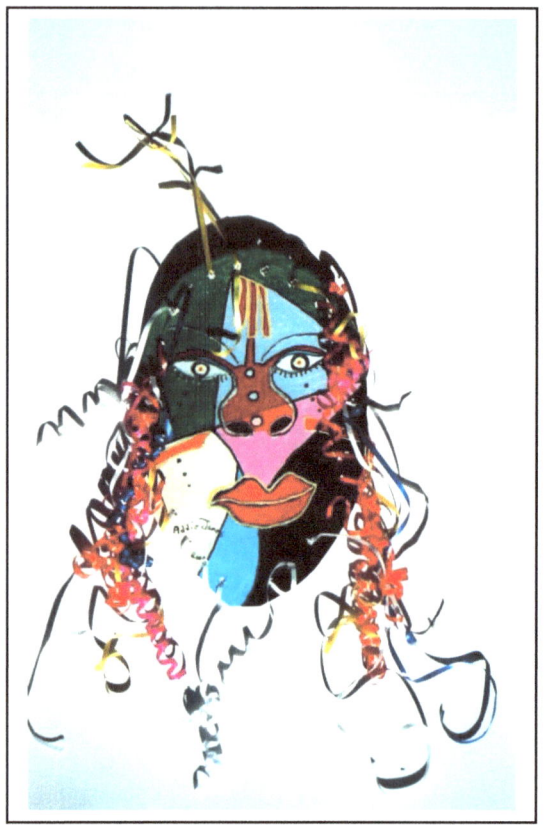

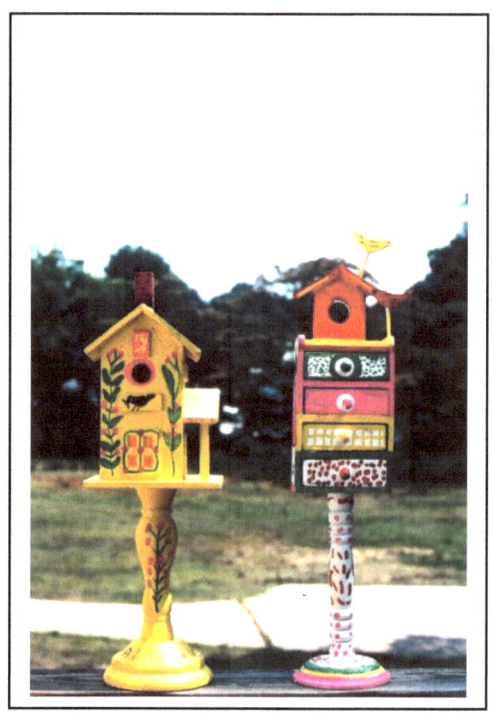

For the Birds, acrylic on wooden houses

Mask Mobile, mixed media on cardboard

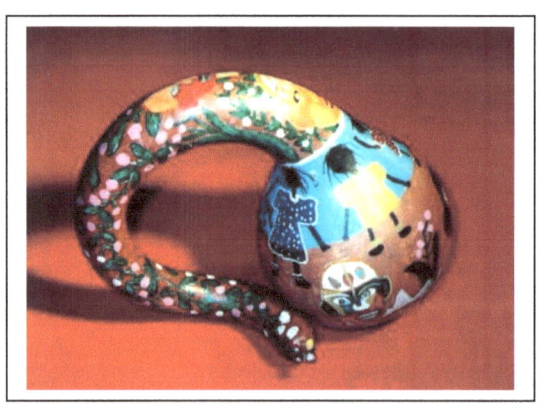

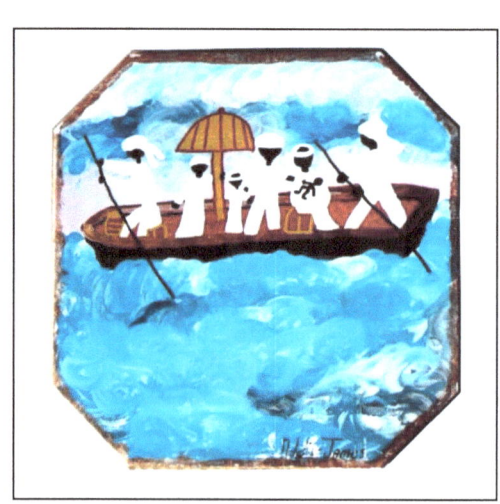

Susan's birthday gourd

Boat Tile

Of all Miss Addie's objects d'art, her hand-painted church fans were the hands-down favorites. These double-sided delights reflected the time-honored Southern tradition from hot summer Sundays when the pew was too hard and the preacher's sermon too long.

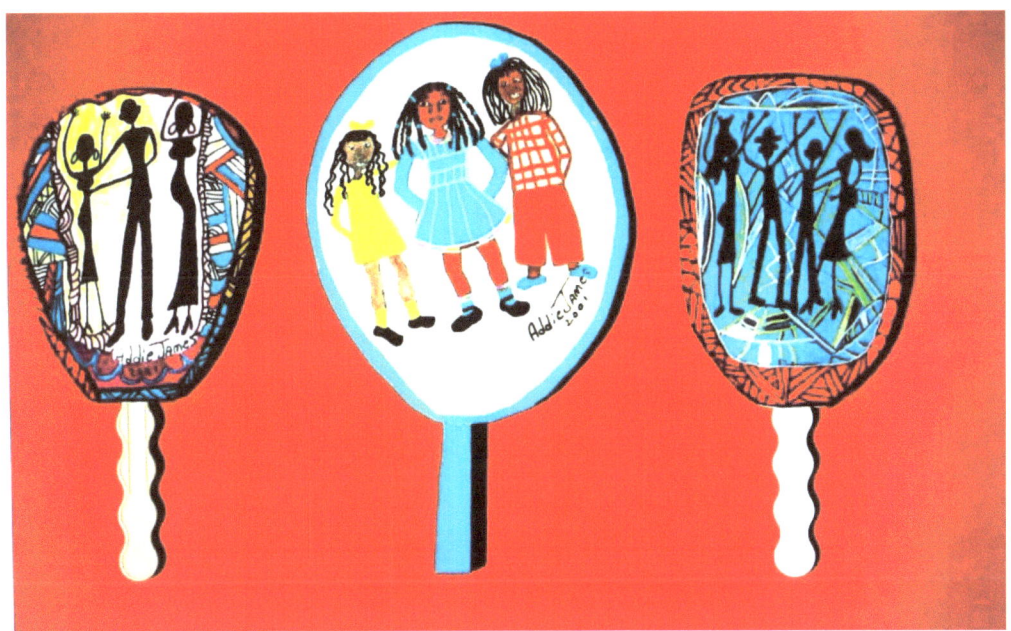

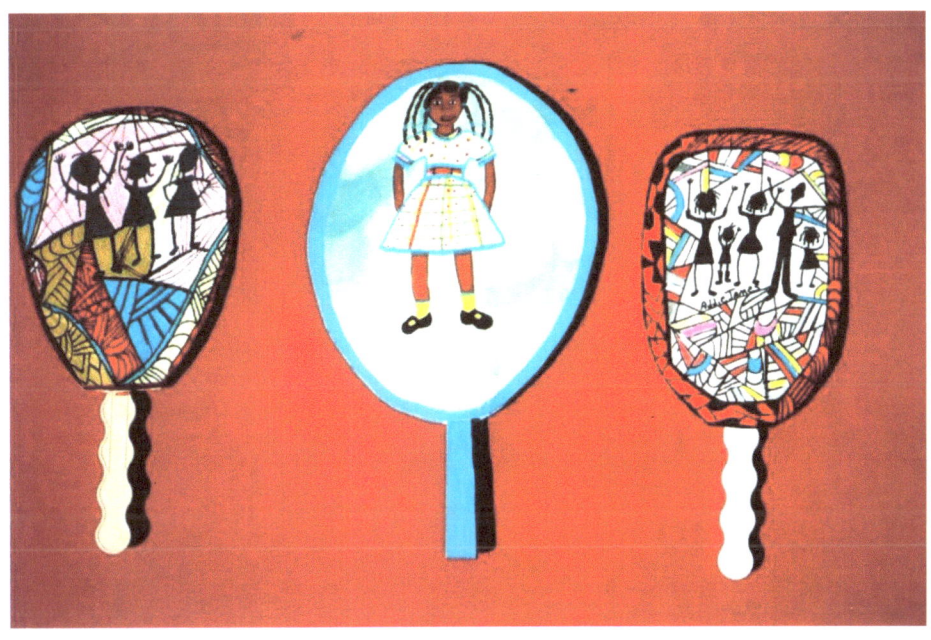

She painted on miniature teacups and discarded canister sets. She painted on golf balls and displayed them in cardboard egg cartons….

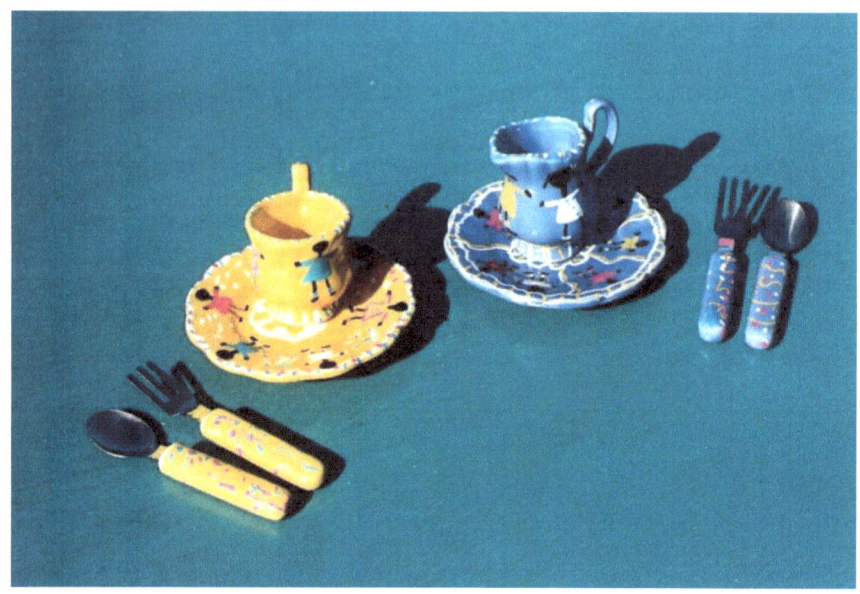

Teacup sets, acrylic on ceramic

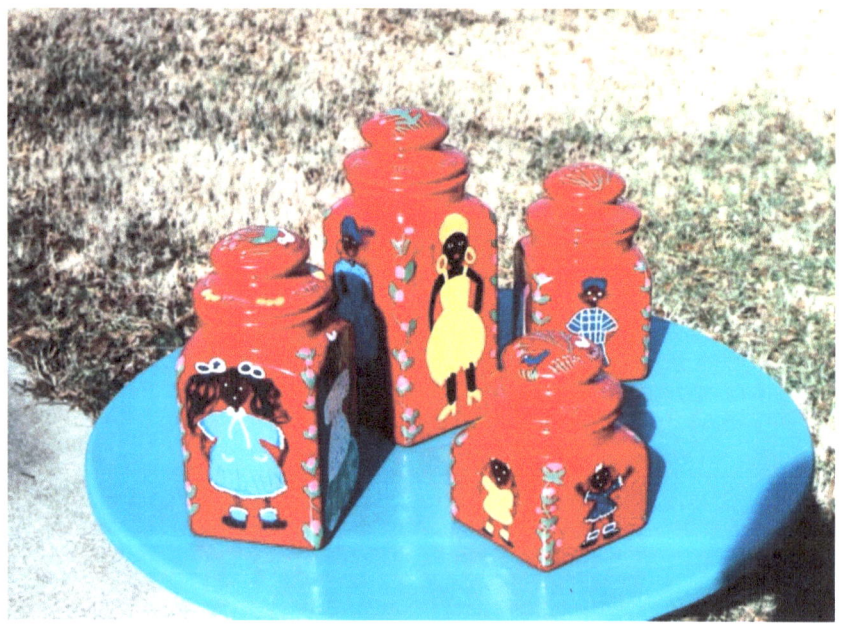

Canister set, acrylic on ceramic

And Oh, those wonderful chairs!

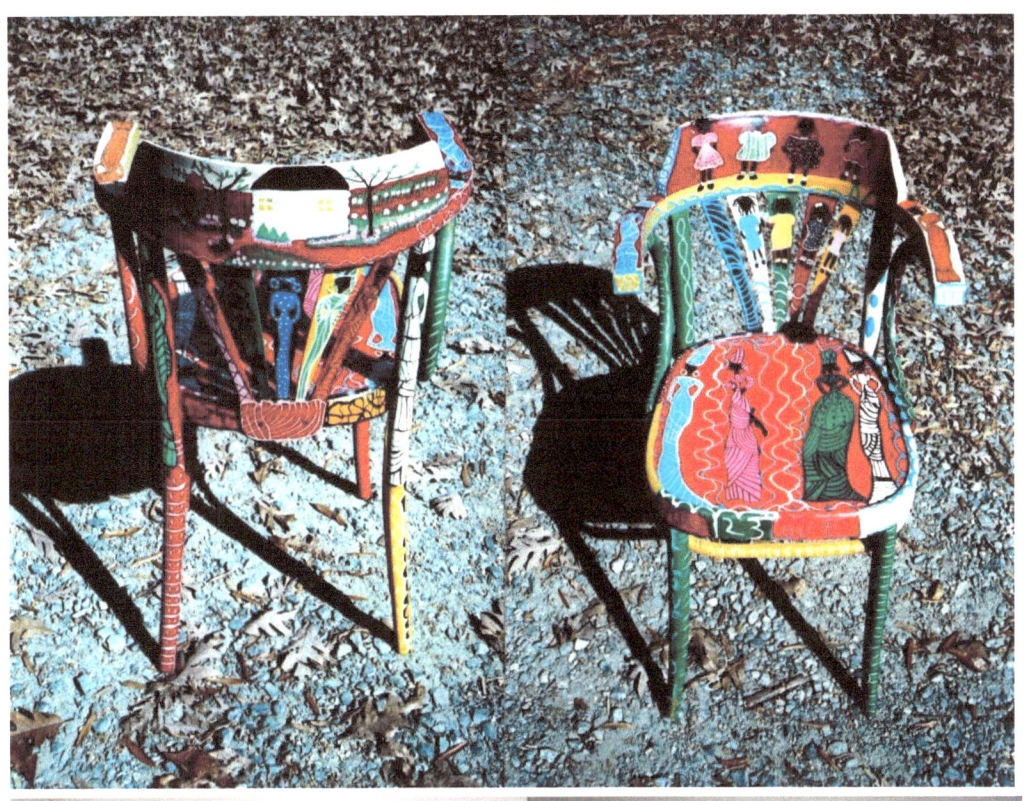

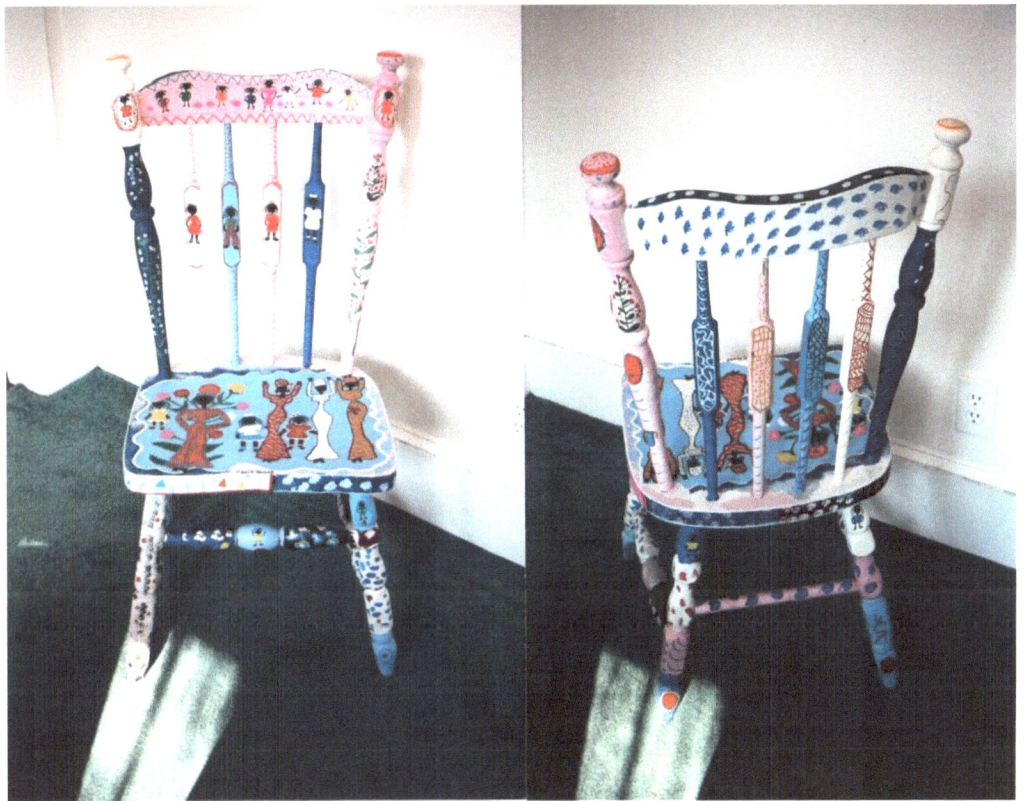

First Miss Addie did the painting, and then she decided to sew the quilt. She used the painting as the centerpiece:

The daddy is reading to his children, and all the other panels are scenes from that family's life.

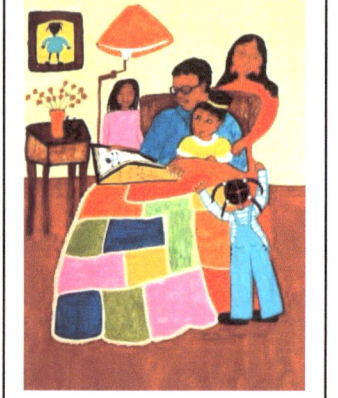

The Quilt
12 x 16
acrylic on mat board

The Quilt that Came to Life, 5 foot by 7 foot mixed media is a tour de force featuring Addie James' many styles: portraiture, fashion, full-blown outdoor scenes, angels, and children growing on trees. After she painted the panels, she invited her daughter, Madaron, to help her hand stitch it together onto navy blue felt. This mother/daughter participation is an old quilting tradition.

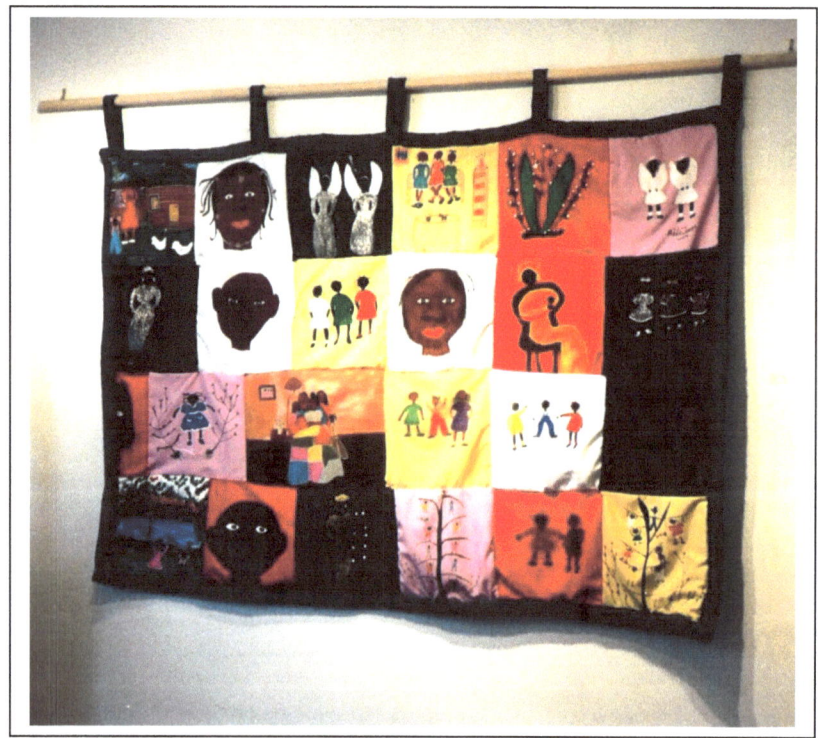

BROTHERS KILLING BROTHERS
Life is not Perfect

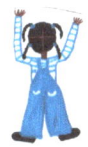

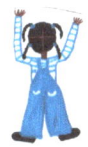

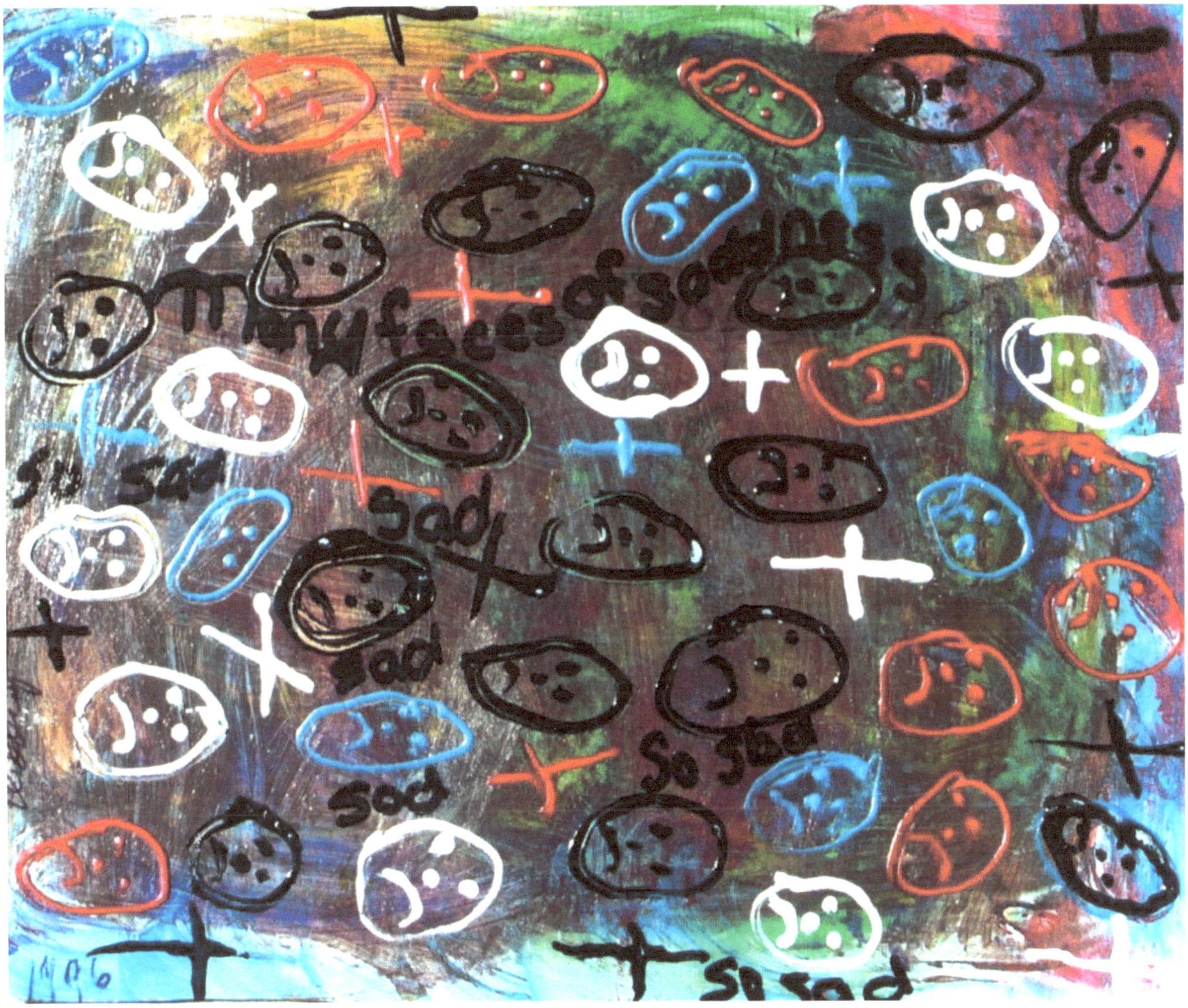

The Many Faces of Sadness, **8 x 10 ½ acrylic on paper**

When we think of Addie James' art, we see a joyous land where happy children frolic in sunshine, where families bond in solidarity, and God presides over a planet at peace. The vast majority of Addie's paintings project harmony because this is the legacy she *chose* to leave to her children. This was her unique gift to a troubled world.

Because Miss Addie made the conscious choice to emphasize the positive, it is easy to forget that her personal life had been an ongoing struggle to overcome poverty, loss, racism, and adversity. She seldom mentioned this. Indeed, she denied it saying God had blessed her. In that respect, her determination to create uplifting images was all the more heroic.

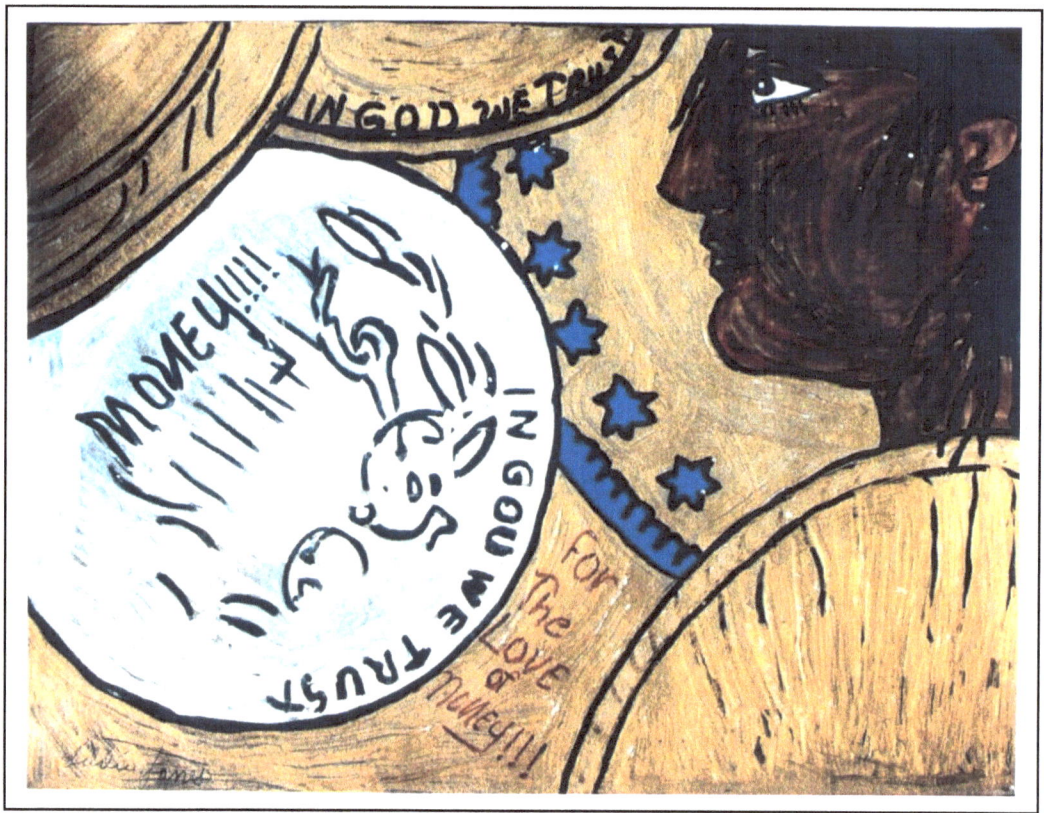

In Money We Trust, **8 ½ x 11 mixed media on paper**

Occasionally Addie produced a painting or poem which reflected her feelings about the *dark side.* These rare offerings gave us some insight about how very much she deplored greed, prejudice, and mindless violence.

Some of these social statements, like *In Money We Trust* and *Hands* were subtle reproaches, in these cases against the evils of avarice. The multi-racial hands grasping towards the dollar bill implied that greed was a sin shared by all cultures.

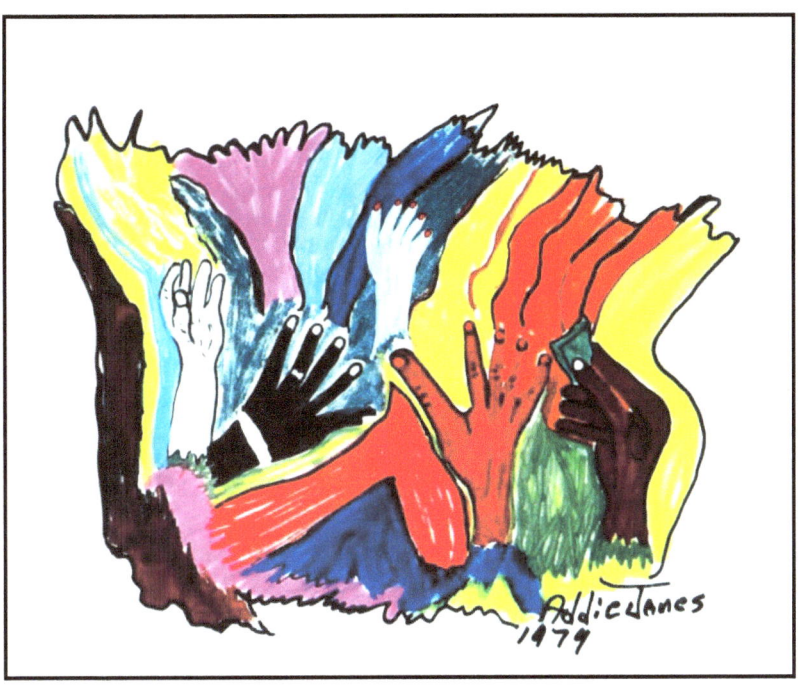

Hands, 10 x 11 ½ acrylic on mat board

Addie James never bowed to racism:

And you know how they used to have to go in the back door in Woolworth's and places? **I never went in the back door.** *Me and my sister, they always let us come in the front door.*

And I remember a big write up about it...about those people going in the front door at some other Woolworth. But me and my sister ALWAYS went in the front door to sit down and eat.

They didn't mess with us. I think about that SO much. And we sat down and ordered food and they just looked at us. **I never went in no back door!**

It was like that mostly places where you went to eat, **but I never went in a back door.**

After Daddy died, me and my sister got part of the social security check every month, and we'd go into town. My mama give us money to buy whatever we want, and me and my sister were always going to Woolworth's and we always sat right there beside those white people and they never said a word.

I don't know what other kids did, but WE DID IT!

151

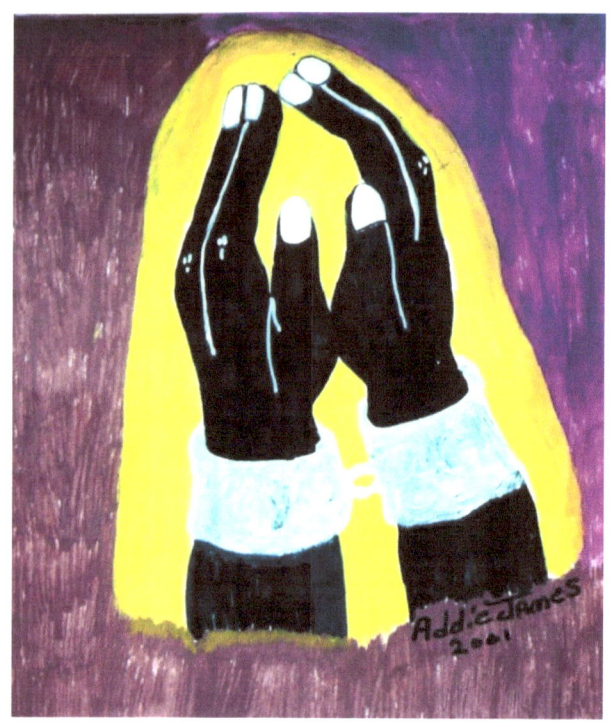

Prisoner's Prayer, 9 x 10 ¼ mixed media on paper

*People said back then times was hard, but you know, **we wasn't brought up to hate black or white.** Mama cared for little white children, and we wasn't taught to hate things! No, we had a GOOD time. We had a GOOD time. And I never met a stranger.*

And those little white boys we took care of...they ate what we ate, like them big meat skins, they loved them, just coming hot out of the oven. We kept the white boys while their mother worked. They didn't want to go home. Sometimes they stayed over night until the next day. We let them stay over night.

*And when I sometimes feel racist things, I don't like it, because **I love everybody. I love black, and I love white.** But my FAMILY is my world, and I'm so grateful.*

***Because when I see people, I don't see colors, I see people.** Anyplace, where you live, or where you work at, it is what you make it.*

> *Now you can stand around in a place where there's a lot of white people and you can be thinking about the old slave days and HATE, or you can stand there with love in your heart, too.*

And what's been in the past is in the past, because we are living in the future and we can't help about those old things.

A person can't help being born white; a person can't help being born black. Just think of love, that's the way I feel about it.

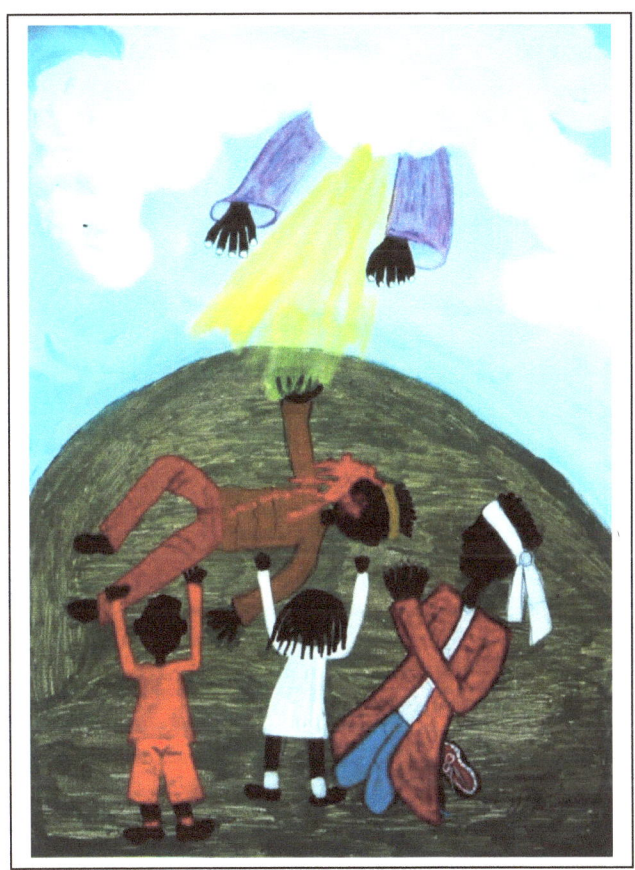

Going to Heaven, 12 x 16 acrylic on paper

You know, there's some people can look at a movie about slavery and they be ready to fight the next day. **Well, my grandma was a slave in South Carolina.** *She used to tell us how she would pick cotton until she felt like she was having heat stroke. She used to tell us about that stuff...slave stories. I tell my grandchildren every story I know...about working on the farm...about how we lived back then.*

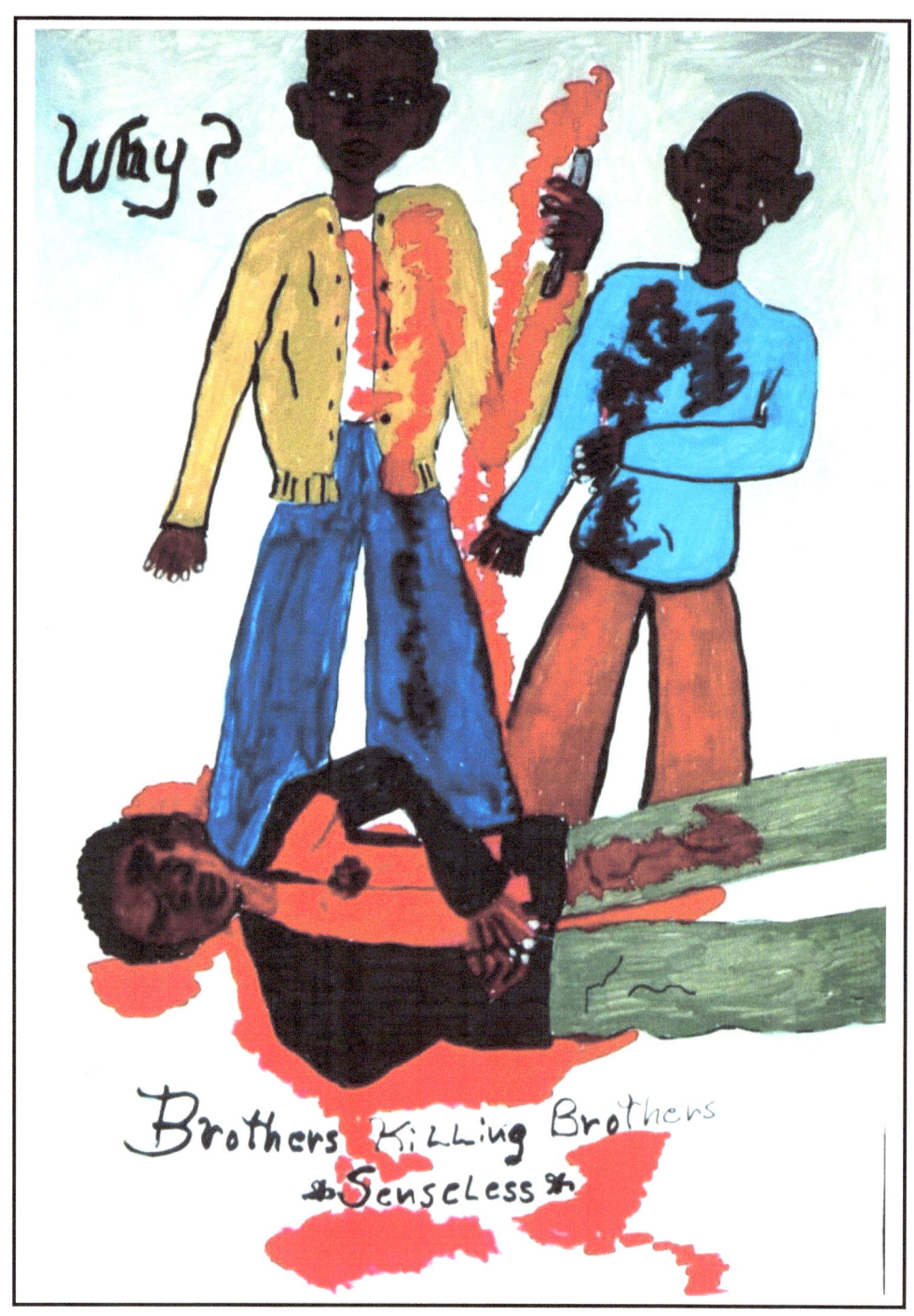

Brothers Killing Brothers, 9 x 13 ½ acrylic on paper

Addie's sense of self-worth, coupled with a tolerance born of her faith, gave her the strength to do battle with racism.

Needless violence, however, especially between brothers, was an evil she could neither abide nor reconcile. *Going to Heaven, Brothers Killing Brothers,* and the furious painting, *Body Parts and Blood,* graphically expressed Addie's anger at gang warfare and the entire drug culture.

Crack Baby
by Addie James

Don't call me that!
I got a right to be here.
I was introduced to crack
Before I was born.
Don't call me that!
Crack Baby is not my name.
When I was born
They didn't put me
 In my mother's arms.
They hooked me up with tubes
And left me alone.
But with the help of God,
This *Crack Baby* lived.
Look at me, I'm proof of that.
DON'T CALL ME THAT!

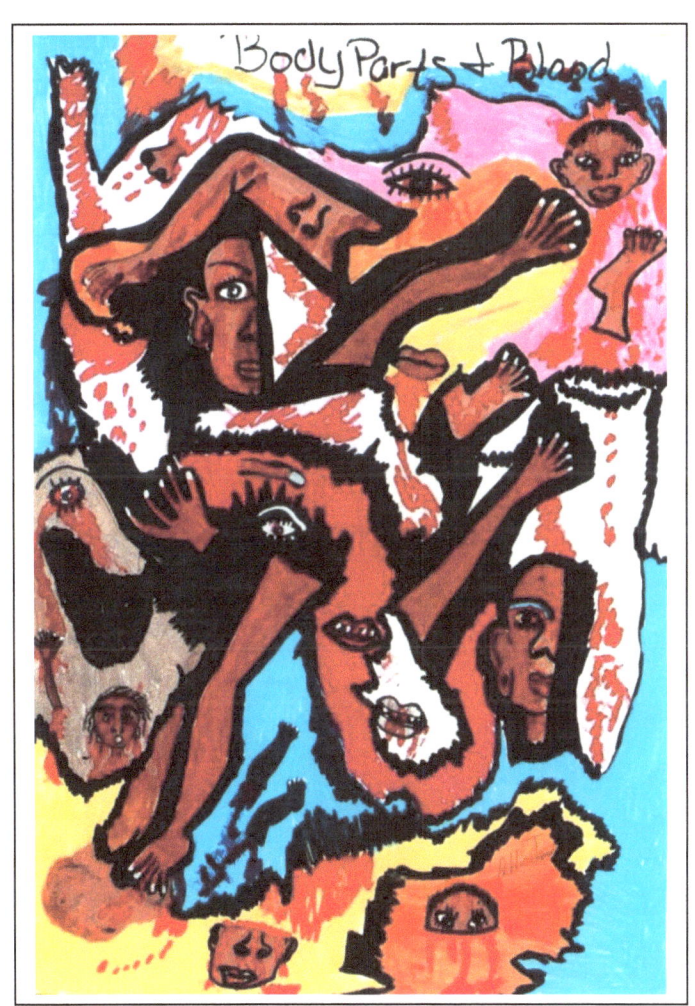

Body Parts and Blood
11 x 17 acrylic on paper

ATTACK ON AMERICA
by Addie James

The day terrorists attacked our jets
And flew into the Pentagon and Trade Centers...
What a sad day!
I thought the world
Was coming to an end.
I was thinking over and over
In my mind...
LORD HELP US!
All and everything began to fall.
I thought just yesterday
The buildings stood so tall.
It's like magic...
Now you see it, now you don't.
So many people lost their lives.
That day it was Mother, Father, Sister, Brother,
And so many more.
If you never called on God, now is the time.
Let us pray!!!

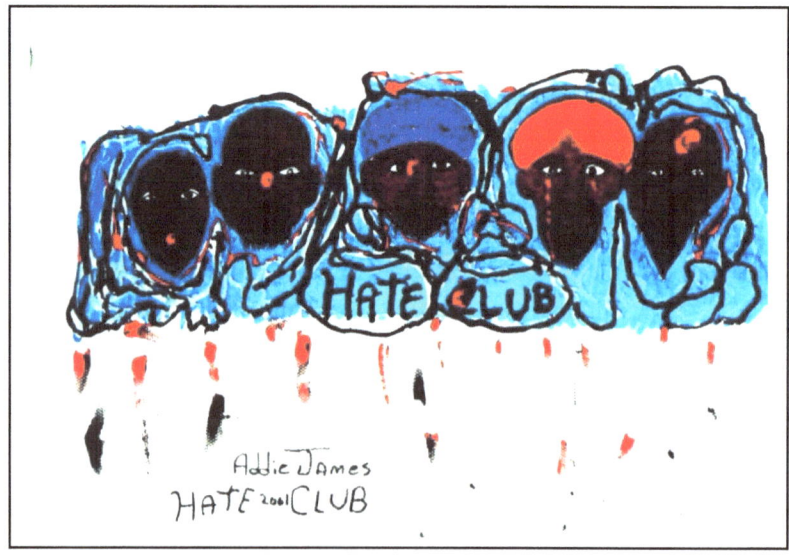

The Hate Club, 11 ¾ x 15 ½ acrylic on mat board

In reaction to the terrorist attacks on September 11, 2001, artists across America spontaneously began painting as an outlet for their fear, their outrage, and an overwhelming sense of impotence. On September 12th Addie James painted *The Hate Club,* and on September 13th she wrote the poem, *Attack on America.*

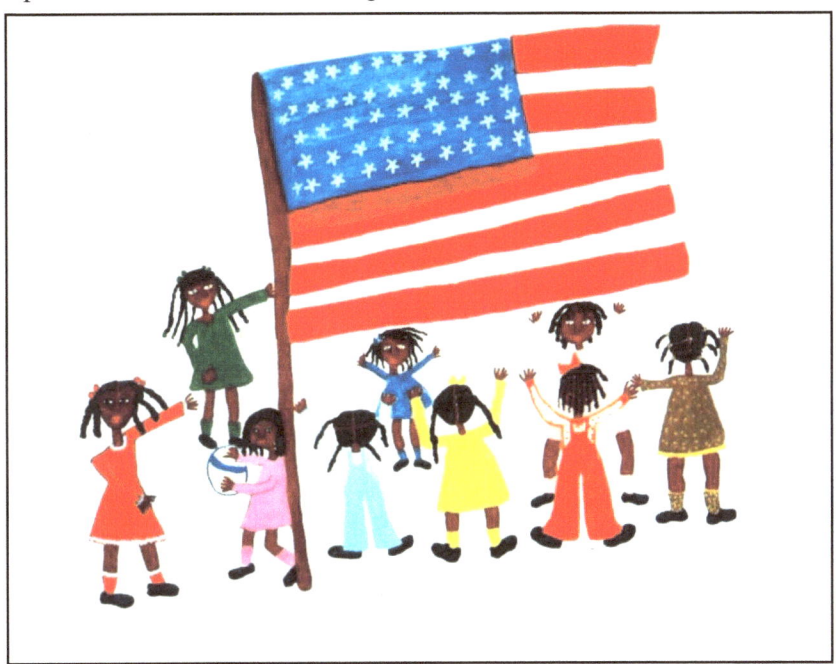

Peace, 16 x 20 acrylic on canvas

Several days later, Miss Addie painted *Peace* and began the universal human process of questioning: **why do bad things happen to good people?**

Sometimes when bad things happen, God is teaching us a lesson. September 11th in New York...? Maybe that happened because we had got away from God too much. We weren't thinking about God. So many people are thinking THEY are God. I think it's a lesson to bring people together with love.

It's a lot to understand, but you got to trust in God. Everybody has to die. If you read the Bible, you know there ain't nothing happening in this world like what's coming. Because we living in the Revelations now, and those bad things are COMING. They're going to happen. They're going to happen. So we better start praying we going to Heaven. **I want to go to Heaven.**

Even if one does not share Addie's views about God allowing the terrorist attacks, does not believe in Judgment Day, or does not share her faith at all… it is still possible to imagine that if there *were* a Heaven, then Addie would surely go there.

One can also celebrate *United Men* even while rejecting the notion of "my country…right or wrong," because Addie's trio of patriots were *bonded by brotherhood, not politics*. As in all her art, these subjects are universally human, beyond all religious or racial considerations, so that they engage and embrace us all.

Thank you, Addie.

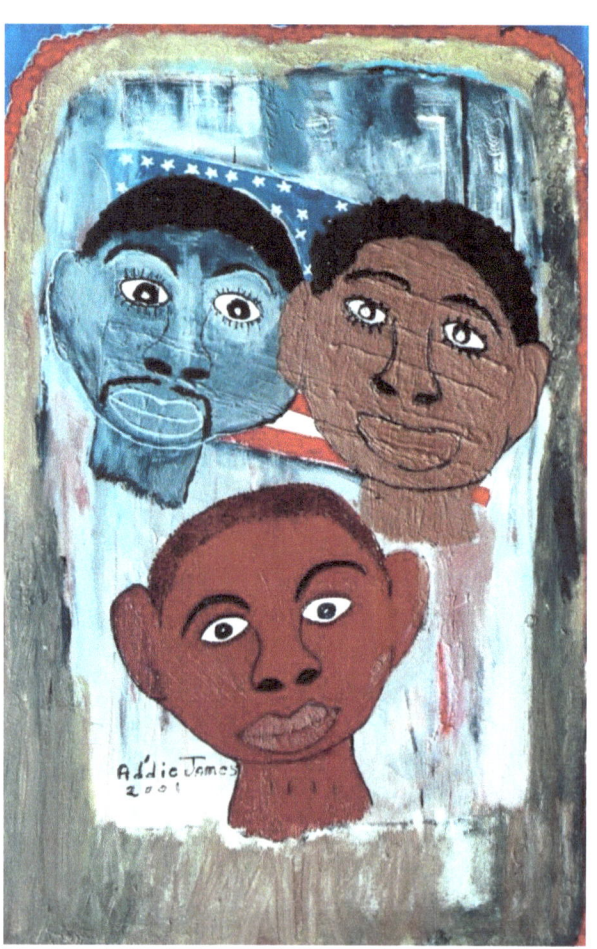

United Men, 24 x 36 mixed media on canvas

Although Addie James did not live to see the final days of Barack Obama's first term or his reelection, she did rejoice in his first historic victory. The event was an amazing affirmation of Addie's belief that everything was good and possible in America…

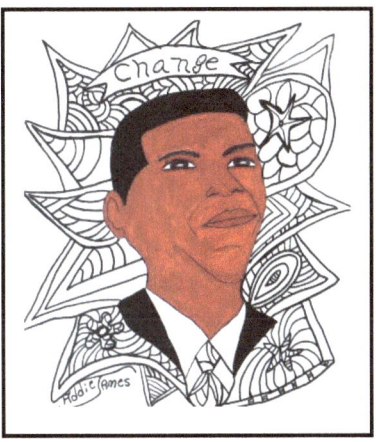

Change
12 x 14
Acrylic on mat board

And during her last One-Woman Show at the gallery, Addie's optimism, faith, and hope for our future was stronger than ever.

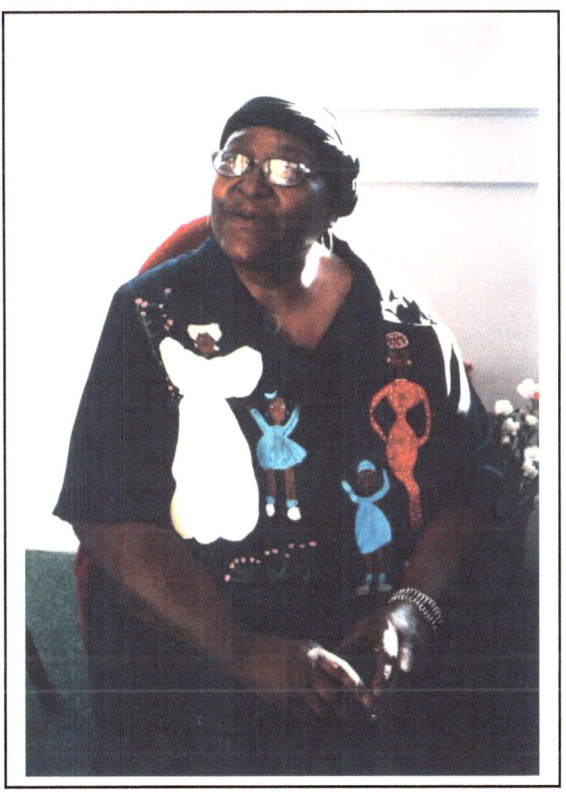

IN MEMORIUM

On Sunday morning, July 17, 2011, our beloved Addie James died at Iredell Memorial Hospital in Statesville at the age of sixty seven. The sudden loss of this amazing human being stunned and saddened not only her family and friends, but also hundreds of collectors who had been charmed and uplifted by her art.

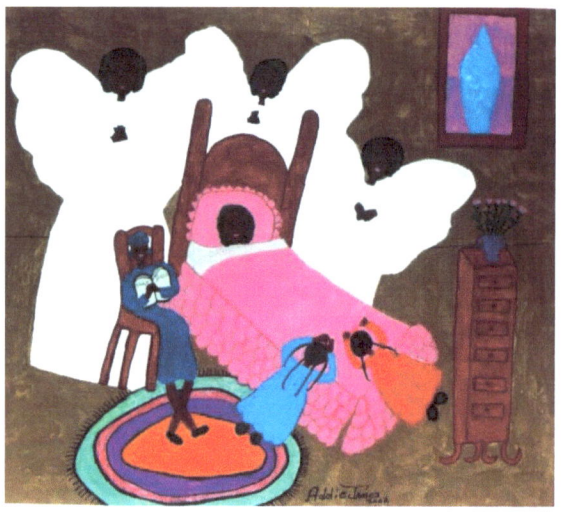

Mary Alice's Angels"
(Angels to See Me Through)

Miss Addie departed this world peacefully, surrounded not only by her family, but most certainly by angels to "see her through."

Since we finished this book together, Addie's life had been filled with both tragedy and triumph. Her little ranch house on Independence Loop had been nearly destroyed by fire, but then rebuilt with the help of a community who loved her. While she battled diabetes, arthritis, gout, and countless other ailments, she retained her ever-present positive attitude.

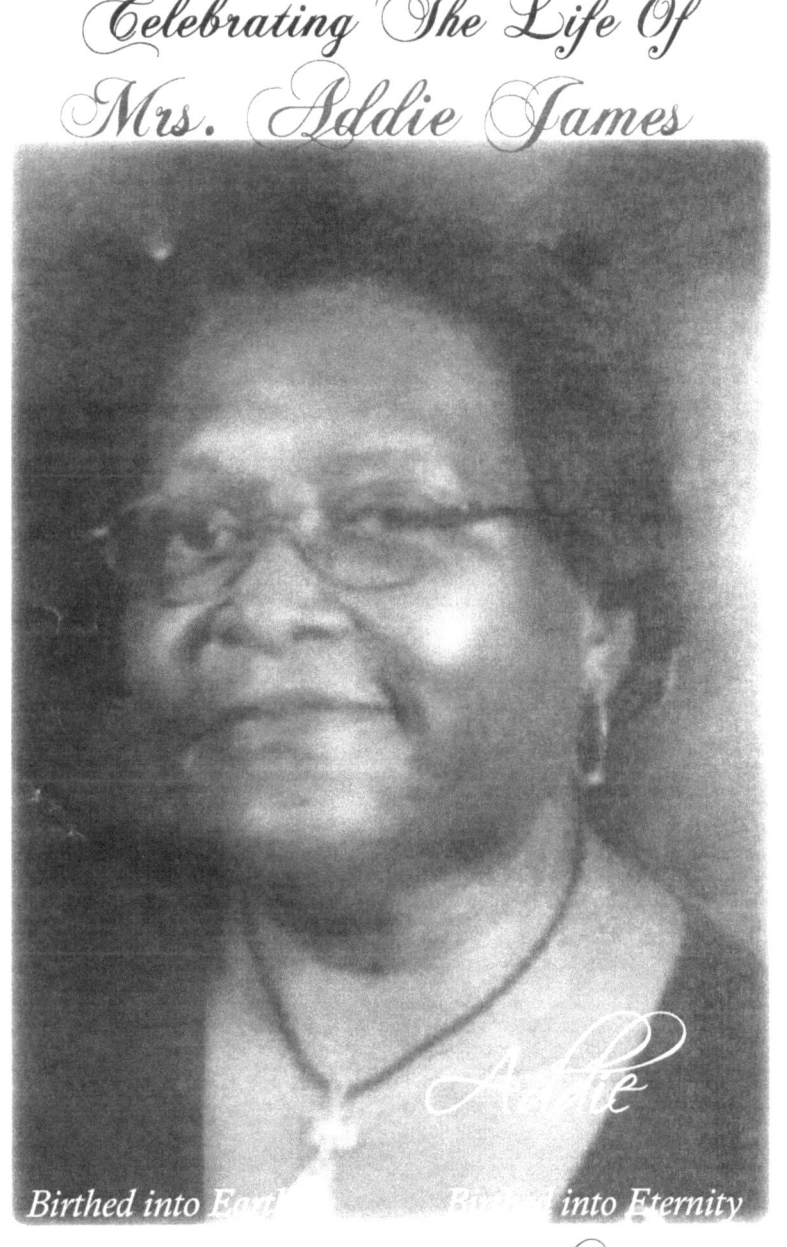

Celebrating The Life Of
Mrs. Addie James

Addie

Birthed into Earth .... Birthed into Eternity

August 11, 1943 .... July 17, 2011

"She left a legacy that colored our world"

Perhaps the most devastating blow to Addie was the loss of her youngest daughter and constant companion, Madaron, who succumbed to breast cancer in August of 2010. By then Addie had buried two of her cherished children and decided to abandon the house where she had raised her large family: "too many memories, too many ghosts."

Living in a rented home where she spent the final months of her life, Addie James' abiding faith kept her spirits high. She took comfort in the fact that her family had blossomed to include ten grandchildren and nine great grandchildren, and to Addie these children were more precious than any material wealth. In addition to our gallery in Davidson, Addie's work was also exhibited in numerous galleries and museums. Her reputation as a treasured North Carolina folk artist was firmly established, and she continued to paint every day. Indeed only two weeks before her death, she called our gallery and asked us to "cut me up some mat scraps to draw on," so as always, Miss Addie's creative drive was a life force as essential as breathing.

Christian Outreach in Statesville hosted a rousing memorial "Celebrating the Life of Mrs. Addie James: Birthed into Earth---Birthed into Eternity…she left a legacy that colored our world." Picture a gymnasium-sized building converted to a church on one of the hottest July days on record. Now observe a seemingly endless sea of faces---black and white---and a colorful fluttering of paper hand fans, some of them painted by Miss Addie. Visualize her coffin surrounded by a lively, impromptu display of the artist's originals and Miss Addie's "Quilt That Came to Life" hung behind the pulpit.

We watched as Wake Forest Professor Mary Dalton's video "*Addie James* Art Unbound" played on an enormous overhead screen. We heard the band, the joyous singing, and were moved to tears by "The Dance of Praise." We listened to the testimony from young people who turned away from destructive habits because Miss Addie put them on a better path, from Pastor Glen Ursy who described Addie eating a rabbit and Mary Bradford who recalled Addie's warmth, humor, and her taste for a chew of tobacco now and then.

Mostly imagine all the arms waving and voices crying hallelujah to celebrate the joy that was Addie's life. That day we were all living inside one of her paintings. And indeed Addie James will live forever in her art.

Farewell. Miss Addie, you have changed us all.

Love, *Kate Merrill*

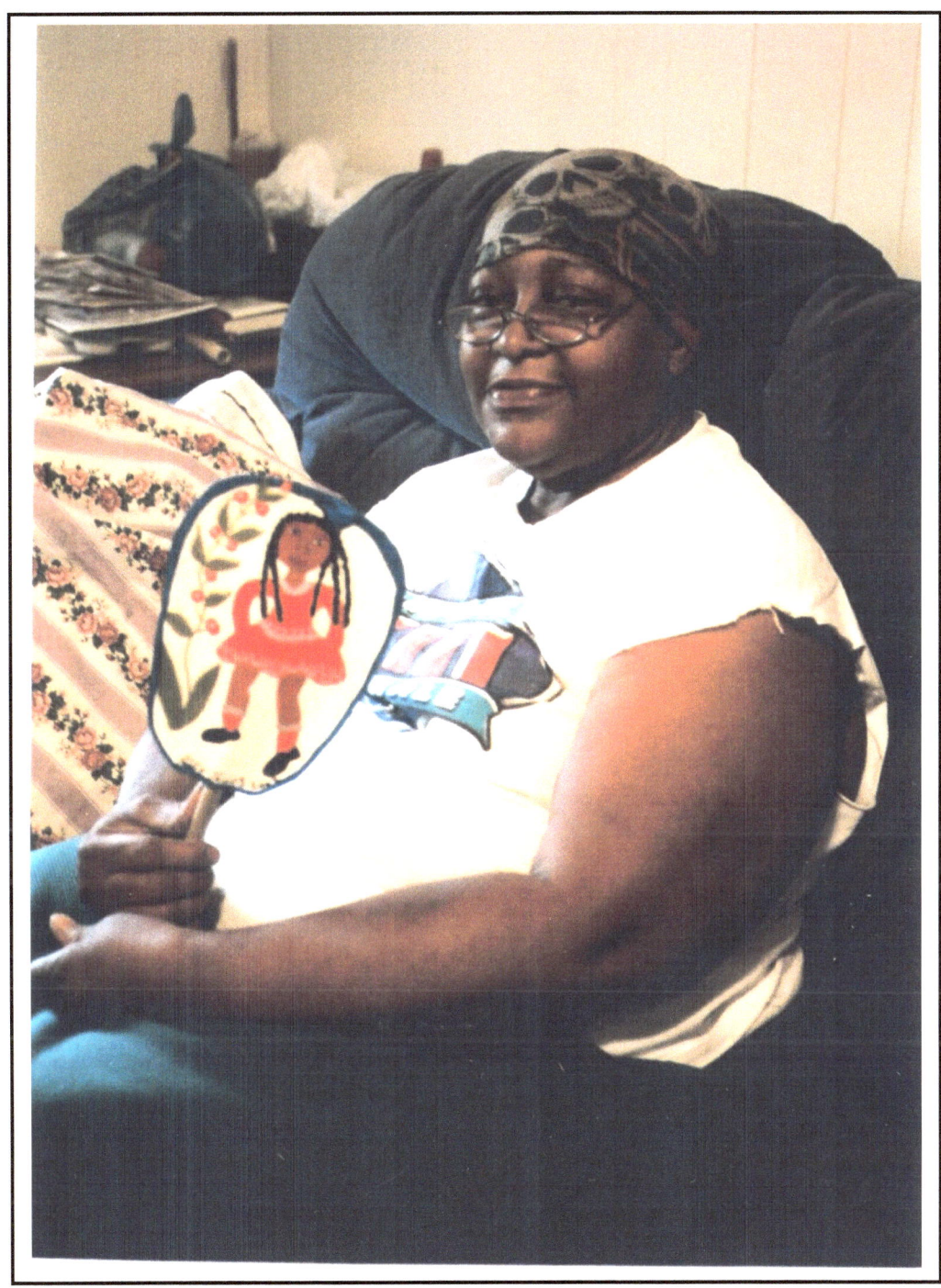

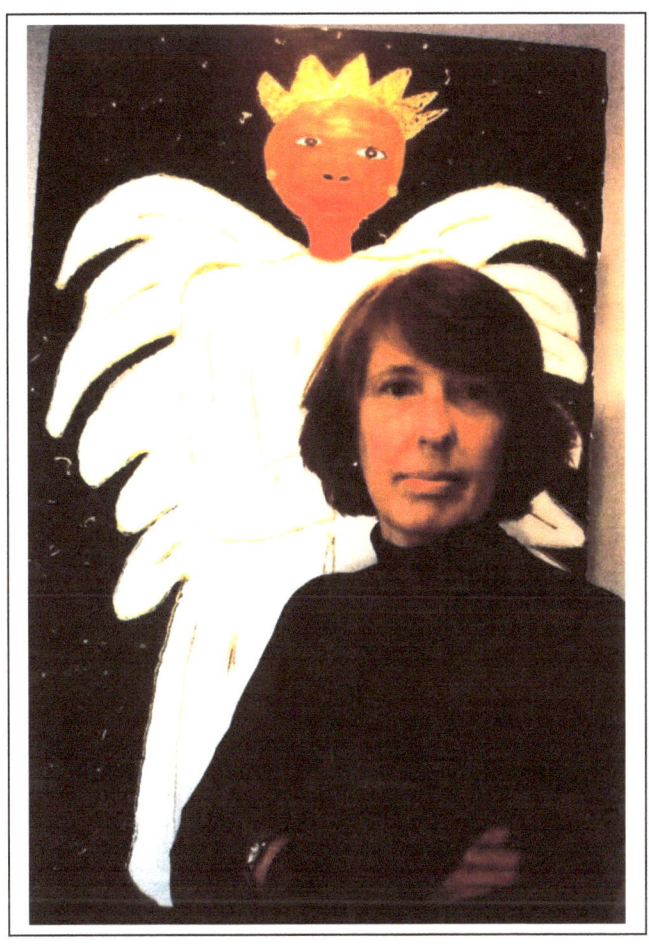

Kate with Addie's Angel
taken upon completion of the book in 2003

A gallery owner since 1970, Kate Merrill has championed dozens of painters with specialties ranging from African American Folk Art to European Surrealism. Her first galleries, THE MERRILL COLLECTION, located in West Chester and Bryn Mawr, Pennsylvania, were among the first in the nation to sponsor Black History Month shows, a tradition carried on by the current gallery, MERRILL-JENNINGS GALLERIES in North Carolina.

In addition to her passion for art, Kate has published both romance novels and mystery fiction, all available for purchase at Amazon and other online booksellers. Her art reviews have appeared in magazines, newspapers, and monthly features.

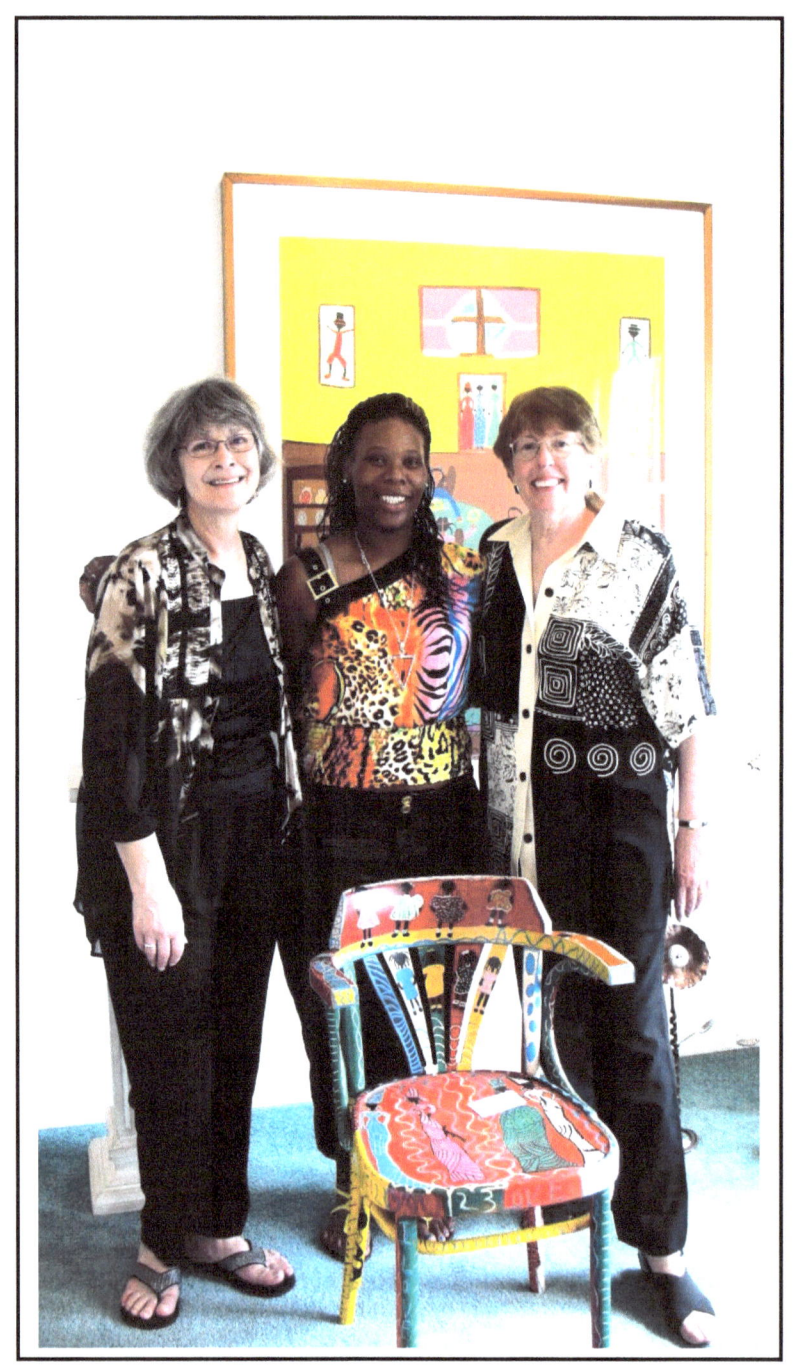

Susan Jennings, Kesha Gillion (Addie's granddaughter)
and Kate Merrill
Memorial Retrospective Show for Addie James
May 5, 2012, Merrill-Jennings Galleries, Davidson, NC

BIBLIOGRAPHY

Black Art and Culture in the Twentieth Century, Richard J. Powell @1997, Thames and Hudson, LTD.

Contemporary American Folk Artists, Eli nor Lander Horowitz and J. Roderick Moore @1975, J.B. Lippincott Company.

I Tell My Heart; The Art of Horace Pippin @1993 Pennsylvania Academy of Fine Arts.

Mainstreams of Modern Art, John Canaday @1959, Holt, Rinehart and Winston.

Miss Addie, the Art of the Smile, Mary C. Curtis, Charlotte Observer, February 10, 2002.

Painting Life Beautiful, Addie James, prepared by Karen Barber for *Angels on Earth,* a GUIDEPOST publication, March-April, 2003.

Statesville City School System is Now Almost 100, Bill Moose, Statesville Landmark and Record, March 3, 1991.

Testimony: Vernacular Art of the African American South, @2001, Harry N. Abrams, Inc.

Touched by an Angel; Statesville Woman Gives Others the Gift of Hope, Carla Froedge, Statesville Landmark and Record, September 23, 2002.

ART AND PHOTO CREDITS

All photography, including the photos of Addie James and her art, were taken and provided by the author, Kate Merrill, unless otherwise specified. Unless indicated, all art pictured is owned by Merrill-Jennings Galleries or was unsold at time of writing this book.

PAGE #

I'VE BEEN THROUGH THE STRUGGLE

9. *I've Been through the Struggle*, Dean Wilke, Concord, NC

11. Addie James as a Child (photo provided by the artist)

12. *Playing at the Swing*

13. *Kids Talking*, America, Oh Yes, Hilton Head, SC

14. *City Playground,* Davidson Elementary School, Davidson, NC

15. *Family Woods,* Dr. Ann Fox, Davidson, NC

16. *Family Farm Work*

17. *Baby and Me,* Dr. Richard Krumdieck, Davidson, NC

18. *Honeymoon,* Liza Sippe

19. *Mother and Daughter*

20. *Mix Up,* Judith Ghoneim, Charlotte, NC

21. *Family Gathering,* Kate Merrill

YOU GOT IT GOIN' ON

23. *You Got It Goin' On,* Ruth Pittard, Davidson, NC

24. *The Woods*

25. *Sasha,* Ramon Figueroa, Jackson, MI

26. *First Christmas Alone,* Rhonda Reddix, Gathersburg, MD

27 *New Home,* Barbara Doyle and Meg Sowicki, Davidson, NC

29. *Party Time with Kids*

30. *Angel with Baby*

31. *David*

32. *Colors*

    Project Kids

33. *The Cotton Patch,* Madeline Kelly, Massachusetts

    Beauty, Sandy Frizzell, Naples, Florida

34. *Monica,* Ruth Pittard, Davidson, NC

35. Alvera Brown Meets Miss Addie (photo)

    Just Like Sisters, Dr. Fred and Kathy Marks, Statesville, NC

36. *Artist's Hand,* Jill Williams, Davidson, NC

LOOK AT ME

37. *Look at Me*

     Look at Her

38. *Nobody But Me*

    Brown Boy

39. *Young Man,* Lee Lewis, Charlotte, NC

40. *Old Times,* Sean O'Neill, Davidson, NC

    Lady in Pink, Randy Blackman, Cornelius, NC

42. *Aunt Addie,* Anita McCurley and Sandra Bromble, Weaverville, NC

    Uncle Benny, Bob and Lisa Barber, Hiddenite, NC

LIFE IN THE COUNTRY

43. *Life in the Country,* Herman McKinney, Huntersville, NC

44. *Springtime,* Alvera Brown, Charlotte, NC

45. *Having a Good Time,* Lizz Slowick, Mooresville, NC

    Bird Nesting, Debra Rossi, Saginaw, MI

46. *Bug and Butterflies,* Virginia Hart, Concord, NC
    Play Time

47. *Girls at the Big Yellow House,* Evelyn Easter

48. *Kids Playing with Dog,* Bruce McMillen, Davidson, NC
    Let's Go Horseback Riding, Shannon Reichly, Charlotte, NC

49. *The Billy Goat,* Jann Bolick, Davidson, NC

50. *A Day at the Lake,* Angela and Ladd Baucom, Davidson, NC
    River Front, George Barnwell, Charlotte, NC

51. *Study for God's Present,* Kathy Holland, Troutman, NC
    God's Present, Cindy Webb

52. *Fun at Home,* Cassandra Burns, New Canaan, CT

LIFE AT HOME

53. *At Home*

54. *TV Time,* Catherine Mowry, Charlotte, NC

55. *My Room,* Chris and Jay Malick, Mooresville, NC
    Red Drawers, Cindy Davenport, Davidson, NC
    Blue Couch, Meg O'Brien, Davidson, NC

56. *Children Waiting on Supper,* America, Oh Yes Gallery
    Cookin' Dinner, Paula Seefeldt, New York, NY

57. *Father Reading Bible to Children,* Ann Grassi, Charlotte, NC

58. *Bedtime*, Eve Dew Danner, Charlotte, NC
    Back in the Day, Bobbi Brownridge

CHILDREN DON'T GO ON TREES

59. *Children Don't Go On Trees*, Gerry Smith. Mt. Ulla, NC

60. *Flower Children...Again,* C. Alexander, Denver, NC

61. *Goin' Dancin',* Eric Vogen, Davidson, NC

Pink Dress, Kay Kincaid, Davidson, NC

62. *Follow the Leader,* Dr. Nancy Fairley, Davidson, NC

Young Tiger Woods, Richard B. Perlman, Longboat Key, FL

64. *Girls in a Puzzle,* Elaine Rhoades, Charlotte, NC

65. *An Angel Over Us,* Edna Jenkins, Mt. Pleasant, SC

Thinking, Eve Dew Danner, Charlotte, NC

66. *Box Kids,* Alexa Kulman

Children at Play, Kay Kincaid, Davidson, NC

68. *Tree Children,* Lizz Slowick, Mooresville, NC

THE FOUR 'F's

FASHION

69. *We Got Class,* Susan Sadler, Cornelius, NC

70. *Polka Dots Hallelujah,* Dr. Richard Krumdieck, Davidson, NC

Shouting Sisters

71. *Fashion Hallelujah Girls*

Three Hallelujah Girls in White, Sandy Frizzell, Naples, FL

72. *Fashions,* Dr. Fred and Kathy Marks, Statesville, NC

Queen for a Day, Glenda Loftin, Denver, NC

73. *Girls' Day Out,* Sean O'Neill, Davidson, NC

74. *Pink N' Polka Dots*

75. *Fashion Show,* Dr. Fred and Kathy Marks, Statesville, NC

76. *Let's Start Fresh,* Mitzi Short, Denver, Co

Come Go With Us

FRIENDS

77. *Ladies' Club,* Angela and Ladd Baucom, Davidson, NC

78. *Comforters,* Loretta Wertheimer, Davidson, NC

79. *New Baby,* Ruth Pittard, Davidson, NC

Boyz, Stuart Warner, Charlotte, NC

80. *Talkin' Trash*

81. *Sorority and Fraternity*

82. *The Faces of Love,* Sean O'Neill, Davidson, NC

Lovers at the Window, Sean O'Neill, Davidson, NC

83. *We Got the Blues,* Gwendolyn Stevens

Saturday Night in the City, Ramon Figueroa, Jackson, MI

85. *Jammin',* Elke Gallagher, Cornelius, NC

FAMILY

86. *Family of Five*

Our Child

87. *Mama's Family,* Andee Byers, Riverton, NJ

88. *Daddy's Girl,* Kristi Weis, Cornelius, NC

Father and Daughter, Sean O'Neill, Davidson, NC

89. *Family Time,* Susan Crawley, Cornelius, NC

First Steps, Rebecca Sullivan, Lexington, NC

90. *Family Life,* Sean O'Neill, Davidson, NC

91. *Family,* DeWitt Crosby, Davidson, NC

92. *We Finally Got Our Baby*

FAITH

93. *Holy Bible*, Mary Dalton, Jamestown, NC

Going to Church, Laura Phillips, Louisville, KY

94. *Gospel Singing*

People

95. *Spirit of the Angel,* Monica Woodward, Huntersville, NC

96. *Hallelujah, It's Snowing,* Sandy Frizzell, Naples, FL

97. *Spirit with Stained Glass,* DiAngelo Dia, Charlotte, NC

98. *Praying Time,* Francis Broadway

99. *Who Broke the Chain?...God,* Ed Kania, Davidson, NC

100. *Spirit in the Wilderness,* Elizabeth Perry

101. *Angel with a Red Rose,* Sean O'Neill, Davidson, NC

103. *Face in the Church Window*

105. *Hebejebe,* Ramon Figueroa, Jackson, MI

106. *Angel at the Crossroads,* Jerome Smith, Coatesville, PA

HALLELUJAH, IT'S CHRISTMAS

107. *Hallelujah, It's Christmas,* Kate Merrill and Susan Jennings

108. *Christ Child,* Susan Goode, Mooresville, NC

109. *Gifts for the Christ Child,* Monica Woodward, Huntersville, NC

110. *Christmas Time at the Yellow House*

111. *Christmas Carols,* Ruth Pittard, Davidson, NC

112. *People Sing at the Ghetto Tree,* Tony Abbott, Davidson, NC

113. *The Gifts,* George Barnwell, Charlotte, NC

114. *The Star,* Susan Goode, Mooresville, NC

      Santa Claus, Janet Perrotti, Charlotte, NC

115. *The Savior,* Susan Goode, Mooresville, NC

HALLELUJAH, IT'S A PARTY

116. *Party,* Patty King, Davidson, NC

117. *Family Celebration,* Sarah Hyde, Charlotte, NC

118. *Strike a Pose,* Leigh Ann Turbeville, Cornelius, NC

      Dance, Barbara Healy Collins, Davidson, NC

119. *Hip Hop,* Joe and Joan Martin, Charlotte, NC

120. *Singing the Blues,* Mr. And Mrs. Greg Cummings, Chesterfield, VA

121. *Makin' Music,* Sally McMillen, Davidson, NC

122. *New Years Party,* Priscilla McCro, Charlotte, NC

123. *Dressed Up For Valentines Day*, Jane Foard, Charlotte, NC

124. *Birthday Party,* Dotti Martin, Mooresville, NC

THE SHADOW PEOPLE...*Thinking Outside the Box*

125. *Three Hallelujah Women,* Catherine Turner, Charlotte, NC

126. *Look Alike Day,* Andrew Seligman

127. *Bird of Time,* Justina Clemons, Davidson, NC

128. *Color My World,* Sean O'Neill, Davidson, NC

129. *Lost Child,* Dr. Marla Chalnick, Davidson, NC

130. *Smiling Abstract,* Adair T. Kenny, Charlotte, NC

   Lost and Found, Sean O'Neill, Davidson, NC

131. *Faces,* Mary Ellen Horn, Cornelius, NC

   Through the Eyes of People, Dr. Marla Chalnick, Davidson, NC

132. *God's Critters,* Sean O'Neill, Davidson, NC

   Apple of My Eye, Ramon Figueroa, Jackson, MI

133. *All God's Creatures,* Tara Reeves, Mooresville, NC

134. *Creatures of the Earth,* Cindy Webb

134. *Creatures of the Earth, Sea, Sky,* Cindy Webb

AFRICA

135. *Maidens Bringing Water,* ERL Originals, Winston- Salem, NC

136. *Tribal Feast,* David Graves, Huntersville, NC

137. *Woman with Jug,* Sean O'Neill, Davidson, NC

   Rhythm, Dr. Fred and Kathy Marks, Statesville, NC

138. *African Trio,* Dr. Fred and Kathy Marks, Statesville, NC

   Rejoice. Lee Lewis, Charlotte, NC

139. *African Beauties,* Ellen Goheen, Davidson, NC

140. *Village People,* Jerome Smith, Coatesville, PA

141. *Dove of Peace*

THE QUILT THAT CAME TO LIFE

142. *Plastic Delights,* Karel Lucardo, Leigh Naab, Beverly, OH

143. *Comedy/Tragedy Masks,* Ramon Figueroa, Jackson, MI

     Comedy/Tragedy Cool Cats, Leigh Naab, Beverly, OH

144. *Mask Mobile,* Kate Merrill and Susan Jennings

     Susan's Birthday Gourd, Susan Jennings

     Boat Tile, America, Oh Yes, Hilton Head, SC

     For The Birds, Pat Foster, Ginger Wilson, Sarasota, FL

145. *Church Fans*(various collectors)

146. *Teacup Sets (yellow)* Ellen Dellinger, Davidson, NC: *(blue)*

     Canister Set, Sandy Frizzell, Naples, FL

147. *Orange Chair,* Kate Merrill and Susan Jennings

     Pink Chair, Dr. Brenda Flannagan, Davidson, NC

148. *The Quilt, (painting)* Katherine Sellers, Davidson, NC

     The Quilt that Came to Life, Bob and Lisa Barber, Hiddenite, NC

BROTHERS KILLING BROTHERS

149. *The Many Faces of Sadness,* Sean O'Neill, Davidson, NC

150. *In Money We Trust*

151. *Hands,* John Hoffman

152. *Prisoner's Prayer,* Jill Williams, Davidson, NC

153. *Going to Heaven*

154. *Brothers Killing Brothers*, Dr. Robert Iovino, New York, NY

155. *Body Parts and Blood,* Sean O'Neill, Davidson, NC

156.   *The Hate Club,* Sean O'Neill, Davidson, NC

157.   *Peace,* Barbara Healy Collins, Davidson, NC

158.   *United Men*

159.   *Change*

       Miss Addie at Merrill-Jennings Galleries (photo)

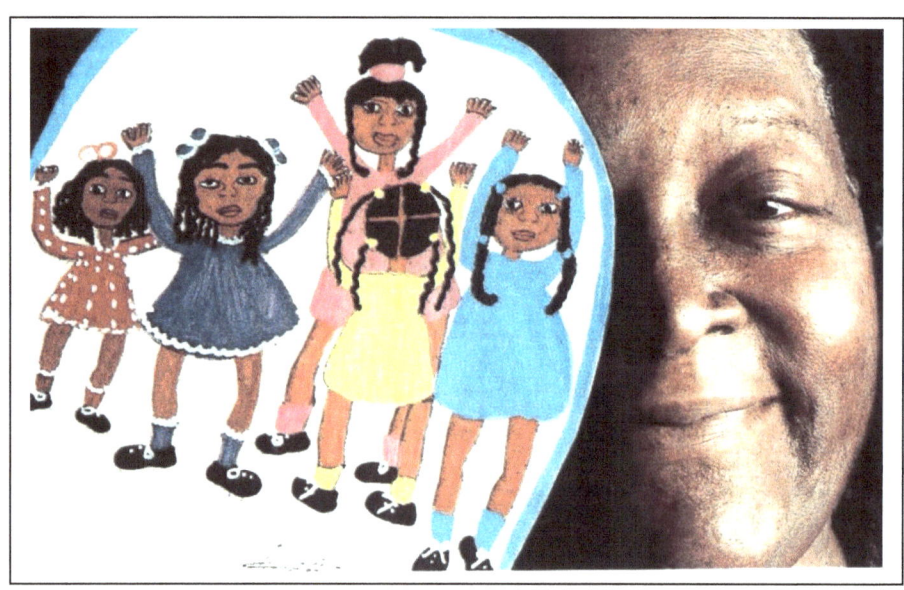